Macroeconomic Uncertainty

MACROECONOMIC UNCERTAINTY

International Risks and Opportunities for the Corporation

LARS OXELHEIM

Scandinavian Institute for Foreign Exchange Research, and The Industrial Institute for Economic and Social Research (IUI), Stockholm

and

CLAS G. WIHLBORG

University of Southern California, Los Angeles

JOHN WILEY & SONS

Chichester · New York · Brisbane · Toronto · Singapore

Library of Congress Cataloging in Publication Data
Oxelheim, Lars, OBS.
 Macroeconomic uncertainty international risks and
opportunities for the corporation.

 Bibliography: p.
 Includes indexes.
 1. Foreign exchange. 2. Hedging (Finance)
3. Risk management. 4. Country risk. I. Wihlborg,
Clas. II. Title.
HG3821.0894 1987   658.1'55   87–8333
ISBN 0 471 91480 0

British Library Cataloguing in Publication Data
Oxelheim, Lars.
 Macroeconomic uncertainty international risks and
opportunities for the corporation.
1. Macroeconomics   2. Managerial economics
 I. Title   II. Wihlborg, Clas
 339'.024658   HB172.5

ISBN 0 471 91480 0

Typeset by Photo·graphics Ltd, Honiton, Devon
Printed and bound in Great Britain by Biddles Ltd, Guildford

FOREWORD

The joint work presented in this book grew out of our independent theoretical and practical work on exchange rate risk and related issues over a number of years. We had both developed frustration trying to come to grips with operational principles for measuring and managing exchange rate exposure. At the same time we were both led to consider a more comprehensive approach to analysing firm exposure in the international environment. Thus started a transcontinent and transatlantic joint venture.

We have worked on this book in Los Angeles and in Stockholm. We are grateful for the use of facilities at the Claremont Graduate School, the University of Southern California, the Industrial Institute for Social and Economic Research (IUI), and the Scandinavian Institute for Foreign Exchange Research, Stockholm.

During the process of writing this book we have developed personal debts and appreciation to a large number of people. Our major intellectual debt is to Professor Thomas D. Willett at the Claremont Graduate School. As the chairman of the economics program there, he helped provide both the intellectual support and the necessary facilities. In Stockholm, Dr Gunnar Eliasson, director of IUI, made facilities available. He and Professor Erik Dahmén also provided intellectual support. We also wish to thank the Banking Research Institute for its role in providing financial support from the Marianne and Marcus Wallenberg Research Foundation, and the Scandinavian Institute for Foreign Exchange Research which

v

partially funded our research. Ms Lori Harnack at the Claremont Graduate School was infinitely patient typing and retyping, and helping administratively in every way. Jacquelyn Huntzinger also helped with the typing of the manuscript. Ms Pamela Martin skilfully provided linguistic assistance. Gustavo A. Ferraro and J. Paolo Gusmao helped create and work out the hedging examples in Chapter IV and the exposure scenarios in Chapter VI. Ms Tijana Zivkov Perl and Mrs Kerstin Wennberg provided valuable research assistance. Ms Zivkov Perl also read and checked most of manuscript.

Remaining errors and omissions are entirely our responsibility.

CONTENTS

LIST OF TABLES

LIST OF FIGURES

LIST OF SYMBOLS

NPV	= Net present value
X	= Net cash flow
x	= Portfolio share
e	= Nominal exchange rate
f	= Forward exchange rate
u	= Real exchange rate
i	= Nominal rate of interest
i^R	= Real rate of interest
d	= Discount rate
P	= Price level index
OP	= Output price index
IP	= Input price index
WP	= Wage index
γ	= Volume effect of price change
$\epsilon^{country}$	= Price elasticity for country
ϵ_t	= Error term
π_t	= Error term
a	= Share of a commodity in a price index
T	= Tax rate
σ^2 and σ_{jj}	= Variance
Cov and σ_{ij}	= Covariance
ρ	= Correlation (Pearson)
E	= Mathematical expectation
$\star$	= Forecast

^	= Rate of change
−	= Bar, which indicates contractual item
t	= Subscript denotes period
US,FC,LC (superscripts)	= Currency denominations
D and F (superscripts)	= Domestic and foreign, respectively
R	= Rate of return
β	= Degree of indexation

CURRENCY SYMBOLS

Country	Currency	Symbol
Austria	Shilling	ATS
Belgium	Franc (commercial)	BEC
Canada	Dollar	CAD
Denmark	Krone	DKK
Finland	Mark	FIM
France	Franc	FRF
Germany (West)	Deutsche mark	DEM
Italy	Lira	ITL
Japan	Yen	JPY
Netherlands	Guilder	NLG
Norway	Krone	NOK
Spain	Peseta	ESP
Sweden	Krona	SEK
Switzerland	Franc	CHF
United Kingdom	Pound	GBP
United States	Dollar	USD
(IMF)	Special drawing rights	SDR
(EEC)	European Currency Unit	ECU
	Local currency	LC
	Foreign currency	FC

I

THE INTERNATIONAL
ENVIRONMENT OF THE FIRM

I.1 EXCHANGE RATE RISK, MACROECONOMIC RISK, AND CORPORATE EXPOSURE

The international financial and trading system has been subject to a large number of shocks since the beginning of the 1970s. The exchange rate environment has been turbulent, and the calls for a return to a fixed exchange rate have been many. Exchange rate risk has become an important issue for management of firms with international transactions. Finance and international business oriented magazines have published a profusion of articles on how to deal with exchange rate risk in corporations. Accounting Standard Boards in the US and other countries have spent considerable effort on developing and revising rules for translating foreign currency items on income statements and balance sheets.

In spite of the extensive preoccupation with exchange rate risk, there is no widely received wisdom among practitioners and academics on how to measure and manage exchange rate risk.

A major theme of this book is that as long as exchange rate changes are viewed independently of other prices, interest rates, and inflation rates, it is impossible to develop a consistent principle for measuring and managing exchange rate risk. The exchange rate is only one of several variables in the macroeconomic system that adjust to different kinds of shocks. Other important macroeconomic variables are inflation rates and interest rates, prices of some commodities like oil, and the aggregate levels of production and demand. These macro-variables are often 'related' to the exchange rate, but there is no clear causal relationship among the different variables. Most of them change in response to monetary and fiscal policy disturbances and to large real shocks in the trading system like oil price changes. This view of exchange rate changes explains why fixed exchange rates cannot be reinstated by some kind of decree (see e.g., Willett, 1986). Exchange rates are turbulent when the international financial and trading system is subject to large and frequent policy disturbances and other economic shocks. Furthermore, the exchange rate rarely changes alone but turbulence in the environment would have impact on price levels, interest rates, and relative prices among commodity groups, as well as on exchange rates. The implication of this view of exchange rate changes is that measuring exchange risk in isolation may lead to a misleading measure of the risk to which a firm is exposed. Therefore, attempts at reducing exchange rate risk may fail to reduce or even increase the total risk to which the firm is exposed. A more comprehensive approach for measuring and managing exchange rate and 'related' risks is called for.

Throughout this book we focus on the measurement and management of *macroeconomic risk*. It refers to risk caused by any uncertainty about the macroeconomic situation characterized by, for example, the level of aggregate demand in a country, the inflation rate, the interest rate, the exchange rate, etc. It should be emphasized, however, that uncertainty may produce profit *opportunities* as well.

All firms in a country have a certain macroeconomic environment in common. Macroeconomic risk, therefore, can be distinguished by the fact that it is not firm-specific or industry-specific. It exists, for example, when there is uncertainty about the general level of demand in the economy. Firm-specific risk, on the other hand, arises as a result of uncertainty about the demand for a firm's specific product relative to other firms' products, while industry-specific risk could be caused by uncertainty about demand for an industry's products relative to other industries' products. An important part of identifying macroeconomic risk is to distinguish it from firm-specific and industry-specific risks. Macroeconomic disturbances, as well as firm- and industry-specific disturbances affect the level of demand and the price of a firm's product but the management implications of falling demand caused by, say, a restrictive monetary policy are different from the implications of falling demand for the firm's product relative to the demand for competitors' products.

Though the macroeconomic environment is the same for a large number of firms the *exposure* to macroeconomic risk depends on the particular product the firm produces. It would depend on whether the firm exports or not, the level of its debt relative to equity, its capital intensity, the extent to which inputs are imported, etc. Thus, exposure is always firm-specific while macroeconomic uncertainty is not.

Macroeconomic risk must be analysed in an international context. Many shocks, such as the oil price shocks, are international. Furthermore, the macroeconomic environments of different countries are strongly interdependent. Inflation is transmitted among countries, and a shock in one country may influence the competitiveness of firms in one country relative to firms in other countries. The level of many macroeconomic variables such as the exchange rate depends on the macroeconomic situation in one country *relative to* other countries. Macroeconomic developments in both the foreign and the home country influence the economic situation in one particular country, and the exposure of any particular firm would depend on whether it has international transactions, and whether it competes in the home market with foreign firms.

A good example of the importance of the macroeconomic environment is provided by the macroeconomic adjustment in the international economy to the large budget deficits in the USA during the early 1980s. The American fiscal policy pushed real interest rates (i.e., interest rates adjusted for inflation) up to levels 4 or 5 percentage points above what was normal during the 1960s and the 1970s. Since financial markets in different countries are closely integrated, the interest rate level rose in the whole OECD area. The capital flows into the USA, caused by higher interest rates and government borrowing, pushed the dollar to new heights. The dollar appreciated by as much as 50 percent in real terms, i.e., after adjusting for inflation differentials, from 1979 to its peak in the mid 1980s. American goods became correspondingly more expensive relative to goods produced elsewhere, or the profit margin for US firms had to be squeezed drastically. As a consequence the US developed a gigantic trade deficit, that made it the largest debtor nation in the world after having been the largest creditor nation. In 1985 and 1986 the dollar started to depreciate while the yen appreciated substantially. These developments have obviously had a strong impact on firms in most countries but the effect varies enormously depending on the product, the degree of international competition in domestic and export markets, and the degree to which production is concentrated in one country.

The particular interest rate and exchange rate effects of the budget deficit in the early 1980s depended on a number of structural and policy factors. For example, with less capital mobility, the US would have borrowed less abroad. The interest rate in the US would instead have gone even higher, while the dollar may have appreciated less. Similarly, under a fixed exchange rate regime the exchange rate could not have appreciated. Therefore, it could not have contributed to creating a current account deficit, which is necessary to accomodate foreign borrowing. Instead the real interest rate would have had to rise further in the US to reduce investments and increase savings. Alternatively, US foreign exchange reserves would have increased, raising the money supply, thereby causing inflation. Different scenarios can be imagined depending on exchange rate regime and policy responses by the monetary authority. In each scenario, the adjustment of the exchange rate, the interest rate, and inflation rates is different. The exposure of any firm, therefore, would depend on what may be called 'policy regime'. An international agreement on pegging exchange rates is a policy regime. Central banks choose a policy regime for monetary policy when they decide to increase the money supply a certain rate instead of setting interest rate targets.

One firm may be interest-rate sensitive while another is exchange-rate sensitive. Yet a third may be hurt, or gain, more by inflation. In each case, the effect of the fiscal policy on the firm depends on the particular combination of interest rate, exchange rate, inflation, and other price effects. We should also emphasize the role of foreign authorities' policies in the adjustment. The effect of US policy on US and foreign firms would depend on the response of foreign monetary and fiscal authorities to US policy.

The above example illustrates that the exposure of one firm to a macroeconomic disturbance depends on three sets of factors. *First,* the *macroeconomic structure*, such as the degree of capital mobility and the relationships among exchange rates, interest rates, and prices, influences the interest rate and price effects of a disturbance. *Second*, the *policy regime* followed by authorities influences the degree to which interest rates, exchange rates, and inflation, respectively, adjust to the disturbance. *Third*, the nature of the firm's product and the *firm's structure* determine its sensitivity to changes in different variables.

In this connection we should again emphasize that profit opportunities arise as well in an uncertain world. The firm that is better able to forecast events may also be able to profit from developments that to other firms are purely unanticipated. As we explain in Chapter II, risk is a measure of the *magnitude* and the *likelihood* of an *unanticipated* event. With this definition, the risk-exposure of a particular firm is partially dependent on the firm's ability to forecast in an uncertain environment.

We mentioned above that exposure depends on macroeconomic structure. It is common in economics and finance to describe structure by means of market equilibrium relationships in goods and financial markets and by specifying adjustment processes towards these equilibria. For exposure analysis the equilibria provide convenient points of reference since, when they hold, there are no profit opportunities and no risk.

We will see that international macroeconomic exposures depend particularly on two equilibrium relationships. One—*Purchasing Power Parity*—refers to the equality of goods' prices across countries when measured in one currency. When there is parity there are no unexploited international trade opportunities and there is no exchange rate risk. Another relationship—*Fisher Open*—refers to the equality of expected returns on financial investments and the equality of borrowing costs across countries and currencies. Oxelheim (1985) demonstrates with data for a large number of countries that there are substantial, at least temporary, deviations from these relationships. It is not clear whether observed deviations imply that it would have been possible to exploit profit opportunities since deviations may not have been foreseeable. However, they certainly indicate that firms face substantial risks of changes in prices, exchange rates, and interest rates in the international environment.

1.2   SOURCES OF MACROECONOMIC EXPOSURE FOR A FIRM

We could go through a number of major economic disturbances
during the last decade and analyse in detail their effects on different
macroeconomic variables, and their contribution to firms' exposure
in different situations. Such an exposé would constitute a thick book
in itself. For our purposes, it is sufficient to mention by examples
the kinds of disturbances in the environment that strongly influence
most firms. Uncertainty about these kinds of disturbances in the
future is accordingly the source of macroeconomic risk. The
examples also demonstrate how important uncertainty about
governments' policies is for the nature and magnitude of macroeconomic risk.

A major macro-disturbance with a worldwide impact during the
last decades was the expansionary policies of the US during the late
1960s in connection with the Vietnam War. The government
employed deficit financing. As opposed to the policy of the early
1980s, the Federal Reserve allowed the deficits to be monetized with
inflation as a predictable result.

The policies conducted by the US during the late 1960s and early
1970s contributed strongly to a second major macroeconomic
event—the breakdown of the Bretton Woods system of fixed
exchange rates in the early 1970s. The US, the UK, and a few other
countries had conducted more expansionary monetary policies than
countries like Germany and Japan. With price levels diverging at
fixed exchange rates, trade imbalances and pressures for exchange
rate realignment grew inevitably until, in 1971, the US devalued
and cut the fixed price relationship between gold and the dollar.
This realignment was insufficient, however, and in 1973 exchange
rates were allowed to float to seek market equilibrium values.

The switch from a fixed exchange rate regime or a flexible (or
floating) regime is a change in the *rules* by which monetary
authorities adjust to disturbances in the economy. Thus, it changes
the relationships between exchange rates, interest rates, and inflation
rates after a disturbance. Uncertainty about such rules or regimes
is an important aspect of political risk.

One can make the argument that as long as exchange rates were
pegged and allowed to change only rarely, it made sense to measure
and manage exchange rate risk as a distinctive risk, separable from

other risks. The reason is that the timing of large exchange rate changes were under political discretion, while inflation rates and interest rates were allowed to change more continuously. Pressures on the exchange rate were caused by other developments but the actual exchange rate change could be seen as an isolated event without simultaneous changes in other variables. Under a regime of floating rates the different macroeconomic variables are allowed to adjust simultaneously and interdependently, however. In our view, exposure management techniques and measurements have not really adjusted to this change from a regime of somewhat adjustable pegged rates to a regime of floating rates.

Another policy regime change that strongly influenced the way in which exchange rates adjust relative to other variables, was the switch towards money supply targeting by central banks instead of interest rate targeting. West Germany started to target the money supply and allow the interest rate to fluctuate, beginning in 1975. Other countries followed to different degrees. The Federal Reserve Board in 1979 started to set and comply with money supply targets, though these targets have subsequently been relaxed.

Major shocks caused neither by fiscal nor by monetary policy authorities during the last decades were the two oil price increases in 1973 and 1979. For industrialized countries these shocks can be compared to substantial decreases in the productivity of the labour force and the capital stock. They were accompanied by large fiscal and monetary policy adjustments in most countries, and gigantic flows in international financial markets as the oil producers' revenues were recycled. The combination of the productivity decreases and policy responses had drastic effects on the level of aggregate demand, inflation rates, interest rates, and exchange rates as well as on the relative prices among different commodities and services. Thus, there were a large number of channels through which the original disturbance affected firms.

The reverse oil price shock, i.e., the fall in prices in 1986 has similarly had important macroeconomic effects and influenced industries and countries to different degrees. In this connection, we may also mention the possibility of a substantial macroeconomic disturbance as a result of the debt problem of many countries. The oil price fall has relieved the pressure on some but worsened the situation for others, notably Mexico. If there were to be a substantial amount of default on loans, the financial repercussions could be severe according to some observers. Bank collapses may trigger central banks' infusion of money into the system or create sufficient uncertainty about the viability of the banking system to dampen economic activity. The specific macroeconomic impact of defaults by countries would, to a large extent, depend on the response of monetary authorities.

The recent deficits in the current account of the US balance of payments have led to demand for protectionism in the US in very severe forms. The success of the protectionist lobby would most likely have very strong macroeconomic effects. Other countries could respond with their own protectionist legislation and, as a result, there could be a substantial worldwide decline in the level of economic activity and growth. The effects on inflation, exchange rates, and interest rates and the specific exposure of firms to protectionist legislation would depend not only on their export and import competition, but on the fiscal and monetary response of political authorities, which would determine the adjustment of exchange rates and related variables.

1.3   RISKS—SOME PRELIMINARY DEFINITIONS

The concept of risk will be discussed in detail in Chapter II. As noted, it refers in general to the magnitude and likelihood of unanticipated changes that have an impact on a firm's cash flows, value or profitability. We discuss in Chapter II how academics and practitioners often mean different things by risk. The use of the concept in the daily language is typically sloppy but in order to derive principles for management of exposure to risk, careful definitions of risks of different kinds are necessary. In this section we simply define and distinguish between the different kinds of macroeconomic risk that will be analysed in more detail in other chapters.

In the first section of this chapter we distinguished between macroeconomic risk as opposed to firm-specific and industry-specific risk. We mentioned that macroeconomic risk depends on uncertainty in the environment of all firms in a country, though the impact on individual firms or their exposure is firm-specific. This definition is not quite sufficient, since the risk of crime, fire, weather changes, nuclear war, earthquakes, etc., are environmental risks to which most firms in a country or a region are exposed. We do not discuss these kinds of risks of nature, war, and human behaviour at all, but limit ourselves to those risks that are related to general and varying economic conditions in countries. These are risks related to uncertainty about variables that are studied in macroeconomics and often seen as business-cycle related. Fiscal and monetary authorities' attempts to control macroeconomic variables are stabilization policies. Trade policy and industrial policy, on the other hand, are typically directed towards specific industries or firms. Only when they have extremely large coverage will there be a macroeconomic impact, i.e., an impact on general business activity, and then to a large extent because fiscal and monetary authorities respond with stabilization policy to reduce unemployment in specific regions or industries.

To clarify the concept further, we may distinguish between the following kinds of macroeconomic risk to which any firm—multinational, exporting or purely domestic—is exposed.

1. *Financial risk* refers to the magnitude and likelihood of unanticipated changes in interest rates and costs of different sources of capital in a particular currency denomination. In this book we emphasize interest rate risk. Interest rate changes may also be related to the general level of demand in an economy. These effects should be considered when measuring exposure to interest rate changes.

2. *Currency risk* refers to the magnitude and likelihood of unanticipated changes in exchange rates and inflation rates, i.e., in the value of foreign and domestic money. We distinguish further between exchange rate risk and inflation risk.

3. *Country risk* (including political risk) refers to the likelihood and magnitude of unanticipated changes in a country's productive development, and of changes in 'the rules of the game', including laws, regulations and policy regimes selected by monetary and fiscal authorities.

These three categories of macroeconomic risk should be distinguished from a firm's *commercial risk*, which refers to the likelihood and magnitude of unanticipated changes in firm-specific and industry-specific prices and demand conditions.

Figure I.1 demonstrates the general relationship between uncertainty about macroeconomic disturbances and cash flow effects on the firm, as well as the categories of risk and their sources. We will elaborate on these relationships in the coming chapters. The figure provides an initial overview.

Starting on the far left we distinguish between domestic and foreign, as well as between policy- and non-policy generated disturbances. In addition there are firm- and industry-specific disturbances. Ideally, we would like to link cash flow effects and risk directly to these fundamental disturbances. This possibility is discussed in Chapter IV. The difficulty of tracing cash flow changes to fundamental disturbances will be shown to depend on the degree of uncertainty about policy reaction to disturbances in the form of monetary, fiscal, as well as industrial and trade policies in the third column of the figure. 'Rules' for policy responses in the form of exchange rate regimes, money supply growth targets, etc., determine how a particular disturbance influences exchange rates, inflation rates, interest rates, and relative prices in the fourth column. Uncertainty about these regimes constitutes one element of political and country risk.

Anticipated changes in the market price variables may lead to profit opportunities of different kinds depending on the nature of market adjustment. As mentioned above, if purchasing power parity holds, good's prices are equalized among countries. Then the exchange rate does not cause profit opportunities. Similarly, if Fisher Open holds, then effective interest rates are equalized and interest rate changes cause no profit opportunities. Inflation does not cause opportunities if all prices are linked perfectly to inflation.

Deviations from the above equilibrium relationships cause profit opportunities, if they are anticipated, while unanticipated changes are the major source of the different kinds of macroeconomic risks in the last column. This column contains also the commercial risk, the source of which is unanticipated relative price changes as a result of firm- and industry-specific disturbances, as well as industrial and trade policies.

The different categories of risk are not independent. Therefore, when measuring macroeconomic risk it is desirable to take into account that relative price changes occur as a result of firm and industry disturbances as well. Furthermore, interdependence arises

Figure I.1 External shocks and the cash flow of the firm

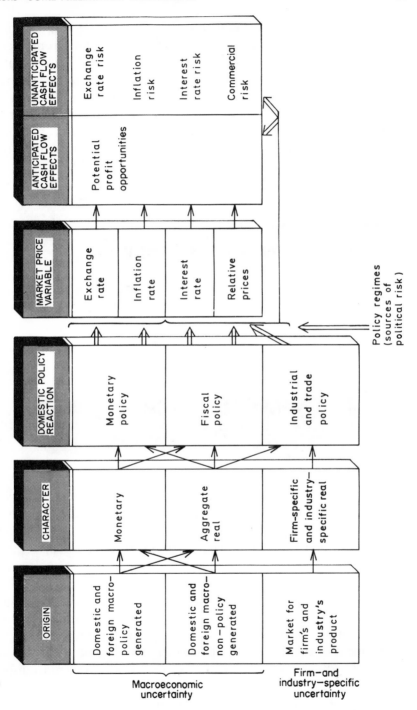

due to the simultaneous adjustment of exchange rates, inflation rates, interest rates, as well as government interventions in markets.

Consider as an illustration Figure I.2. This figure demonstrates the potential substitutability among risks and that country risk may be seen as more comprehensive than the other categories and, in fact, may influence the nature of the others as well as the extent to which firms are exposed to the other risks. The reason is, as we have mentioned, that policy authorities' behaviour influences the relative adjustment and variability of different variables to specific shocks. Furthermore, regulation and laws such as exchange controls influence the extent to which firms can avoid exposure.

Figure I.2   Macroeconomic risk

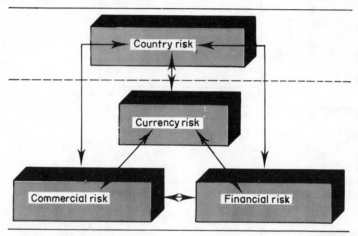

Source: Oxelheim (1985).

The above categorization is rather crude and we shall see that there are other ways of distinguishing between macroeconomic risks. The best categorization of risks would in general depend on how we can best determine operational measures and management strategies for them.

Of the four risk categories above, currency risk and, specifically, exchange rate risk has received the most attention. As we demonstrate in Chapter III, most current approaches to managing this risk presume implicitly or explicitly that exchange rate variability is independent of the variability of other macroeconomic variables. In general, handling any risk-category separately would seem to imply that the changes emanating from unanticipated fluctuations in that source are believed to be independent of other risk-sources.

Analysing exposure and risk management in a comprehensive manner implies not only the recognition of the interdependence among different types of risk, but also the importance of understanding the time horizon over which risks influence the firm, and the channels through which they impact on value and cash flows. The time horizon over which risks impact on the firm may be compared to its planning horizon and objective in terms of net present value of cash flows, short-term cash flows, or cash flows within a cutoff date.

In Table I.1. we list channels through which macroeconomic disturbances impact on firms of different kinds. In our analysis in later chapters, we emphasize that the impact through these channels may offset or enhance one another. Therefore, it is important to take a comprehensive view, not only of different kinds of related risks, but also of all different channels through which changes in the macroeconomic environment impact on the firm.

Table I.1   Type of company and channels of risk

	Type of Company			
Channels of risk	Multi-national with export and import	Domestic with export and/or import	Domestic with financial operations in foreign currencies	Strictly domestic
Monetary and negotiable securities in foreign subsidiaries	X			
Real asset in foreign subsidiaries	X			
Current and future remittances from foreign subsidiaries	X			
Export and import	X	X		
Claims and debts in foreign currencies	X	X	X	
Inventory	X	X	X	X
Domestic sales and purchases	X	X	X	X
Loans and deposits in domestic currency	X	X	X	X

Source: Oxelheim (1984a).

I.4   AN OUTLINE OF THE CHAPTERS

The chapters build on each other but we have made an attempt to make each self-contained so that the reader may select any one chapter of specific interest. To the extent an argument builds on material in previous chapters the text will say so.

Chapter II contains a review of financial theory of risk. It is an elementary review and the reader who is well-versed in the capital asset pricing model (CAPM) for the pricing of risk in financial markets can easily skip this chapter. We also discuss, from the point of view of different stakeholders, reasons why firms would be concerned with the variability of their cash flows or value. Firms may then be classified by their risk-attitude.

Chapter III reviews traditional approaches to measuring and managing macroeconomic exposure. In particular, different measures of exchange risk are discussed and we analyse the relationship among such concepts as transaction, translation, and economic exposure. We demonstrate in examples what is accomplished by conventional hedging techniques. Though the emphasis in this chapter is on exchange rate risk, we discuss also the measurement and management of financial risk—in particular interest rate risk—and country risk. The chapter brings the reader up to date on exposure measures as well as on techniques for managing exposure by means of financial instruments. In appendices we summarize theory and empirical evidence on equilibrium relationships in international goods and financial markets.

Chapter IV develops alternative ways for measuring macroeconomic exposure, recognizing the interdependence among different variables as well as among different kinds of cash flows. We emphasize that political risk, i.e., uncertainty about the behaviour of policy authorities, may create a fundamental problem in measuring risk from historical and current data. In this chapter we demonstrate also in principle and in examples how financial market instruments can be used to hedge risk, thereby decreasing the firm's exposure to unanticipated shocks in the macroeconomic environment. An appendix contains an illustration of the proposed method of exposure measurement using data from Swedish industry.

Chapter V demonstrates how exposure management strategies could be developed with knowledge of the firm's objective, its risk-attitude, time perspective, the structure of its cash flows, and international price and interest rate relationships in goods and financial markets. We analyse first how specific cash flows depend on prices, exchange rates, and interest rates, and how exposure depends on the degree to which purchasing power parity holds, i.e., the degree to which exchange rates reflect relative price levels between countries. We distinguish here between *commercial cash flows* from the firm's primary business operations and *financial cash flows*. A second important distinction is between *contractual cash flows* on which the monetary values are predetermined, and *non-contractual flows*, the magnitude of which depends on future price and interest rate changes. For management purposes we also distinguish between *adjustable* and *non-adjustable flows*.

After discussing alternative objectives of a firm, we demonstrate how rules for managing exposure—exposure management strategies—are determined such that they are consistent with the objective of the firm. Thereafter, information needs associated with each strategy can be determined.

If the desired strategy demands information that is unavailable or too costly to collect, we reverse the analysis and determine what type of strategy could be accomplished with available data. This analysis enables the firm to evaluate how much the desired objective must be compromised given available data or by choosing simplified strategies and thereby lowering costs.

Chapter VI contains a scenario analysis of a hypothetical firm. Such an analysis constitutes an additional method for measuring exposure, when historical data analysis is unreliable. We demonstrate how the impact on the firm of monetary and fiscal disturbances depend on the macroeconomic structure, i.e., on the way in which prices, exchange rates, and interest rates adjust to a disturbance.

Chapter VII is the final analytical chapter. The important issues of evaluation of managers and strategy, and feedback between different decision-makers involved in implementation are discussed. Organizational issues of centralization versus decentralization are briefly touched upon in this connection. The key issue in this chapter is the development of evaluation methods such that the incentives of managers are consistent with the overall objective of the firm. Few firms seem to have developed systematic methods for evaluating their exposure management strategies. This is clearly an important task but it is also a difficult one, and it presumes that firms form explicit objectives for their exposure management related to their overall objectives.

Chapter VIII, finally, contains a concluding comparison of alternative methods for measuring exposure. We discuss relative advantages of traditional methods, and of our proposed methods for estimating sensitivity coefficients, as well as of the scenario approach for estimating the impact of macroeconomic disturbances on the firm. In this chapter we also summarize the different steps the firm needs to take in order to develop a systematic and feasible exposure management strategy.

II

CORPORATE RISKS: WHO CARES?

II.1 INTRODUCTION

Recent turbulence in world goods and financial markets have resulted in increased fluctuations in firms' earnings. These fluctuations, emanating from unanticipated changes in market conditions, constitute the basic element of corporate risk. In this chapter we discuss the concept of risk in more detail and look at reasons why corporate management may want to reduce the impact on the firm of increased uncertainty in the environment.

Section II.2 reviews the concept of risk in finance. In Section II.3 we present elementary financial theory of the trade-off between risk and return for individual investors (shareholders). Section II.4 contains a discussion of the different stakeholders in a company and how their attitudes influence what is seen as an acceptable trade-off between risk and return. We ask here whose objective will guide the corporate handling of risk?

II.2 CORPORATE RISK

The concept of risk is often used differently by practitioners and academics. This confusion of language frequently leads to misunderstandings. For example, one may read in the newspaper 'there is a substantial risk that the pound will be devalued by 10

percent over the next few months'. The meaning of this statement presumably is that there is a strong likelihood the pound
will be devalued. In the academic's language there is, in this
situation, an *expected devaluation* while risk refers to the problem
that the timing and the magnitude of the devaluation is uncertain.
Essentially, it seems that many practitioners evaluate risk in
terms of potential changes relative to today's values of variables
while in academic language risk is evaluated relative to *anticipated*
changes in the values of variables like the exchange rate. Risk
is then a measure of the likelihood and magnitude of *unanticipated*
changes. When the academic states that risk may be irrelevant in
the choice of currency denomination of a loan, it is not implied that the anticipated devaluation should be disregarded, but
only that the borrower should act as if the measure of the anticipated devaluation is certain. In other words, the likelihood and
magnitude of changes larger or smaller than anticipated are
disregarded.

It is clearly essential that we define the concept of risk used in
this book. We largely follow the definition used in finance and
economics since it enables us to better discuss how to design
operational strategies for dealing with uncertainty in the macroeconomic environment. It is important to keep in mind that changes
in variables may be anticipated or unanticipated and that *risk is a
measure for unanticipated changes*. Anticipated change is measured by
the *expected* change which is normally evaluated through *forecasting*.
In general, the management of uncertainty involves both the
forecasting of variables such as exchange rates or inflation rates, *and*
an evaluation of the likelihood that the forecast may be wrong, that
is, that unanticipated changes will occur. In this book we are most
concerned with the process of risk evaluation and will discuss only
briefly methods of forecasting.

At this point we should mention that the presence of uncertainty
is not necessarily negative. It also presents opportunities for both
individuals and firms, especially for those able to forecast better
than others. The forecaster could naturally wish the impossible,
i.e., that a forecast is certain, but then it is unlikely that the forecaster
could profit from it. Thus, in the uncertain environment the firm
looking for profit opportunities must also face the possibility that
the outcome differs from the forecast. In essence, risk-management
deals with this· issue before the outcome is known.

The value, cash flows, and profits of a firm are influenced by changes in macro-variables such as interest rates, inflation rates, and exchange rates and also by changes in prices and volumes on the company level. Changes in these variables could become sources of unanticipated changes in the company's future cash flows and therefore in value and profits. From a *stockholder's* perspective, investment in the firm's shares is, therefore, risky. The changes may also impact on other stakeholders in the firm, as discussed in Section II.4. To clarify the concepts initially we limit the discussion to shareholders.

The risk for the stockholders of investing in shares in a firm may be seen as the spread of possible future returns on these shares around an expected return. For a stockholder, risk is often evaluated in light of the existing portfolio, as will be seen later. The risk of investing in a firm's shares depends then on the contribution of these shares to *portfolio risk*, i.e., the spread of possible future returns on the whole portfolio. Initially, we discuss the risk associated with a specific asset as if this asset constitutes the whole portfolio.

The spread in future returns due to unanticipated changes in firm value is often captured by the *standard deviation* and *variance* of a *probability distribution of returns*. The variance of the return is the expected squared deviation from the expected return or:

$$\text{Variance }(R) = \text{the expected value of} \tag{II.1}$$
$$(R - R^\star)^2 = E[(R - R^\star)^2] = \sigma_R^2$$

where:

R = actual return, and
$R^\star$ = expected return (the sum of probability weighted possible returns)

The standard deviation is the square root of the variance:

$$\text{Standard deviation of } R = \sqrt{\text{variance }(R)} = \sigma_R.$$

Variance and standard deviation are often used as measures of risk for individual assets as well as for portfolios of assets. When these measures of risk are applied to individual assets, rather than a portfolio, one disregards the possibility that risks on different assets may offset each other.

Sometimes a distinction is made between risk and uncertainty, in which case risk refers to the variance of a known probability

distribution of outcomes while uncertainty exists when the probability distribution is unknown. There are instances when it is
meaningful to make such a distinction, as we shall see in Chapter
IV.

If we have only a few possible outcomes it is easy to demonstrate
the concepts of risk, standard deviation, and variance. Consider the
following example. A manager is offered the chance to play a simple
game where the outcome is determined by flipping two coins. The
individual starts by investing $100. For each head that comes up
the starting balance plus 30 percent is paid and for each tail that
comes up the starting balance less 20 percent is paid. The following
possible outcomes with adjacent probabilities can be identified:

Head–head	gain 60 percent with a probability of $\frac{1}{2} \cdot \frac{1}{2} = \frac{1}{4}$
Head–tail	gain 10 percent with a probability of $\frac{1}{2} \cdot \frac{1}{2} = \frac{1}{4}$
Tail–head	gain 10 percent with a probability of $\frac{1}{2} \cdot \frac{1}{2} = \frac{1}{4}$
Tail–tail	lose 40 percent with a probability of $\frac{1}{2} \cdot \frac{1}{2} = \frac{1}{4}$

The manager can now use this matrix for the decision, but listing
all possible outcomes in real life could be extremely cumbersome,
to say the least. Therefore, statistics such as expected value, variance,
and standard deviation serve a useful purpose by capturing a large
amount of information in a single measure. When they are known,
it is possible to estimate the probability that the outcome will be
below or above a certain value.

In our example we can calculate the *expected return* as the sum of
the probability-weighted possible returns in the following way:

$$E[R] = R^\star = (0.25 \times 60) + (0.25 \times 10)$$
$$+ (0.25 \times 10) - (0.25 \times 40) = +10.$$

Table II.1 demonstrates the calculation of the *variance of returns*, i.e.,
the risk associated with the game. We can note that risk measured
this way implies nothing about the expected outcome. Thus, we
cannot state that the risk of a loss of a certain amount is some
figure. However, as was mentioned, one can estimate the probability
of a loss.

The variance is equal to 1250 and hence the standard deviation

Table II.1 Outcomes, probabilities, and the variance

(1)	(2)	(3)	(4)	(5)
Percent rate of return R	Deviation from expected return $R-R^\star$	Squared deviation $(R-R^\star)^2$	Probability	(3) (4) squared deviation probability
+60	+50	2500	0.25	625
+10	0	0	0.5	0
−40	−50	2500	0.25	625
	0		1.0	$1250 = \sigma_R^2$

is $\sqrt{1250} = 35.4$. The standard deviation is comparable with the expected return, so we can summarize the game as having an expected return of 10 percent and its risk may be captured either by the standard deviation of 35 percent or the variance of 1250. If the outcome of the game is certain, the standard deviation (and the variance) is zero and there is no risk.

As previously mentioned, the variance of future outcomes can originate in many different sources. Two sources not mentioned above are accidents and criminal activities. These sources were the first to be explicitly handled by *risk management*. Today there is some confusion around the concept of risk management, since it can refer to either a program for insurance against fire, crime, or accidents, or to a program for handling the unanticipated effects of changes in the company's environment. In this book, we focus on the latter category of risk management, and exclude pure commercial risks—for instance, the obsolescence of the company's products due to the introduction of a better product by its competitors—and emphasize risks emanating in the macroeconomic environment that tend to affect all firms but to different degrees and in different ways.

II.3 THE TRADE-OFF BETWEEN RISK AND RETURN, AND THE PORTFOLIO APPROACH

One can view a company's portfolio of assets and liabilities as a number of contracts for which the future outcome is uncertain. In the case where the company is owned by domestic residents, the risk of a certain contract, from the owner's point of view, has two parts. One is the *unique risk* that is peculiar to that contract, and the other is the *market risk* that emanates from market-wide variations and affects all contracts held by domestic residents. If exchange rate fluctuations are the only source of risk, and companies and individuals may choose contracts of different currency denominations, then market risk is due to factors influencing all exchange rates while unique risk influences only one exchange rate. Investors are able to eliminate unique risk (unsystematic risk), but they cannot eliminate market risk (systematic risk). The owners' portfolio variance, which could be lowered by adequately increasing the number of stocks and therefore the number of contracts, is the average covariance among all the different contracts. The covariance is a measure of how asset returns covary due to market risk. (It will be defined further below.) If stock returns in the portfolio do not covary, it would be possible to eliminate all risk by holding a sufficient number of stocks. In this case, stock returns are independent. The covariances are zero and there is no market risk. If, for example, all exchange rates change independently, then it would be possible to put together a portfolio of currency contracts on which the aggregate exchange rate variance approaches zero as the number of currencies increases.

There is a market relationship between the risk associated with a specific asset and its return. Pricing of risk depends not on assessed variance alone, however, but on the contribution of an asset to the total risk of asset-holders' portfolios. Markowitz (1959) laid the foundation for the modern theory of asset pricing of risk when he showed how an investor can reduce the standard deviation of portfolio returns by choosing stocks that do not covary perfectly for the portfolio. He extended the analysis to formulate principles for the selection of 'efficient portfolios'.

Efficient portfolios are those in which return cannot be increased without increasing portfolio variance, and variance cannot be lowered without reducing expected portfolio return. Underlying this concept of efficiency is the assumption that investors like high expected returns and dislike risk. Their concern is with risk on the *total* portfolio. The relevant risk, from the investor's point of view, for a specific asset is, therefore, the asset's addition to portfolio risk.

In order to decrease this additional portfolio risk an investor would be willing to pay by sacrificing expected return.

Let us take an example where the investor has two stocks under consideration to form a portfolio. One has an expected return of 25 and a standard deviation of 10. The other has an expected return of 40 but a standard deviation of 25. In this situation, the investor would not invest in only one stock unless he or she were totally uninterested in the variance (*risk-neutral*). If the investor is *risk-averse* and concerned about both expected return and portfolio variance, then he or she will build up a portfolio of the two stocks. Suppose the investor chooses to hold 50 percent of available wealth in each. The expected portfolio return will equal the average of the expected returns. Thus:

$$\text{Expected portfolio return} = 0.5 \cdot 25 + 0.5 \cdot 40 = 32.5.$$

In general, the expected return on a portfolio is a *weighted average* of the expected returns on the individual stocks.

The portfolio variance depends on the variance of each stock and the covariance between the two stocks. The portfolio variance can be written for these two stocks as:

$$\text{Portfolio variance} = x_1^2\sigma_1^2 + x_2^2\sigma_2^2 + 2x_1x_2\cdot\rho_{12}\sigma_1\sigma_2$$

$$= .5^2 \cdot 10^2 + .5^2 \cdot 25^2 + 2 \cdot .5 \cdot .5 \cdot \rho_{12} \cdot 10 \cdot 25 \quad \text{(II.2)}$$

where:

x_i = proportion invested in stock i,

σ_i^2 = variance of return on stock i,

ρ_{ij} = correlation between returns on stock i and j.

The correlation is $+1$ if the two assets' return always moves in the same direction and always in the same proportion relative to each other, it is -1 if they always move in opposite directions, and relative changes are constant, and it is 0 if returns are completely independent, or more exact, if there is no linear relationship between returns. The covariance between the stocks is $\rho_{12}\sigma_1\sigma_2$; it depends on the correlation as well as on the variability of each asset's return. In our example, suppose that the two stocks covary so that the coefficient of correlation is equal to 0.7. Then the portfolio variance is 268.75. Thus, the standard deviation is 16.4. Note that portfolio expected return, as well as the variance, lies between the values of the two individual assets in this case. It is possible, however, to reduce portfolio variance below any asset's specific variance if the correlation coefficient is sufficiently low.

Assume now that the investor holds a portfolio consisting only of asset 1 with an expected return of 25 and a standard deviation of 10. What is the contribution to portfolio variance of substituting asset 2 with a standard deviation of 25 for asset 1 on the margin, i.e., when substituting a small amount. Initially, the variance is σ_1^2. After substitution of, say, one percent of wealth, portfolio variance is $(.99)^2 \cdot \sigma_1^2 + (.01)^2 \cdot \sigma_2^2 + 2 \cdot .99 \cdot .01 \cdot \sigma_1\,\sigma_2\,\rho_{12} = 101.5375$ and the relative increase in portfolio variance is:

$$\frac{(.99)^2 \cdot \sigma_1^2 + (.01)^2 \cdot \sigma_2^2 + 2 \cdot .99 \cdot .01 \cdot \sigma_1 \sigma_2\, \rho_{12} - \sigma_1^2}{\sigma_1^2} = \frac{1.5375}{100} \qquad \text{(II.3)}$$

The expected portfolio return increases from 25, when asset 1 alone is held in the portfolio, to $(.99 \cdot 25 + .01 \cdot 40) = 25.15$. Thus, we notice that portfolio return increases by .6 percent, portfolio variance increases by 1.5375 percent, while portfolio standard deviation increases by .765 percent when asset 2 is substituted for one percent of the original portfolio with asset 1.

When pricing the risk of specific assets, we would expect that investors evaluate the increase in portfolio variance (standard deviation) from a marginal portfolio change as in the above example, rather than evaluating the relative variances of individual assets. It is irrelevant to the investor that the variance of asset 2 is 6.25 times the variance of asset 1, since this figure does not indicate the increase in portfolio variance. The figure neglects the covariance among assets. If the investor in our case is willing to increase portfolio variance by 1.5375 percent for a .6 percent increase in expected return, then the investor substitutes asset 2 for asset 1 in the portfolio.

For a marginal change in the portfolio, the increase in portfolio risk of adding asset 2 is actually proportional to $\sigma_1\sigma_2\rho_{12}/\sigma_1^2$, i.e., the relative covariance between the new asset and the original portfolio. In equation II.3, which represents the variance increase of a substitution of one percent of the portfolio, we can observe that the expression is approximately equal to $2 \cdot .99 \cdot .01 \cdot \sigma_1\sigma_2\,\rho_{12}/\sigma_1^2$, since $(.99)^2$ is close to 1 and $(.01)^2$ is close to 0.

Figure II.1 Efficient portfolios

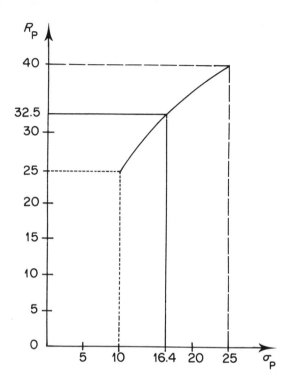

The lesson of this example is that from an investor's perspective we can express *the marginal risk of asset* j *as the relative increase in portfolio variance of a marginal increase in the proportion of asset* j *in the portfolio.*

The substitutability between risk and expected return on the portfolio of our two assets is illustrated in Figure II.1. Three points were identified above. These are $E[R_p] = 25$, $\sigma_p = 10$ for asset 1 above, and $E[R_p] = 40$, $\sigma_p = 25$ for asset 2 above, and $E[R_p] = 32.5$, $\sigma_p = 16.4$ when the portfolio is equally divided between the two assets. Notice that the curve connecting the points is not linear due to the covariance between the assets.

Which portfolio to choose depends on the *risk attitude* of the investor or of those whom the investor represents. By moving along the curve in Figure II.1, a suitable trade-off can be found.

The methods can easily be extended to a portfolio containing n securities. In this extended case we have the following expressions:

$$\text{Expected portfolio return} = \sum_{i=1}^{n} x_i R_i \qquad (\text{II}.4)$$

$$\text{Portfolio variance} = \sum_{i=1}^{n} x_i^2 \sigma_i^2 + \sum_{i \neq j}^{n} x_i x_j \rho_{ij} \sigma_i \sigma_j. \qquad (\text{II}.5)$$

Figure II.2 shows the choice situation when a larger selection of risky securities is involved and we introduce the possibility of borrowing and lending at a risk-free interest rate.

The shadowed area shows the possible combinations of expected returns and standard deviations for different portfolios of risky securities. If the investor likes high expected returns and dislikes high standard deviations, portfolios along the curved line are preferred to those below and to the right of it. Markowitz called

Figure II.2 Efficient portfolios with risk-free borrowing/lending

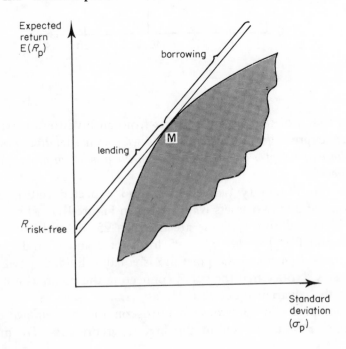

portfolios along the line *efficient portfolios*, as previously mentioned.

In practice calculations of expected return and variance with many risky securities can be cumbersome. A variance–covariance matrix as in Figure II.3 illustrates the principle. Securities 1 through n are listed horizontally and vertically. Each entry is the covariance between the row and column securities, weighted with the proportions of the two securities in the portfolio. In the diagonal entries the variances of individual security returns can be observed. The sum of all entries is the portfolio variance and the sum along each row is the contribution of each security to the portfolio variance. This contribution is the weighted sum of the covariances between the security and all other securities. The average of these covariances is the covariance between the security and the whole portfolio. (Notice that the notation for variances and covariances has been adjusted to what is common in matrix notation.)

With the help of a computer, given the variances (σ_{ii}) and covariances (σ_{ij}), portfolio variance can be calculated for different

Figure II.3 A variance-covariance matrix

	1	2	. . . .	n	Sum
1	$X_1^2 \sigma_{11}$	$X_1 X_2 \sigma_{12}$		$X_1 X_n \sigma_{1n}$	$\sum_{j=1}^{n} X_1 X_j \sigma_{1j}$
2	$X_2 X_1 \sigma_{21}$	$X_2^2 \sigma_{22}$		$X_2 X_n \sigma_{2n}$	$\sum_{j=1}^{n} X_2 X_j \sigma_{2j}$
.					
.					
.					
.					
.					
n	$X_n X_1 \sigma_{n1}$			$X_n^2 \sigma_{nn}$	$\sum_{j=1}^{n} X_n X_j \sigma_{nj}$

Total portfolio variance $= \sigma_p^2 = \sum_{i=1}^{n} \sum_{j=1}^{n} X_i X_j \sigma_{ij}$;

$\sigma_{ii} = \sigma_i^2 =$ variance of return of security;

$\sigma_{ij} = \text{cov}(R_i, R_j) =$ covariance of return of securities i and j.

combinations of the securities. The efficient portfolio is that which gives maximum expected return for a given risk. Quadratic programming then can be used to obtain the desired portfolio given an objective in terms of risk and return.

In the n-asset case, the proportion of the risk contributed by an individual stock j can be measured by $x_j \cdot \sigma_{jp}/\sigma_p^2$ (where $\sigma_p^2 = \sigma_{pp}$), i.e., the proportion invested in the stock times its relative covariance with the portfolio. The total proportion of risk accounted for by all stocks in the portfolio must equal 1.0. If the ratio σ_{jp}/σ_p^2 is greater than 1, the return on stock j is unusually sensitive to changes in the average portfolio rate of return. A marginal increase in our holding of that stock will, therefore, increase portfolio risk. Suppose that our portfolio is the so-called *market portfolio* or the average portfolio held by all investors. For the market portfolio the variance is σ_M^2 or in matrix notation σ_{MM}. For any asset j, the relative contribution to market portfolio variance is called asset j's beta value. In this case,

$$\text{beta}_j = \beta_j = \frac{\text{cov}(R_j, R_M)}{\sigma_M^2} = \frac{\sigma_{jM}}{\sigma_{MM}} \qquad (\text{II.6})$$

where M refers to the market portfolio. Beta is a measure of a stock's relative marginal contribution to the risk of the market portfolio. Stocks with beta greater than 1 have an above-average impact on market risk and stocks with beta less than 1 have a below-average impact. As mentioned market risk is sometimes called systematic or non-diversifiable risk.

When the market portfolio is truly international then market risk depends on factors that influence all securities' rates of return across all countries. On the other hand, if security markets are segmented and each country has its own market portfolio, then market risk depends only on national factors. The business cycle in a country may be such a national factor. If business cycles are not coordinated across countries, then an international portfolio could reduce portfolio variance, since the international market portfolio would be subject only to the global average of national business cycles.

Investors may also have the possibility of lending and borrowing at a risk-free rate of interest. The most efficient combinations of risk and return are no longer restricted to the curved surface in Figure II.2 in this case. Instead, the risk-free alternative can be combined with a particular portfolio of risky securities, represented by the point M in Figure II.2, to reach portfolios along the line from $R_{\text{risk-free}}$ through M. The implication of the existence of a risk-free asset/liability is that the investor may first select the 'best' portfolio combination of common stocks at M and then determine the *size* of this portfolio by borrowing or lending so as to obtain the desired risk-return *combination*. This addition to the principles of Markowitz was pointed out by Tobin (1958). The portfolio at M becomes the market portfolio.

Further work on optimal portfolio composition was done in the 1960s by Lintner (1965), Mossin (1966), Sharpe (1964), and Treynor (1965) who developed the ideas behind the *Capital Asset Pricing Model* (CAPM), a widely used model for the pricing of risk. CAPM has the advantage of being simple and intuitively appealing. The basic idea is that in a competitive market, the expected risk premium, i.e., the required expected return in excess of the risk-free rate, varies in direct proportion to beta. We can now recognize the beta from our discussion above and write the expected risk premium for asset j as follows:

$$E[R_j] - R_F = \beta_j(E[R_M] - R_F) \qquad \text{(II.7)}$$

where R_F is the risk-free rate and R_M is the market portfolio rate of return.

For illustration, assume the risk-free rate is 7 percent, the average market rate of return is 15 percent and β_j for a particular security is 1.75. Then, in equilibrium, the expected rate of return on security j is $7 + 1.75 (15-7) = 21$ percent.

Finally, it is important to note that in the CAPM investors do not receive a risk premium for bearing a firm's unique or unsystematic risk. The reason is that such risk can be diversified away. Market risk, on the other hand, cannot be diversified away and each asset would be priced such that investors are compensated for its contribution to market risk.

A further advancement to modelling asset pricing is the Arbitrage Pricing Theory (APT) developed by Ross (1976). According to this theory the risk-premium is determined by unanticipated fluctuations in a number of factors in the firm's environment. A coefficient for each factor's influence on the firm's rate of return can be estimated. In the CAPM, there is only one factor: the market rate of return.

A factor in the APT may be any economic variable that influences firms' rates of return to some degree. The coefficient captures the covariance between the factor and the rate of return. In the following chapters we will employ a methodology similar to the APT to determine the exposure of a firm to macroeconomic disturbances.

II.4 STAKEHOLDERS AND FIRMS' RISK-ATTITUDE

Risk-averse stockholders prefer a diversified portfolio of securities in order to reduce risk of different kinds. This does not imply that *firms* should diversify their holdings of contracts with different currency and country risk. The reason is that in efficient capital markets, corporate diversification is redundant, since individual investors can diversify risk themselves. The key to this argument is that in efficient markets, by definition, investors do not face higher transaction and information costs than corporations.

Since investors can gain access to financial markets in many countries through, for example, investments in mutual funds it is probably realistic to assume that costs of diversification for individual investors are not generally higher than for firms. Thus, if *stockholders* were the only stakeholders in firms and markets were completely efficient, then firms would not have to be concerned about risk in their decisions. Instead they would focus on maximizing the expected return on investments. Firms' contribution to portfolio risk of stockholders would nevertheless enter their investment decision through the discount rate that is applied to projects of different kinds. The discount rate (the required rate of return on investments) would depend on the risk-premium that stockholders demand on projects of different kinds. In the CAPM this risk premium is described as in equation II.7, and the discount rate to be applied on the project would be the risk-free interest rate plus the project risk-premium, which would depend on the project's beta-coefficient.

The above argument for firms not concerning themselves with risk-diversification in business decisions has been used to argue further that firms should be risk-neutral when choosing among, for example, assets and liabilities in different currency-denominations. By a risk-neutral attitude then, we mean that a firm always chooses the asset (liability) with the highest (lowest) expected return (interest cost), and that it does not consider the variance of the return (cost) in its decisions. This definition is somewhat misleading, however, since it could imply that firms observing speculative or arbitrage opportunities would take advantage of them. But, if firms would get involved in such activities, their betas would no longer be constant from stockholders' point of view. Therefore, if shareholders were not perfectly informed about firms' speculative and arbitrage activities they could not obtain their desired diversification of different kinds of risk in financial markets.

Efficiency of capital markets implies only that firms disregard risk in decision *directly related* to their area of business. They would not, however, get involved in speculative or arbitrage activities. For example, they would not borrow in one currency to invest in another purely to take advantage of an expected return differential.

In the following we define as *risk-neutral* a firm which maximizes its profits, cash flows, value, or any other target-variable in decisions within its normal area of business. If shareholders are the only stakeholders, the risk–neutral firm maximizes the market value of equity. The *risk-averse* firm, on the other hand, considers also the variance of its target variable.

On what grounds would firms be risk-averse and try to reduce the variance of, say, cash flows or market value? To answer this question we consider other stakeholders in firms. *Holders of the firm's debt* in the form of bonds and bank loans are one group of stakeholders. It is now widely recognized among financial theorists that if the costs of defaulting in the form of explicit bankruptcy costs and constraints on the use of assets are substantial, then rate of return variance should be a management concern even if it is the shareholders' interests which are ultimately in the managers' minds. The reason is that this variance could be related to the probability of default and, therefore, the probability that debt- and stockholders will suffer the direct costs associated with, for example, bankruptcy proceedings (see Dufey and Srinivasulu, 1983).

Another important group of stakeholders is the *employees*. Individuals often put a value on earnings stability and especially job security. Accordingly, direct costs may be associated with unanticipated fluctuations in a firm's output level. A stable and predictable output level simplifies personnel planning as well. Fluctuations in a firm's optimal output level due to changes in sales price, demand or direct costs could, accordingly induce it to take action that reduces the impact on output of these fluctuations. In the case where adjustment costs are extremely high, the firm may keep output constant at the cost of lost customers or excessive inventories. In some cases a firm may avoid markets with large demand fluctuations if there are competitors with lower adjustment costs. In general, the higher the costs of adjusting output, the more we would expect the firm to behave in a risk-averse manner in markets where there is substantial uncertainty about market conditions. Risk-averse behaviour could take the form of a preference for long-term contracts fixing price and/or quantity or a lower production level to avoid inventory costs (see, e.g., Shapiro and Titman, 1984). The exact form of risk-averse behaviour may differ among firms. It suffices here to establish that labour-related costs may induce the firm to avoid fluctuations in output and employment.

Relations to *customers* and *suppliers* could analogously induce risk-averse behaviour with respect to the firm's commercial operations. In these cases the value of the firm to shareholders increases by a reduction in uncertainty about the firm's optimal *output* levels, since cost savings are associated with less output fluctuation. However, reducing uncertainty about the future *value* of many financial assets and liabilities would not necessarily be in the shareholders' interest.

Government authorities may also be considered stakeholders. Authorities depend on corporate taxes and have a stake in their stability. Furthermore, the propensity of a government to deliver beneficial transfers and services to firms could be seen as a function of employees' satisfaction with the company as expressed politically through powerful labour organizations.

The final, but certainly not the least important, group of stakeholders is the *management* of the firm. As is well-known in the so-called principal-agent literature, managers' objectives are not always in line with shareholders' objectives. Managers are often evaluated in a short-term perspective based on available information in the firm. Long-term considerations cannot be afforded by the manager if, for example, available accounting information refers only to the most recent decisions. Hence, he or she wants performance to look as good as possible in the short run. There may also be a bias in the firm's evaluation process against decisions that could look unfavourable in the short run even if there is equal chance of a favourable outcome. Ex post losses may cause higher personal costs to a manager than the benefits associated with ex post favourable outcomes.

These internal reasons for risk-averse behaviour by managers are not valid economic reasons for such behaviour as are default costs and employee-related adjustment costs. Rather, it is induced by imperfect information and evaluation systems within the firm. We will return to the importance of such systems in Chapter VII, where we discuss their role in designing an exposure management strategy that is consistent with the firm's overall objectives.

In most of this book we take the widely accepted view that firms behave in a risk-averse manner with respect to cash flows and/or market value, but we discuss also the cases where the firm is risk-neutral, and when risk-aversion is limited to the interest of employees.

III

MANAGING CORPORATE MACROECONOMIC EXPOSURE—A REVIEW OF CURRENT APPROACHES

III.1 INTRODUCTION

In Chapter II we demonstrated how risk and opportunities can be defined based on economic and financial theory, and that there are reasons for a firm's management to be concerned about variance in cash flows, value and/or output. The complexity of the task of measuring and managing risks in the international monetary system has generally been met by relatively simple rules. In this chapter we survey the most frequently used approaches to exposure management and offer our own interpretations and criticism. The reviewed approaches are all *partial* in the sense that they deal with one type of risk independent of others. In particular, foreign exchange rate risk has received substantial attention by both practitioners and academics.

The emphasis on exchange rate risk can perhaps be explained by the relatively recent breakdown of the fixed exchange rate system under which this risk was clearly associated with large discretionary adjustment of pegged rates. During this period most central banks followed a policy of pegging the interest rate. This policy continued even under the flexible exchange rate system at least until the mid-1970s, when a few central banks started to follow money supply rules and interest rate variability became more prominent. Price level variability, similarly, did not receive substantial attention in most countries until after the oil price shock.

After more than a decade of more or less flexible exchange rates the limitations of traditional partial approaches to exchange rate management have become obvious as we argued in Chapter I. Today managers are better educated to handle exposure of different kinds and new approaches to exposure management are developing which make use of recent improvements in computer support. This enables firms to be more ambitious in their management of exchange rate exposure. However, as we shall see, even the most recent approaches are partial.

There are still reasons to take seriously the traditional approaches presented in this chapter. It is possible that after a comprehensive evaluation of risk a partial approach will be found sufficient for a particular firm. However, such a decision should be based on deliberate exclusion of certain factors from exposure analysis based on knowledge about the relative importance of these factors. We return to these issues in Chapters IV and V.

Section 2 contains a description of current practices of measuring exchange rate exposure. Then in Section 3 we describe briefly current management practices and recent developments in exchange rate exposure management. Practices in dealing with financial—primarily interest rate—and country risks are reviewed in Sections 4 and 5, respectively. Finally, drawbacks of using a partial approach are discussed in Section 6.

III.2 CURRENT EXCHANGE RATE EXPOSURE MEASUREMENT PRACTICES

Three common measures of exchange rate exposure are (a) transaction exposure, (b) translation exposure, and (c) approximations of economic exposure. After describing each of these measures we discuss the relationship among them. We also devote one subsection to recently developed exchange risk measures. These are more consistent with financial theory since they utilize variance as a measure of risk.

III.2.a   Transaction Exposure

This type of exposure refers to uncertainty about the domestic currency value of a specific future cash flow in a foreign currency. Transaction exposure, therefore, refers to uncertainty about cash profits due to unanticipated exchange rate fluctuations.

The exposure of a strictly home-based company that contracts a loan on the international capital market is easily understood. Similarly, the importing company is exposed to exchange risk when it is invoiced in the supplier's currency, and an exporter is exposed when a delivery must be paid for at a later date in a currency other than the domestic currency. In all three cases we know which party is exposed to exchange rate uncertainty, and the strength and duration of the exposure can be measured fairly easily.

It is more difficult to determine the exposure to exchange rate risk of a company which has extensive international operations, or one which, over and above its export and import activities, possesses overseas assets not normally intended to be transferred, as well as debts in a number of currencies. Thus the multinational company has additional risk to consider apart from the risk facing domestic companies whose international activities are limited to exporting and importing.

Most often the concept of transaction exposure is reserved for *contracted* flows in foreign currencies. This limitation is obviously not necessary, but taking non-contracted cash flows into account demands a substantially larger information base. A consequence of this limitation is that transaction exposure usually takes only a small fraction of the exposure of a firm's commercial operations into account but emphasizes *financial commitments in foreign currencies*. Some future commercial cash flows can naturally be contracted for in money terms in advance of delivery of goods, and it is possible that financial flows are not definitely contracted for in money terms at the time a loan is taken. Nevertheless, as a rough approximation, financial flows are *contractual flows* while most commercial flows are *non-contractual*. Often, an expected cash flow is initially a non-contractual expected sale or purchase, which at the date of delivery becomes a contractual financial flow in the form of accounts payable or receivable. A simple example of how to measure transaction exposure is provided in Table III.1. As is often the case, transaction exposure is here limited to contractual flows.

Table III.1   Measuring transaction exposure in a foreign currency (FC)

	Quarter			
	I	II	III	IV
Accounts receivables from exports	40	50	60	30
Accounts payable for imports	−20	−30	−30	−30
Foreign interest payments (net)	−10	−10	−10	−10
Amortization of foreign debt (net)	0	0	−50	0
Net exposure before covering	10	10	−30	−10
Sale or purchase of foreign currency in forward markets	−10	−10	20	0
Net exposure	FC 0	FC 0	FC−10	FC−10

Net exposure before covering is estimated in the given currency
denominations of contracts. Thereafter, the desired exposure must
be decided on before offsetting covers can be undertaken by entering,
for example, forward market contracts. In the case of transaction
exposure for contractual flows, nearly exact *covers* can be obtained
by entering forward contracts when the exact day on which each
cash flow will occur is known. (There is always a credit risk
associated with accounts receivable.) If more extended definitions of
transaction exposure are used, including non-contractual commercial
flows, then exact covers cannot be obtained but the cover decision
must be based on expectations of cash flows. The distinction between
contractual and non-contractual flows may be somewhat vague. We
include in our definition of non-contractual flows those that are
expected in the future for which no commitments have been made,
as well as those for which commitments have been made but the
price or volume remains undetermined.

III.2.b   Translation Exposure

Translation exposure is most often an accounting concept, though
one could theoretically define a corresponding economic concept.

We discuss the relationship between accounting-based and economic exposure in Section III.2.d. Accounting translation exposure in a particular currency (often called simply accounting exposure) may be defined as the *net balance sheet position* in a foreign currency. Since translation gains are estimated over reporting periods, exposure is often measured as a period average. Furthermore, a firm's translation exposure in a particular currency refers usually to the *consolidated* balance sheet of a multinational corporation in quarterly or annual reports to stockholders.

Translation exposure can be seen as a measure of a *latent risk*. In the short term, translation gains or losses on exposure have no cash flow effects, i.e., they are *not realized* over the reporting period. Cash flow gains or losses occur, however, if the firm is liquidated, or they will occur in the future when assets and liabilities produce cash flows. Thus, ideally, translation exposure should capture the sensitivity of economic value, in the form of either liquidation value or the present value of future cash flows, to exchange rate changes.

It is not easy to evaluate the different methods of calculating translation exposure since many conflicting elements enter the analysis as we shall see below. It is possible that exposure cannot be determined satisfactorily by one method; a combination of methods may be needed, or at least a method may have to be adapted to a particular country or industry. Developments in accounting seem to be moving in that direction. Perhaps it is even time to question the validity of the whole idea of 'consolidated' accounts and of their purpose, as formulated in the following definition, for instance:

> The purpose of consolidated statements is to present, primarily for the benefit of the shareholders and creditors of the parent company, the results of operations and the financial position of the parent company and its subsidiaries essentially as if the group were a single company with one or more branches or division.
> (Accounting Research Bulletin, No. 51, Financial Accounting Standards Board, 1975)

Table III.2 shows different translation rules in use internationally. All items are translated either at the *current rate* on the translation

Table III.2 Balance sheet translation rules

	Current/non-current	All-current (closing rate)	Monetary/non-monetary	Temporal
Asset:				
Cash	C	C	C	C
Securities				
–historical cost	C	C	C	H
–market price	C	C	C	C
Receivables				
–current	C	C	C	C
–long-term	H	C	C	C
Inventory				
–historical cost	C	C	H	H
–market price	C	C	H	C
Fixed assets	H	C	H	H
Liabilities:				
Current payables	C	C	C	C
Long-term debt	H	C	C	C
Equity★	Residual	Residual	Residual	Residual

C: Translated at current exchange rate.
H: Translated at historical exchange rate.
★ Includes the translation gain or loss.
Source: Oxelheim (1985).

date or *the historical rate* on the day an asset or liability was acquired. We will first describe different methods of translation and thereafter compare the resulting exposure with economic exposure. However, the purpose of a translation method may not be to obtain a measure of economic value or economic exposure. We return to this discussion below. The most common translation methods in use internationally are the monetary/non-monetary method, the current method, and the current/non-current method.

Under the *monetary/non-monetary method*, monetary balance-sheet items (cash, bankholdings, and most claims and debts) are translated at the rate pertaining on the closing date. Non-monetary balance-sheet items (inventories, machines, real estate) are translated at the historical rate, that is, the rate applying when an asset was acquired. On the income statement, earnings items are translated at the rate on the transaction date. The average rate for the year can be used as an approximation. For depreciation the same rate is used for the translation as for the asset in question. The monetary/non-monetary method can be regarded as compatible with accounting based on the historical cost concept. Therefore, the method is approximately equal to the temporal rate method in the United States. There, in line with the recommendation of FASB (Financial Accounting Standards Board) Statement No. 8, the temporal method was used until 1982 and is still in use under certain circumstances after FASB 52 was substituted for FASB 8. We return to the contents of the more recent rule below.

The temporal method (the monetary/non-monetary method in the US) has been criticized for the possibility of error that arises because physical assets and inventories are evaluated at historical rates, while other items such as the long-term debts contracted in order to finance these acquisitions are translated at the rate on the closing date.

According to the monetary/non-monetary method only monetary items are regarded as subject to exchange rate exposure. Under the *current method*, on the other hand, the complete net asset position in foreign currency is exposed. This method is sometimes referred to as the closing-rate method since all assets and liabilities on the balance sheets of foreign subsidiaries are translated at the rate pertaining at the closing of the accounts. During the 1970s the current method has been the most common translation method in the UK. In the UK companies are able to choose which translation method they prefer, though since 1977 the choice has been limited by law to the current method and the monetary/non-monetary method. The most recent recommendation in the UK is similar to the method implemented in the US under FASB 52. In accordance with these recommendations, companies translate all assets and liabilities at current, rather than historical, rates.

According to the third method—the *current/non-current method*—current assets and short-term debt on the balance sheets of foreign subsidiaries are translated at the closing rate, while fixed assets and long-term debt are translated at historical rates. This latter characteristic of the current/non-current method has given rise to a good deal of criticism, since long-term debt is subject to exchange rate changes to the same extent as short-term claims and debts, according to some observers. The method is sometimes referred to as the working-capital method.

It can be noted that the monetary/non-monetary method always yields a more positive result than the current method in any year during which a foreign currency has been devalued. In the years immediately following, the reverse will apply, since the method only affects the distribution over time, and the total effect of exchange rate changes over time is the same regardless of which method is used.

In many countries it has been recommended, and under FASB 52 it is the rule, that all claims and debts in foreign currencies are evaluated at the closing rate, while exchange gains and losses are in general deferred. Such a procedure is an answer to some of the criticism of FASB 8 that evaluation at the closing rate without any possibility of apportionment to different periods can give rise to unacceptable fluctuations in results from year to year, which in turn can give the company's stakeholders an incorrect picture of the real trends.

Appendix III.1 contains an example illustrating the major differences between FASB 8 and FASB 52. The first and older method is, as we noted, similar to the monetary/non-monetary method, while the second method is a current method in most cases. However, when applying FASB 52 there can be a choice of 'functional' currency for a foreign subsidiary. For example, if the subsidiary operates in a hyperinflationary environment, or most of its transactions are dollar-denominated, then the US parent may choose to use dollars as the subsidiary's functional currency. In this case there is a translation problem only for the subsidiary. Since according to FASB 52 the subsidiary should use the temporal method to translate into the functional currency, FASB 52 becomes similar to FASB 8 in the consolidated dollar statement when the dollar is the subsidiary's functional currency.

There are additional differences between the two methods. In particular, translation gains or losses do not, as the main rule, appear on the consolidated income statement but go to a special reserve account under FASB 52, while under FASB 8 translation gains or losses appear both as parts of net consolidated income *and* the change in owners' equity. Under FASB 52 these unrealized gains or losses appear only as changes in owners' equity.

The reserve account procedure is clearly sensible when the exchange rate fluctuates around a constant value, since then translation gains or losses will never be realized. However, if there is a trend in the exchange rate, or for a country with hyperinflation, or if it changes permanently, then it may be sensible to account for expected future cash flow effects in the income statement at the time the exchange rate changes as under FASB 8.

The example of translation exposure worked out in Appendix III.1 demonstrates that translation gains, net income, and changes in owners' equity are very sensitive to the choice of translation method. One may therefore wonder if any one particular method captures the firm's true economic exposure to a larger extent than the others. If no method captures economic exposure, one may wonder what value translation methods have since the choice of method does not influence tax payments or other cash flows in any way. Most countries, including the US, tax income from foreign subsidiaries at the time dividends are remitted and the rules for taxation of foreign source income are independent of the accounting translation rule chosen. We return to the issue of the relevance of accounting methods after discussing economic exposure next. In Section 4 of this chapter we will also discuss methods of hedging translation exposure.

III.2.c   Economic Exposure

The idea of economic exchange rate exposure is to obtain an estimate of the *sensitivity of a firm's economic value to changes in exchange rates*. The economic value depends on the expected ability of the firm to produce cash flows in the future. The final effect of an exchange rate change obviously cannot be known until time has elapsed, but at the time a disturbance occurs, managers, shareholders, and other stakeholders should have some more or less explicit judgment of its impact on the firm.

Measures of economic exposure will be discussed in detail in the following chapters, but we may note here that ideally exchange rate exposure should be evaluated in terms of exchange rate effects on the present value of future cash flows. Lessard (1979), Wihlborg (1980a), Oxelheim (1981), and Glick (1986) as well as major textbooks on international business management by Aliber (1978), Eiteman and Stonehill (1982), Feiger and Jacquillat (1982), Jacque (1978), Levi (1983), Prindle (1976), Ricks (1978), Rodriguez and Carter (1976), and Shapiro (1983) agree on this point but execute the concept in different ways. Many firms seem to have some concept of economic exposure in the form of an adjusted accounting translation method. For example, a firm may consider its inventory exposed, but not its plant and equipment. In this case it would measure economic exposure as under FASB 8, but its inventory in foreign subsidiaries is added to the FASB 8 exposure. This method of measuring exposure for a particular balance sheet position has the drawback that it implicitly implies that a certain exchange rate change has the same effect on the values of all exposed assets and liabilities while, in fact, the sensitivity of value varies among assets and liabilities.

Table III.3 Characteristics of foreign exchange exposure

Type Characteristics	Translation exposure	Transaction exposure	Economic exposure
Latent or active	Latent	Active	Active
Static or dynamic	Static	Static	Dynamic
Goal orientation	Book value	Economic/book value	Economic value
Focus	Assets/debts	Cash flow	Cash flow/value
Period	Limited	Limited	Unlimited
Data base	Book items (plus estimated items from forecast)	Book items (in its broader definition also including estimated items from forecast)	Book items plus estimated items from forecast taking elasticities into account

Source: Based on Oxelheim (1985).

Table III.3 shows how economic exposure is often viewed in practical exposure management relative to transaction and translation exposures. It can be seen that economic exposure, as well as the other types, is estimated from a data base provided by given accounting systems. We argue in Chapters IV and V that a well-developed economic exposure concept should not be constrained by accounting principles since it should be forward looking.

We can illustrate the economic relevance or irrelevance of accounting based concepts of exchange rate exposure by a few simple examples. In the process, we note that there is a common pitfall in exposure analysis in equating the search for a relevant translation rate (i.e., current, historical or another rate) with the search for a method to evaluate exposure. The choice of a translation rate could be, for example, to obtain a measure of the (accounting) value of foreign assets that is comparable to the (accounting) value of domestic assets. The dollar value so estimated may or may not be a good exposure measure and the value may not correctly reflect the economic value of foreign assets unless those assets also have been correctly evaluated in economic terms.

Levi (1983) and Oxelheim (1983) compare the income statement effects of exchange rate changes under different accounting methods for translation of specific foreign currency items. Their criterion for evaluating the methods is *comparability*—from an economic point of view—of income or cost on a translated income statement with income or cost from a comparable domestic asset or liability. For example, assume that a firm has the choice between borrowing in domestic and foreign currency. The interest cost in domestic currency is 10 percent while the interest cost in foreign currency is 20 percent, and the expected depreciation of the foreign currency is 10 percent. Over the year, if the exchange rate behaves as expected, the income statement under FASB 8 will include the outright interest cost as well as the exchange rate loss. However, if the loan is not paid back within the year, then under FASB 52 a translation gain will appear in owners' equity but *not* on the income statement.

Which method is superior from an economic point of view? This depends on whether the exchange rate change is expected to be *permanent* or *transitory*. If the change is expected to be permanent then FASB 8 provides a good effective interest cost comparison, while if the change is expected to be reversed before payment of the loan, then the income statement under FASB 52 provides a better effective cost comparison.

Assume next that plant and equipment with similar capabilities are located in different countries and that the firm uses historical cost accounting at home. In this case an exchange rate change has no effect on the income statement regardless of whether FASB 8 or FASB 52 is used. In the first case the historical exchange rate is used for translation, so no translation gains or losses occur. Under FASB 52 translation effects occur, but they appear only in a reserve account and in owners' equity. Does the relative dollar value of the equipment located in different countries change with the exchange rate? Assume first that the exchange rate change corresponds to domestic inflation. Historical cost accounting will then lead to a false (underestimated) dollar value of the plant and equipment when it is located at home. A comparable underestimation of the dollar value of the foreign equipment occurs if translation is done with the historical exchange rate (as under FASB 8). If, instead, the current exchange rate is used (as under FASB 52), the dollar value of the foreign equipment is better estimated but the value of the foreign equipment *relative to* domestic equipment is overestimated.

On the other hand, if the exchange rate change is real so that the purchasing power of foreign currency increases, then there may be a real gain in having the equipment earning cash flows in the foreign currency. Specifically, if the exchange rate is expected to be permanent, the relative value of foreign equipment changes with the exchange rate. Accordingly, the balance sheet under FASB 52 provides a better estimate of the relative dollar values even with historical cost accounting, though the income statement will not reflect the value changes until gains are realized.

When analysing economic value and changes therein it is convenient to use a present value formula:

$$PV_0^{US} = E_0 \left[\frac{X_1^{US}}{(1 - d) P_1^{US}} + \ldots + \frac{X_n^{US}}{(1+d)^n P_n^{US}} \right] \qquad (III.1)$$

where:

E = expectations operator; subscripts refer to time period; superscripts refer to country (currency in which valuation occurs)

X = a cash flow

d = the (real) discount rate

P = the price level

US   = shareholders' country of residence.

The effect on the present value in dollars (PV_0^{US}) of exchange rate changes will now depend on the following factors:

i.   The type of cash flows.

ii. The nature of exchange rate changes.

iii. The timing of cash flow remittances.

iv. The expected degree of permanence of exchange rate changes.

We will discuss these factors one by one in order to better understand *economic (exchange rate) exposure, which can be defined as* $\hat{P}V_0^{US}/\hat{e}_0$, *i.e., the change in the US value of the firm of an (unanticipated) exchange rate change.*

i The type of cash flows in any period From monetary assets or liabilities payable in foreign currency there is a fixed foreign currency cash flow ($\overline{X}^{FC}$) each period. On the other hand, production from given real assets tends to increase in value with foreign inflation, so that in period t the foreign currency cash flow is $X_0^{FC} \cdot P_t^{FC}$, that is, the initial cash flow in foreign currency multiplied by the price level in period t (assuming the initial price level is one).

ii The nature of exchange rate changes In general, an exchange rate can be written as $e_t \equiv (P_t^{US}/P_t^{FC}) \cdot u_t$ for period t where u_t is the real exchange rate or deviation from Purchasing Power Parity (PPP).

Using this expression and equation III.1, the value of a foreign currency *monetary asset* (M) or liability can be written as:

$$PV_0^{US}(M) = E_0\left[\frac{\overline{X}^{FC} \cdot e_1}{(1+d)P_1^{US}} + \dots + \frac{\overline{X}^{FC} \cdot e_n}{(1+d)^n P_n^{US}}\right] \quad \text{(III.2)}$$

or

$$PV_0^{US}(M) = \overline{X}^{FC} \cdot E_0\left[\frac{u_1}{(1+d)P_1^{FC}} + \dots + \frac{u_n}{(1+d)^n P_n^{FC}}\right] \quad \text{(III.3)}$$

Monetary assets are exposed to real exchange rate changes and changes in the price level in the currency of denomination. Their values are independent of domestic inflation, unless real exchange rates and price levels are correlated.

The value of *physical assets* (Ph) can be written as:

$$PV_0^{US}(Ph) = E_0\left[\frac{X_0^{FC} \cdot P_1^{FC} \cdot e_1}{(1+d)P_1^{US}} + \dots + \frac{X_0^{FC} \cdot P_n^{FC} e_n}{(1+d)^n P_n^{US}}\right] \quad \text{(III.4)}$$

or

$$PV_0^{US}(Ph) = X_0^{FC} \cdot E_0\left[\frac{u_1}{(1+d)} + \dots + \frac{u_n}{(1+d)^n}\right], \quad \text{(III.5)}$$

assuming the volume of cash flows from the real assets are known. (We relax this assumption in later chapters.)

The values of real assets depend here only on expected real exchange rate changes.

iii The timing of cash flow remittances

The above expressions are written as if cash flows were exchanged into US dollars every period. Assume instead that there is great flexibility in the timing of remittances *and* that the firm will be able to evaluate whether it is a good or bad time to remit, i.e., that the firm has some forecast ability with respect to real exchange rate changes. It is not able to forecast at time 0 the exact dates and rates at which remittances will occur, however. In that case we could value the cash flows in equation III.5 at a relatively favourable average real exchange rate. Exposure to unanticipated exchange rate changes would clearly be smaller since the variance of real exchange rates evaluated at time zero exaggerates the variance of the dollar value of future cash flows.

A more general approach to expressing the present value of a foreign subsidiary would be to multiply the present value of the subsidiary in foreign currency with an estimated translation rate (e_T), which represents a weighted discounted sum of future expected exchange rates at times remittances actually take place. For example, the value of a foreign currency monetary asset can be expressed in the following way:

$$PV_0^{US}(M) = e_{T,0}\bar{X}^{FC}E_0\left[\frac{1}{(1+d)P_1^{FC}} + \ldots + \frac{1}{(1+d)^nP_n^{FC}}\right] \quad \text{(III.6)}$$

The value of a foreign subsidiary as a whole may be expressed as

$$PV_0^{US}(\text{subsidiary}) = e_{T,0} \cdot PV_0^{FC}(\text{subsidiary}). \quad \text{(III.7)}$$

The translation rate $e_{T,0}$ is evaluated at time zero and depends on the expected timing of remittances, and on the ability of the firm to forecast and avoid periods of unfavourable exchange rates. Using expressions III.6 and III.7 it becomes clear that the subsidiary's exposure depends on two factors. First, it depends on the exposure of the subsidiary evaluated as any foreign company.

Second, it depends on the sensitivity of the rate $e_{T,0}$, the average translation rate, to changes in the current exchange rate e_0. In other words, exposure to current exchange rate changes depends on $\hat{e}_{T,0}/\hat{e}_0$. To analyse this sensitivity further, we must examine the expected degree of permanence of exchange rate changes.

iv **The expected degree of permanence of exchange rate changes** Assume first that the foreign subsidiary is to be sold in the near future. Then it is clear that the translation rate $\hat{e}_{T,0}$ is almost equal to the current exchange rate e_0 (i.e., $\hat{e}_{T,0}/\hat{e}_0 = 1$). In other words, the dollar value of the firm changes in proportion to the current exchange rate. The exposure based on current-rate accounting is essentially a 'liquidation value exposure' in this sense.

Even if the subsidiary is not going to be sold, but there is an expected *permanent* exchange rate change (or at least a change expected to remain for the lifetime of the asset) then $E_0[\hat{e}_1]/\hat{e}_0 = \ldots = E_0[\hat{e}_n]/\hat{e}_0 = \hat{e}_{T,0}/\hat{e} = 1$.

On the other hand, if there is an expected *temporary* exchange rate change so that $E_0[\hat{e}_1]/\hat{e}_0 = 1$, but $E_0[\hat{e}_2]/\hat{e}_0 = \ldots = E_0[\hat{e}_n]/\hat{e}_0 = 0$, *and* remittances will occur over all future periods, then there is little reason to change the translation rate (i.e., $\hat{e}_{T,0}/\hat{e}_0 \approx 0$), since only a small part of remittances are expected at the rate existing on the valuation date.

We expect real exchange rate changes to be less permanent than changes in price levels, since goods markets over time tend to return towards PPP (see Appendix III.2). The extent to which shareholders should be considered seriously exposed to exchange rate changes would accordingly depend on the length of time needed to restore PPP, the forecastability of deviations from PPP, and the degree of flexibility of remittances. In other words, the exposure of these subsidiaries may well be approximated by the exposure of an identical corporation owned by shareholders in the host country under some circumstances.

The choice of an exchange rate at which to translate is equivalent to the search for $e_{T,0}$ above, *if* the purpose of translation is to express the economic value of the firm. Oxelheim (1981) and Wihlborg (1980a) argue that if the exchange rate tends to fluctuate around purchasing power parity, an estimated exchange rate consistent with PPP could be a convenient translation rate for assets and liabilities held by foreign subsidiaries as well as for the income statement. Alternatively, Oxelheim (1983) suggests that the translation rate at the end of a period is set so that the exchange rate change for translation purposes is equal to the interest rate differential at the beginning of the period. In efficient markets this rate is an approximation for the expected rate. If a forward market exists for the currency, then the forward rate observed at the beginning of the period could be used for translation purposes. In either case, only unexpected gains and losses are deferred until the time cash flows occur, while the income statement and the balance sheet reflect expected gains and losses.

III.2.d The Purpose of Accounting Rules and the Relationships Among Exposure Measures

In the above analysis of economic exposure we demonstrated that translation exposure based on any of the existing accounting rules cannot capture economic exposure consistently. It may be unfair, however, to ask this of an accounting rule. Such a rule should be designed to inform stockholders and financial markets about the impact of exchange rate changes on the firm's value. However, economic value depends on expectations, which may differ among individuals. Thus, the purpose of a rule could simply be to provide the best possible information to market participants. Different individuals may then form their own judgments and expectations about the impact of exchange rate changes on a firm.

We cannot go into all the facets of how to provide financial markets with information here, but the necessity that any rule be clearly understood and its objective clearly defined is obvious. For example, the objective may be to capture changes in the value of exchange rates in the parent company's currency. Such value changes differ from *real* value changes for shareholders, however, since inflation must be taken into account to determine real values, and the consumption bundle differs among shareholders, especially when they reside in different countries. A translation rule could never take all such real value changes into account, but if shareholders can interpret the data given in nominal terms, then individuals may determine exposure themselves.

Another possible objective of accounting rules may be to make changes in income and/or changes in owners' equity comparable among subsidiaries in different countries. In this case, translation rules should perhaps not capture economic value, since accounting principles used for each subsidiary in their respective currencies do not. Instead, translation rules should be made consistent with other accounting principles.

From an information signalling point of view the all current method could be superior to other methods since it is very simple and market participants can more easily infer from the income statement and the balance sheet in domestic currency what the firm's position is in foreign currencies. With the temporal method, on the other hand, the information content of the translated balance sheet is less since different items are translated at different rates.

Ultimately, the actual choice of translation rule may not be very important for market valuation when market participants learn to understand it and learn to extract information from it. Then market participants can reinterpret the accounting data themselves and form their own valuation. Empirical evidence is contradictory on this point, however.

In addition to the relationship between accounting (translation) and economic value, it is important to understand the relationship between transaction exposure on the one hand, and economic and translation exposures on the other. Are, for example, transaction and translation exposures complementary or substitutes? Can they be added together to obtain a measure of economic exposure? These issues can be discussed by considering the differences between locking in dollar values of transactions, accounting values, and economic values, respectively. In Section III.3 we discuss how such operations are done.

To an important extent the answers to the above questions depend on whether translation exposure is viewed as a measure of the value of the expected foreign currency position. Equation III.2 shows that economic value consists of the present value of a number of cash flows through time. Economic *exposure* is more properly a sensitivity measure for the economic value. In Figure III.1 we define *transaction exposure* in the conventional way as the cash flows in foreign currency in each period. The *translation exposure* here is the foreign currency present value of cash flows, while *economic exposure* is defined as the sensitivity of the dollar value of the firm to an exchange rate change during a period. Economic exposure defined this way can take into account that a near-term change may or may not be expected to be permanent.

Figure III.1   Exposures of value and cash flows at time 0

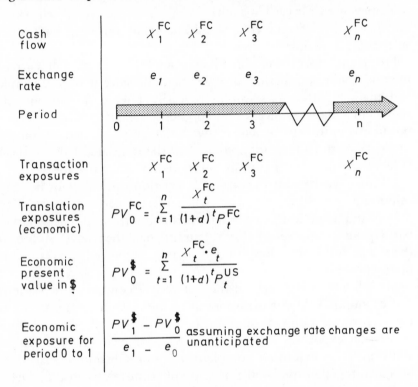

To an extent there is substitutability between transaction and translation exposure. The firm that locks in the dollar value of all future transactions $(X_1, \ldots, X_n)$ is obviously not economically exposed to exchange rate changes at all. Reducing *translation* exposure to zero for one period by locking in the dollar value in one period of the foreign currency value of the firm may overprotect against economic exposure. The reason is that exchange rate changes are sometimes perceived to be temporary in which case the present value in dollars of all future cash flows does not change in proportion to the exchange rate. However, if all exchange rate changes are expected to be permanent (if, for example, the exchange rate follows a random walk), then reducing translation exposure in Figure III.1 to zero is equivalent to reducing economic exposure to zero. In this case, economic exposure can be reduced to zero *either* by locking in the dollar value of all transactions $(X_1, \ldots, X_n)$ or by consecutively eliminating translation exposure one period at a time. On the other hand, if all exchange rate changes are expected to be temporary (if, for example, there exists a constant long-run equilibrium rate) then eliminating translation exposure (PV_0^{FC}) would in fact cause economic exposure. Partial reduction of translation exposure would instead eliminate economic exposure and serve as a substitute for eliminating transaction exposure.

Let us assume instead that the firm's concern is with accounting value. Even in this case there may be some substitutability between translation and transaction exposure, if accounting principles reflect correctly the transaction exposure for the near future, i.e., if all transaction exposures appear on the balance sheet. Then the firm could evaluate its total accounting exposure as the sum of transaction exposures for the near future (for example, X_1^{FC} in Figure III.1) and the translation exposure *net* of near-term transaction exposures. On the other hand, if the transaction exposure of the firm, as described in Subsection III.2.a does not appear on the balance sheet, then transaction and translation exposures are linked in a more complicated way. For example, it is common that transaction exposures for near-term cash flows are evaluated relative to each subsidiary's home currency, while accounting exposure is always evaluated relative to the parent's currency. Then, eliminating transaction exposure in a foreign subsidiary could increase the accounting exposure of the parent. In general, translation and transaction exposures should not be considered independent if current assets and liabilities are included in the definition of translation exposure.

III.2.e Recent Developments in Measuring Exposure

For practical reasons the textbook procedures for measuring foreign exchange risk are not always followed. The point of departure in practice is the currency position, namely, the company's net claims or net debts in a given currency expressed in its own base currency. But the position only expresses the size of the risk exposure, while the time dimension is ignored. As we mentioned above, economic risk should be linked to the pattern of fluctuation in the relevant exchange rate given the time dimension of claims and liabilities. Nevertheless, working solely with the currency position provides a first indication of the risk dimension in the company, as the position can be compared with such quantities as total corporate foreign exchange flows, turnover, exports, and imports.

The currency position as a useful and practical approximation of exchange rate exposure must be used with discrimination since it does not take into account the magnitude and likelihood of exchange rate changes as expressed by a variance. In practice there are rarely any variance calculations; instead, the exchange risk is often expressed as the probability of the company suffering exchange losses of a certain size. Although symmetry would require it, exchange opportunities are rarely used as a measure of possible exchange gains. As mentioned in Chapter II, foreign exchange risk, as referred to in everyday speech, generally reflects the likelihood that a particular exchange rate movement will occur leading to a loss of a certain size.

There is an element of surprise built into the term 'risk'; it refers to the likelihood and magnitude of unanticipated deviations from forecasts, and these may be positive or negative. Therefore, we would expect that the concepts developed in financial theory and reviewed in Chapter II could form a basis for defining exposure.

In this section we briefly explain an exposure measure suggested by Adler and Dumas (1980), Hodder (1982), and Garner and Shapiro (1984). It is related to the concept of asset risk from the stockholders' point of view, i.e., the beta measuring the contribution of a particular asset's return pattern to portfolio variance. Assuming that a firm is concerned with cash-flow variance or value, exchange risk from a firm's point of view could be defined in an analogous fashion as the contribution of exchange rate fluctuations to a firm's cash flow- or value-variance. Since the value depends on expected cash flows, a suitable starting point is to determine cash flow exposure to exchange rate changes.

The suggested exchange rate exposure measure is defined as the covariance between the exchange rate and the firm's cash flows relative to the variance of total cash flows, i.e.:

$$\text{cash flow exposure} = \frac{\text{cov}[e_t, X_t]}{\text{var}[X_t]} \tag{III.8}$$

This measure can obviously be applied on components of cash flows as well. For example, exchange rate exposure of business operations may be estimated separately from the exposure of financial cash flows. Similarly, different time horizons can be used to measure exposure on a monthly, quarterly or annual basis.

An important advantage of this exposure measure is that it includes *volume* effects as well as *price* effects of exchange rate measures. Volume effects may be very important for exporting firms or firms facing substantial competition from foreign firms.

The above exposure measure would also include cash flow effects due to, say, interest rate changes which often accompany exchange rate adjustment. This may or may not be an advantage depending on whether the firm analyses its financial exposure to interest rate changes independently of exchange rate exposure. We return to this issue in Chapter IV.

A cash flow based exposure measure such as equation III.8 is an economic exposure measure. It is entirely independent of accounting principles, as it should be from the stakeholders' point of view. To obtain a measure of exposure of a firm's economic value, the cash flow measure would have to be combined with knowledge of intertemporal relationships among exchange rates and cash flows.

There are also disadvantages to the measure defined in equation III.8. In particular, we can question if a stable exposure coefficient of this kind exists. This issue is the subject of Chapter IV.

How can we estimate an exposure measure that includes a large number of price and volume effects? The most simple way, suggested by Garner and Shapiro (1984), would be to run a regression on historical data like the following:

$$X_t = a_0 + a_1 e_t + \epsilon_t \qquad (III.9)$$

where a_0 and a_1 would be estimated and ϵ_t is an error term capturing variations in cash flows that are not linearly related to the exchange rate. In equation III.9 the coefficient a_1 is actually the exposure coefficient defined in equation III.8. For example, if $a_1 = 200$, then a one-unit increase in the exchange rate causes a \$200 increase in cash flows. In other words, the exposure coefficient measures cash flow sensitivity to exchange rate changes. Naturally, the variables could be defined in log form in which case we obtain a coefficient that measures an elasticity, namely, the percentage change in cash flows from a one-percent exchange rate change.

Knowledge of a coefficient like a_1 enables the firm to cover exposure through forward markets or in other ways. Given the coefficient, it is easy to calculate the size of the forward contract that would leave cash flows unaffected by exchange rate changes. In Chapter IV we discuss the use of exposure coefficients for purposes of covering and hedging. In the appendix to that chapter we also compare measures of exposure using equation III.9 for actual firms to more refined measures developed in Chapter IV. In that chapter we discuss how a regression to measure exposure should be specified for the exposure coefficients to remain stable over time. Otherwise historical data cannot be used to measure exposure. Instead, judgment of exposure must be based on current information inside the firm.

III.3 AN OVERVIEW OF EXCHANGE RATE MANAGEMENT PRACTICES

Exposure management consists of (a) choosing an exposure measure, (b) defining an operational strategy and organization for handling exposure consistent with the firm's objective, and (c) selecting tools such as forward cover for obtaining a desired exposure. After a brief review of firms' exposure concepts we discuss in Subsection (a) how firms currently deal with transaction exposure. In Subsection (b) translation exposure is discussed and in Subsection (c) we review recent developments in exposure management.

In a study of firm practices Rodriguez (1980) concluded that 'economic exposure has come to mean different things to different people. However, the term is usually identified as a measure reflecting the true impact of exchange fluctuations, in contrast to the "paper impact" of translation exposure.'

Rodriguez discovered, nevertheless, that 86 percent of the companies studied found translation exposure to be the most relevant exposure measure. However, Oxelheim (1984a) in a study of Swedish firms, discovered that almost all companies gave priority to transaction exposure. Many argued that market value stabilization was their objective, though as we shall see in Chapter V this objective and the management of transaction exposure are not always consistent. Doukas (1983) found that a shift occurred among US firms after the introduction of FASB 52, which happened after

Rodriguez's study. His results show that once translation gains and losses were removed from consolidated income with the introduction of FASB 52, only a small percentage of US firms continued to hedge translation exposure.

III.3.a   Current Practices in Managing Transaction Exposure

We turn now to the way exchange risk is often managed at different planning levels in a firm and ways in which companies often handle this perceived risk. The studies referred to make clear that even if market value stabilization is the stated objective, firms usually avoid becoming involved in attempts to estimate economic value and rely on accounting numbers in the form of transaction exposure, translation exposure or both.

Let us assume that transaction exposure is the major concern. Then Figure III.2 may be used to describe the time aspect of an exposed export or import transaction.

Figure III.2   Time aspects of transaction exposure

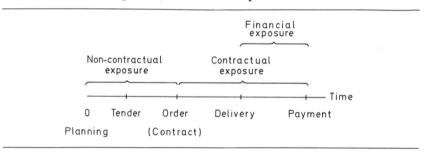

At time 0 planning of exports or imports starts and tenders may be taken after a few months. At this time the firm gets a non-contractual exposure which becomes more probable at the time of tender. At order-time, exposure may shift to a contractual exposure if price is determined at this time. Otherwise, the exposure becomes contractual at delivery when it also changes to become financial.

Assume now that transaction exposures have been determined in different currencies for a multinational corporation. Usually firms with centralized exposure management will then wish to obtain a picture of the total transaction exposures in different currencies.

This exposure could include more or less firm contractual and non-contractual exposures as described in Figure III.2. A matrix, as in Table III.4, may then be created. It shows *cross-border* transactions in all currencies for a particular time period and distinguishes between *intra-company* transactions and *external* transactions. It also distinguishes between receivables (+) and payables (−).

This particular type of transaction exposure matrix presumes that all payables and receivables *within* each country are denominated in the local currency. These claims and liabilities are therefore implicit in the matrix.

Take the US company: among its cross-border transactions $10 are external receivables denominated in dollars, while $5 are intra-company receivables denominated in dollars. We observe that the Swedish and the UK subsidiaries hold the corresponding dollar-denominated intra-company payables. The total *intra-company* position in each currency is by definition zero.

Reading horizontally we have the currency denomination of each subsidiary's cross-border flows. For the US subsidiary the total cross-border position is +29 in dollar equivalents at the forward rate at the time. Thus, there must be a negative intra-country position of $−29 for the US subsidiary. The total foreign currency position of the US subsidiary is 14 since 15 of the total amount 29 in cross-border flows are dollar denominated. Thus the dollar column net position (15) is deducted from the total cross-border position (29) to obtain the position in non-local currency, i.e., the exposure of the US subsidiary (14).

Reading vertically we see each country's cross-border position in a particular currency. Intra-company positions cancel. The total external dollar denominated cross-border position of the MNC is +10. To obtain the exposed position vertically for the whole MNC, we must add the net dollar position inside the US. This position is the negative of the cross-border position of the US subsidiary since against each cross-border inflow (source) there must be an intra-country outflow (use). The cross-border position for the US subsidiary was added up horizontally to +29. The negative of this figure is moved down to the net intra-country position in dollars. Finally, we obtain the net position in dollars for the whole MNC by adding the MNC's cross-border position in dollars and its intra-country position in dollars. Doing the same for each currency we

Table III.4 Cross-border transactions matrix
$ equivalents evaluated at forward rate

	$		SEK		£		Cross-border position of subsidiaries in country	In non-local currency
	Ext.	Intra.	Ext.	Intra.	Ext.	Intra.		
USA (+)	10	5	0	8	0	6		
(−)	0	0	0	0	0	0		
net	+10	+5	0	+8	0	+6	Sum net +29	$ +14
SWE (+)	0	0	5	0	0	0		
(−)	0	−3	0	−8	−3	0		
net	0	−3	+5	−8	−3	0	Sum net −9	SEK −6
UK (+)	0	0	5	0	0	0		
(−)	0	−2	0	0	0	−6		
net	0	−2	+5	0	0	−6	Sum net −3	£ +3
Total cross-border position in currency	+10	0	+10	0	−3	0	17	
Net intra-country position	−29		+9		+3			
MNC net position in currency	−19		+19		0			

obtain an exposure for the whole MNC of −19 in dollars and +19 in dollar equivalent Swedish kronor (SEK).

The centralized firm can now become completely *covered* by selling SEK in an amount of 19 dollar equivalents for dollars in the forward market. This transaction creates a negative SEK position and a corresponding positive dollar position of 19 in the forward market.

In the decentralized firm, each subsidiary deals with its exposure relative to the local currency. For the US company the total foreign currency exposure is 14 on the far right. Looking inside the table we observe that of these 14 a position of +8 is held in SEK and +6 in pounds. Table III.5 summarizes exposures and the forward market transactions that balance all exposures. The end result of complete cover of transaction exposure is the same in the two cases, but in the centralized case the MNC has economized on transaction costs to banks. Additional reductions of transaction costs are obtained by intra-company netting.

Advantages or disadvantages of centralization, which are discussed further in other parts of this book, depend on the firm's general exposure objective. If there is a well-defined MNC objective for

Table III.5 Centralized and decentralized cover of transaction exposure

	Centralized:
Exposure:	$ −19
	SEK +19
Cover:	Sell SEK for $19 in forward market
	Decentralized:
US exposure:	SEK +8
	£+6
cover:	Sell SEK for $8 in forward market
	Sell £ for $6 in forward market
Sweden exposure:	$ −3
	£ −3
cover:	Buy $3 for SEK in forward market
	Buy £3 (dollar eq.) for SEK in forward market
UK exposure:	$ −2
	SEK +5
cover:	Buy $2 for £ in forward market
	Sell SEK 5 (dollar eq.) for £ in forward market
Total transactions:	$ bought 19; SEK sold 19; £ bought 8, £ sold 8
(27 $-equivalents)	

total exposure in each currency, then centralization is clearly advantageous. Such a central objective may be formed by weighing expected gains of holding each currency against risk. Only a centralized finance function can have the necessary expertise or authority to forecast exchange rates and identify profit opportunities. On the other hand, we argued above that with a flexible remittance policy each local subsidiary's exposure can be evaluated as for a local firm. In this case, exposure decisions may best be taken on the local level, given broad guidelines and exchange-rate forecasts from a central level. The central function would then determine the timing of remittances.

Different degrees of centralization are possible. For example, each subsidiary may be allowed to determine its exposure by selling currencies to or buying currencies from a central finance office. This office may then determine the desired total exposure and enter external forward markets accordingly. However, this method works only if the central office obtains information on the total exposure in each subsidiary.

In addition to *external* tools for influencing exposure, like forward contracts, a firm has a number of *internal* tools available. For example, during the planning stage of business operations there is flexibility in the choice of country in which to place orders or in which currency to invoice. Short- and long-term borrowing can be obtained in a multitude of currencies, payments can lead or lag, and so forth. Typically a number of *internal* tools for adjusting positions can be used at a lower cost than external. Therefore, internal tools may be used first. Thereafter the *residual* risk can be covered in external financial markets by means of money market or forward market contracts. The meaning of a money market contract is simultaneous borrowing in one currency and depositing in another. Table III.6 lists a number of tools and measures by which exposure can be adjusted.

In all cases the costs and returns associated with covering transactions must be evaluated. These costs are of two kinds. First, interest costs (returns) and expected exchange rate costs (returns) will vary depending on the method of obtaining a desired currency position. For example, by lagging a payment a cash discount may have to be given up. Second, outright transaction costs must be paid for external measures.

The concept of *cost of cover* in forward markets has been used with different meanings. Some authors mean by the cost of forward cover the forward premium on buying the foreign currency for future delivery rather than immediate delivery. However, when the firm faces the choice of covering or not covering, the *opportunity cost* of covering is really the difference between the forward rate and the expected future spot rate. This cost may be positive or negative. Many observers argue in fact that it is zero as a result of speculators' activities. These may equalize the forward rate and the expected future spot rate (see Appendix III.3). It should be noted that covers do not always refer to known future cash flows. As Figure III.2 illustrates, transaction exposure may refer to an expected payment for sales or purchases. After delivery of goods a firm is exposed to credit risk of non-payment. Therefore, the firm must focus on covering *expected cash flows*. It is then possible that actual cash flows in a foreign currency differ from the size of the forward contract.

Let us now take a closer look at the type of exposure management decisions that would be taken at different levels in a firm. The first and highest decision-level is to determine an exposure management *strategy*, i.e., a systematic rule for making currency decisions. We can distinguish among:

1. aggressive strategy (expected value maximization)
2. laissez faire strategy
3. cover everything strategy (variance minimization)
4. selective covering strategy (expected value/variance trade-off)

The first strategy implies that the firm uses exchange rate forecasts in order to always hold the currency with the highest expected return. The second strategy implies that there is no covering of exposures that arise as a result of normal operating decisions. Both these strategies presume little concern for risk and the second is usually based on the belief that markets are efficient *and* that Fisher Open holds (see Appendix III.3), in which case the forward rate is the best possible exchange rate forecast. The third and fourth strategies presume 'risk-averse' behaviour, i.e., the firm is willing to pay a cost for decreasing exposure. The always cover strategy can be based on either 'risk-paranoid' attitudes or on milder risk-aversion coupled with the belief that the forward rate is equal to

Table III.6   Tools with which transaction exposures can be adjusted

Internal group/company tools

1.   Change in contract currency
2.   Matching of revenues and costs in current operations (structural matching)
3.   Total matching of revenues and costs in current operations with revenues and costs in the financial side of the group
4.   Change in payment rhythm internally (leads/lags parent company/subsidiary)
5.   Change in payment rhythm externally (leads/lags parent company/other foreign stakeholders)
6.   Advance payments in other forms
7.   Allocation of responsibility for borrowing and payments between parent company and foreign subsidiary
8.   Structural changes in debts/claims among currencies (weak currencies versus strong)
9.   Currency reserves (for example with internal forward hedging)
10. Export financing arrangements in the group
11. Internal pricing routines (transfer pricing)
12. Adjustment in level of inventories
13. Change in credit conditions for foreign suppliers or foreign customers
14. Cross-matching based on correlation
15. Change in prices in export markets
16. Change in prices in local markets

External group/company tools

17. Forward market transactions
18. Foreign loans
19. Swap arrangements (parallel loan/deposit)
20. Sell future receivables
21. Arrangements for financing exports
22. Factoring
23. Leasing
24. Currency options
25. Financial futures
26. Interest rate options

---

the expected future spot rate. Then some risk aversion would induce the firm to always cover. The selective covering strategy is the most difficult to implement, but it is the one that would be consistent with some risk-aversion and a belief that the firm's forecasters can 'beat' the forward rate on the average.

At the highest policy level it may also be necessary to determine how decisions on exposure management should be delegated among subsidiaries and in general the degree of centralization of financial decisions.

On the second more *tactical* level the principles for fulfilling the objectives of the exposure strategy would be determined and delegation of authority to personal areas of responsibility made. For example, under the selective covering strategy an important problem is to determine how optimal exposures can be estimated and what expertise the firm has or must purchase. Should a sophisticated mean-variance analysis of risk be implemented taking into consideration variances and covariances among returns on different currency positions? Alternatively, 'rules of thumb' can be developed in the form of limits to positions in different currencies. Such limits may be proportional to the expected extra return relative to some standard from holding a currency.

The third level is purely *operational* and implements the strategy. Given the data available on interest rates, prices, expected exchange rates, forward rates, etc., the manager on this level decides which positions should actually be taken, implementing the model for determining desired exposures. On this level a choice among different kinds of covering may also be taken. This choice would depend on the transaction costs involved in using each tool for covering. The cheapest way to cover in terms of transaction costs is normally to *match* positive and negative positions in a currency. If two currencies tend to move together it may be advantageous to match a positive position in one of these currencies with a negative position in the other currency. As we noted, transaction costs are not the only costs to consider. Interest costs on different financial instruments must also be considered.

Finally, an important part of exposure management is the evaluation of decisions made at different levels since evaluation will influence managers' behaviour. In Chapter VII we discuss in more detail how evaluation can be conducted in such a way that managers obtain incentives which are consistent with the firm's objective.

III.3.b Current Practices in Managing Translation Exposure

We assume now that the firm's concept of exposure refers to translation exposure. This kind of exposure is not covered but *hedged*. 'Cover' is usually reserved for activities that fix the domestic currency value of known or expected future cash flows, while the firm can 'hedge' in order to reduce uncertainty about the *value* of assets and liabilities even when gains or losses due to uncertainty are not going to be realized within the planning horizon, nor at the time the hedge-contract matures.

Translation exposure refers usually to uncertainty about a foreign asset's domestic currency value on a consolidation date for which balance sheets are made public. In Figure III.1 we referred to the translation exposure at time 0, but the concern may be with translation gains or losses between time 0 and time 1, if the latter is the consolidation date. In this case, gains or losses depend on the average translation exposure for the period. Gains and losses before the consolidation date may potentially be realized on later dates, or they may never be realized.

A simple way of hedging the balance sheet is obviously to adjust the currency denomination of exposed assets and liabilities until they are balanced. For example, under FASB 8 monetary items including long-term debt are exposed while plant and equipment are not. Therefore, US firms could avoid exposure in foreign subsidiaries in an accounting sense by raising long-term debt in dollars. After the switch to FASB 52, under which all assets are exposed, long-term debt in a foreign currency would balance plant and equipment in foreign subsidiaries. In hyperinflationary countries, however, the functional currency under FASB 52 is dollars. Then, as noted above, exposure becomes as under FASB 8, and firms are again induced to borrow in dollars in order to avoid translation exposure.

It is more interesting to analyse in detail the nature of a hedge in forward and money markets. Assume, for example, that we are in the firm described in Appendix III.1. We observe that at the end of year 1 and on 1/1 year 2, the exposure of the foreign subsidiary is FC 500 under FASB 52. The exchange rate is $1/FC. The forward rate on contracts maturing at the end of the year is $1.05/FC. Since the FC exposure is positive, we try to hedge by selling FC 500 for delivery on 12/31 of year 2. Table III.7(a) illustrates what happens in this situation. In the left column we have actual outcomes on the consolidation date. The second column shows the translation gain or loss associated with each outcome. Thereafter, we have the cash gain or loss on the forward contract that must be fulfilled on

Table III.7(a)   A hedge
Hedging FC 500 on 1/1 by selling FC 500 for delivery on 12/31.
Forward rate = $1.05/FC

Outcome on 12/31	Translation gain (loss) on FC 500 exposure	Cash gain (loss) on forward contract	Translation gain + cash gain
$1.10/FC	$50	$(25)	$25
$1.05/FC	$25	–	$25
$1.00/FC	–	$25	$25
$ .95/FC	$(25)	$50	$25

Table III.7(b)   A double hedge
Selling FC 1000 on 1/1 for delivery on 12/31 tax rate: 50%.
Forward rate = $1.05/FC

Outcome on 12/31	Transl. gain(loss)	After tax cash gain on double hedge	PV of after tax cash gains after 12/31*	Transl. gain + after tax cash gain on hedge	PV of after tax cash gain + after tax cash gain on hedge
$1.10/FC	$50	($25)	$25	$25	0
$1.05/FC	$25	–	$12.50	$25	$12.50
$1.00/FC	–	$25	–	$25	$25
$ .95/FC	$(25)	$50	$(12.50)	$25	$37.50

*Assuming: (i) translation exposure (FC 500) is the present value (PV) of taxable cash flows in foreign currency after 12/31. This column is 50% of the translation gain/loss; (ii) exchange rate changes are expected to be permanent.

12/31. For example, if the exchange rate turns out to be $1.10/FC, then the contract can be fulfilled only by the purchase of FC 500 at the spot rate $1.10/FC while, according to the forward contract, the firm receives $1.05/FC when the foreign currency is delivered. Thus, there is a cash loss of 25. The last column in the table demonstrates that the sum of the translation gain (loss) and the cash gain (loss) is constant. This total gain or loss with hedging is equal to the translation gain that would occur if the actual spot rate at the end of the year is equal to the forward rate. Thus, *the balance sheet value of the foreign assets is locked in at the forward rate.* If the forward rate had been below $1/FC, it would not have been possible to lock in a gain, but instead a loss would have been locked in at least insuring the firm against even larger losses.

It is noteworthy that hedging accounting exposure leaves the firm exposed to cash gains and losses on the forward contract against unrealized losses and gains on the translation exposure. There is, in other words, a mismatch of maturities, though in an accounting sense the firm is not exposed. The hedging may, nevertheless, make economic sense if the unrealized translation gains or losses are expected to be realized in the future when the assets and liabilities produce cash flows.

There has been some debate about whether the forward contract should be doubled in size relative to exposure in order to hedge translation exposure. The reason would be that cash gains (losses) are taxable (tax deductible) while there are no tax effects from translation gains or losses. We show the accounting and economic results of a double hedge of the translation exposure in Table III.7(b). If the firm is concerned only about accounting net worth, then doubling the contract would clearly be necessary to hedge accounting net worth as shown in the column for translation gain plus after tax cash gain on the hedging contract. On the other hand, if the translation exposure is viewed as economic exposure, then there is no reason to double the forward contract as shown in the last column of Table III.7(b). In this case, assuming exchange rate changes are expected to be permanent, and translation exposure is the present value of future cash flows, a translation gain is the present value of expected future cash flow gains. When actual cash flows occur they will be taxed, or when losses occur they will be deductible. Thus, the present value of after-tax expected cash flow gains is half of the translation gain. Accordingly, with the double hedge cash gains/losses on this forward contract are more variable than the present value of after tax expected cash flow gains, and the firm's transaction exposure is increased. In this case, a regular forward contract as in Table III.7(a) would be sufficient to hedge the firm's value and fix it at a value corresponding to the forward rate, even when taxes are taken into account.

The term hedge of translation exposure has sometimes been misused to represent a forward contract that creates a gain equal to an expected translation loss. Assume, for example, that the *expected* (on 1/1) exchange rate (for 12/31) is one of those listed in the first

Table III.8 **'False hedging'**
Forward contract size that equates expected cash
gain with expected translation loss on FC 500.
Forward rate: $.95/FC. Spot rate: $1.00/FC

Expected spot rate	Expected transl. loss	Forward contract (C)
$1.00/FC	–	0
$ .975/FC	$12.50	500
$ .95/FC	$25	∞
$ .90/FC	$50	−1000

column in Table III.8. Assume now that the forward rate on 1/1 is
$.95/FC. We can ask what size foreign currency forward contract
(C) would create an expected gain equal to the expected translation
loss. The following formula can be used to determine this contract:

− (Expected translation loss) = desired cash gain on forward
contract = C · (Expected spot rate − forward rate).

For example, if the expected spot rate is .975, then C = 12.50/
(.975−.95) = 500. Thus, the firm would buy FC 500 in the forward
market. Table III.8 illustrates that this kind of 'false hedging' is
highly speculative, if possible at all. Clearly if the forward rate is
equal to the expected future spot rate, then there is no way to offset
the expected translation loss. If the expected rate is .975, the firm
must buy FC 500 adding to its exposure which is already FC 500.
Therefore, this kind of activity may actually increase the firm's
exposure to unanticipated exchange rate changes. In times of
substantial exchange rate uncertainty the activity is obviously
dangerous, especially since expected rates often deviate little from
forward rates. Large contracts are then necessary to create this
'hedge' in an expectational sense. One may, of course, also ask why
the forward contract size would be limited to the size of the exposure
if the firm has some faith in its forecast.

We have demonstrated two important facts about the role of the
forward rate in exposure management. First, *the forward rate is the
only exchange rate at which the domestic currency value of an exposed
position can be locked in.* Second, *there is no way in which expected losses
can be offset, if market expectations, as reflected in the forward rate, are
equal to the firm's expectations.*

We should finally mention that money market contracts can be used as an alternative to forward contracts for hedging as well as covering. For illustration, denote by i^{FC} the FC interest rate. In our case, a money market hedge would consist of borrowing FC 500/ $(1 + i^{FC})$ and depositing this amount of dollars at the interest ràte i^{US}. There is now a liability payable in an amount of FC 500 at the end of the year. This liability offsets the asset exposure. Notice that at the end of the year the cash gain on the money market hedge is:

$$\left\{ \frac{FC\,500}{(1+i^{FC})} \cdot [e_{1/1}(1+i^{US})/e_{12/31}] - FC\,500 \right\} e_{12/31},$$

where e is dollars/FC in the spot market on the date referred to by the subscript. We can compare this cash gain with the forward market cash gain:

$$FC\,500\,(f_{1/1} - e_{12/31}).$$

This comparison reduces to the following expression for choosing the money market contract in favour of a forward market contract:

$$\frac{1 + i_{US}}{1 + i_{FC}} \text{ larger than } (f_{1/1}/e_{1/1}). \tag{III.10}$$

This expression is simply a deviation from interest rate parity (IRP). IRP is an equilibrium covered arbitrage condition in international financial markets. (For further description see Oxelheim, 1985, and Appendix III.3). If IRP holds, money market hedges and covers are equivalent to forward market hedges and covers. Since among major currencies IRP holds well, the choice between the two instruments normally comes down to a comparison of transaction costs. Such a cost in money markets is the difference between borrowing and lending rates, while in the forward market the cost is the bid-ask spread.

III.3.c   Recent Developments in Exposure Management: Futures, Options, and Swaps

In this subsection we emphasize new financial instruments for dealing with exposure and new forms of organization that expand a firm's ability to manage exposure.

Among financial instruments it is particularly futures, options, and swap markets that increase the portfolio of exposure management tools. At the International Mercantile Exchange in Chicago futures contracts in a number of currencies are traded. However, for a firm trying to cover a particular transaction, futures markets offer hardly any advantage relative to forward markets. In the former, price changes on contracts have to be reflected in the cash deposits of the parties to a contract, and there are contracts for specific amounts and dates only.

A more important hedging instrument is the foreign currency option. Markets for *options* (the right to buy or sell a currency for another at a specific price on a specific date) in a number of currencies and maturities have developed during the last few years. An option functions as an *insurance* against unfavourable price movements as opposed to a forward or futures contract, under which the firm loses the opportunity to take advantage of favourable price movements. For example, if a firm buys at a certain price a 30-day (call) option to buy pounds at a 'striking price' of $1.05, then if the pound reaches $1.06, the firm exercises its option, and sells the pound in the spot market with a one cent profit on the contract. On the other hand, if the price reaches only $1.04 the firm does not exercise its option.

An American importer that must buy and deliver one pound in 30 days could make sure that the price of this pound will not exceed $1.05. If it reaches $1.06 the option is obviously exercised, while if it reaches only $1.04 the importer buys the pound in the spot market at this more favourable price. Such an option is naturally not free, but may cost, say, two cents per pound. Then, the importer has in effect made sure that the pound price will not exceed $1.07 (1.05 + .02). The option price will increase with the variability of the pound price. Variability increases the price of the option since increased variability increases the probability that the striking price will be reached before the striking date.

The opposite of a call option is a put option which implies the right to sell one unit of a currency for another at a fixed price.

In a situation when the expected future spot rate, the forward rate, and the striking price are $1.05, the cost of an option, i.e., an insurance against unfavourable price movements, is going to be much more expensive than a forward contract. The cost of the latter is simply the bid-ask spread while the cost of taking an option is the option price, which may be several percentage points of the striking price *plus* the bid-ask spread in the option market. The option price is going to be higher the more valuable it is.

A disadvantage of options is that there is not a continuum of striking prices, maturities, and contract sizes. However, banks offer to an increasing extent more flexible option contracts since they can match many customers' needs and go to the option market with the net position of their customers.

Among financial instruments we should also mention *swaps* of different kinds. The term is used for a large number of different contracts which involve the simultaneous buying and selling of one currency for another. Swaps in forward markets refer to two opposite positions with different maturities. The more interesting swaps are tailor-made transactions between a bank and a firm or between two firms with a bank as a possible intermediary. In general such swaps are designed to avoid exchange controls, to alleviate political risk, or to overcome information problems in capital markets. Two firms in different countries with access to local credit markets, but without access in the foreign market, could each borrow in local currency and 'swap' obligations for payments on the loans. Thereby, the two firms gain access to foreign currency loans and/or access to credit conditions in foreign markets.

A particular kind of swap is a parallel loan. For example, a US firm may lend to a US subsidiary of a Brazilian corporation while the Brazilian parent lends to the Brazilian subsidiary of the US corporation. The two firms agree on terms at which the relative value of the two loans can be determined in the future. Indirectly, swaps may help relatively unknown subsidiaries gain access to the respective local capital markets or, depending on the contract terms, it may be the case that they indirectly are able to borrow in their parents' markets. There is no cross-border transaction in this type of swap; all firms hold assets or liabilities in their local currencies, and the relatively well-known parent companies stand as the borrowers in the capital markets.

A large number of different swap transactions for different purposes can be identified. Some of them have the purpose of changing the terms of interest payment in a specific currency. We return to these in Subsection III.4 where Table III.9 lists the different types of swaps.

Among recent developments in the organization of exposure management are the creation of specific finance subsidiaries, designed to increase a multinational corporation's ability to handle exposure, and the increased tendency towards centralization of decision-making in exposure management.

The finance subsidiaries may have very limited functions, such as reinvoicing or refinancing, or corporations may create their own merchant banks performing a large number of activities that otherwise would be handled through banks.

A 'reinvoicing vehicle' is simply a non-producing subsidiary through which all intra-firm trade is formally channelled. In other words, an exporting subsidiary in country A and an importing subsidiary in country B may ship goods directly to each other, but the exporting subsidiary invoices a third subsidiary in C, which reinvoices the importing subsidiary in B. The amount of trade credit internally in the multinational corporation doubles. The ability of the firm to give intra-company loans by leading and lagging payments expands accordingly.

'Refinancing vehicles' are similar, but a wider range of financial activities passes through them. For example, trade with other firms may be reinvoiced in such a way that subsidiaries avoid taking exchange risk and the buying firm can also be offered an exchange risk-free contract. Instead, exchange risk is centralized to the refinancing vehicle.

The centralization versus decentralization of exchange rate risk management is a key issue in many firms. The financing and reinvoicing vehicles described above offer means of centralization. The extreme case of an internal 'merchant bank' constitutes the centralization of an even larger number of financial activities including activities often handled by external bank contacts. For example, a firm's internal bank may issue commercial papers, take 'deposits' of excess cash from subsidiaries, lend to other subsidiaries in their local currencies, invest in financial instruments without going through middlemen, or even become traders in foreign exchange markets.

In general the level of centralization depends on the firm's perceived advantages such as the ability to match exposures comprehensively, scale advantages when buying or selling foreign currency, and better utilization of the firm's expertise on, for example, exchange rate forecasting. Centralization also offers the advantage of global tax planning and cash flow planning to avoid exchange controls.

The disadvantages of centralization are the great demand for information that is often dispersed, and possible ill effects on motivation and incentives in the firm. The relative weights of the advantages and disadvantages may depend on the firm's concept of exposure. For example, consolidated transaction exposure can only be evaluated at a centralized level, while local transaction exposures may be determined easily on the local level.

Exchange controls and tax planning are bound to have strong effects on the organization of exposure management. Even though it is theoretically possible to manage taxes and currency exposure separately, it is almost inconceivable that a firm with an advanced centralized tax management system will not manage exposure concurrently. The reason is that many cash flow adjustments for tax purposes have exposure consequences. Similarly, the avoidance of exchange controls in a particular country by means of intra-company trade, and lending and borrowing in different ways may force the firm to take positions in specific currencies. Furthermore, the existence of controls may prevent a subsidiary from obtaining a desired currency position on its own, while a central finance office can acquire positions on behalf of the subsidiary.

There has been a tendency towards increased centralization during the last decade. In the US this tendency was reinforced by increased concern with translation exposure after the introduction of FASB 8 (Evans et al., 1978). In spite of the lack of concern of Swedish companies over such exposures, Oxelheim (1984a) found that an increasing number of firms in Sweden favoured centralization because of improved global tax planning, knowledge concentration, and other financial economies of scale.

III.4 PRACTICES IN INTEREST RATE RISK MANAGEMENT

The assets of a firm may be financed by debt or equity. From the stockholders' point of view, uncertainty about the future cost of debt is a source of risk. Two common rules of thumb for a long time were to match the maturity of debt with the life span of the assets it was financing, and the currency of debt with the currency of cash flows from sale of products. However, starting in the mid-1960s in the US, relatively high and uncertain inflation meant the real cost of long-term debt became uncertain, while cash flows from sales were better protected against inflation. Furthermore, inflation rates among countries diverged under flexible exchange rates in the 1970s and became uncertain to different degrees. Accordingly, the task of choosing the cheapest source of debt in terms of maturity as well as currency became more complex.

An *ex post* analysis of effective interest costs in different currencies—costs including exchange rate changes—indicates that only over very long time periods are relative costs equalized (see Oxelheim, 1985 and Appendix III.3). Similarly, the relative advantage of short- and long-term loans changes substantially over time. Whether markets are strongly efficient in such a way that expected interest costs are equalized across currencies and maturities remains an open question. There is little doubt that firms perceive profit opportunities in their choice. Furthermore, even if no expected profit opportunities exist, risk-averse firms would be concerned with uncertainty about real interest costs.

The real interest cost on a loan is the nominal cost minus inflation. Thus, the real cost can be locked in *ex ante* only if the nominal interest cost can be linked to a relevant measure of inflation from the firm's point of view. Such a measure may differ substantially from commonly used price indices to which interest costs in some currencies are linked. For the sake of discussion we disregard perfectly inflation-linked debt, which is extremely rare.

A firm with a long time horizon for the use of its assets faces, when taking a loan, a combination of real interest rate risk and the inflation risk associated with a particular currency denomination. When inflation was low and believed to be relatively certain, the major concern was real interest rate risk. Such risk could be avoided by issuing relatively long-term debt on which the interest rate was fixed. However, when it is not known whether the inflation rate is going to be 5 percent or 10 percent on the average over the next decade, real interest costs become highly uncertain on fixed interest rate loans.

A response to high inflation uncertainty has been increased use of roll over credits and flexible interest (floating rate) loans on which the interest rate may be reset every six months or so based on short-term interest rates. Since inflation can be forecast rather well for a period of six months, borrowers and lenders can reduce their exposure to inflation risk by shifting to such flexible rate securities or to a series of short-term securities.

The drawback of flexible interest loans is that the six-month interest rate may change as a result of real interest rate changes in the economy. In general, the more short-term interest rate fluctuations depend on real factors such as fiscal policy, savings propensity, or aggregate investment, the more favourable are long-term loans from a risk point of view. On the other hand, when the basic real rate of interest is stable and short-term nominal interest rate fluctuations reflect inflation expectations, then short-term loans become relatively favourable. It should be noted that lenders would react in the same way as borrowers to both real interest rate and inflation risk. Thus, increased risk of either kind induces both borrowers and lenders to shift maturity preferences the same way (see, e.g., Wihlborg, 1978).

Interest rate risk with its source in either the real interest rate or the inflation rate can be diversified by creating an international portfolio of securities or debt. Under the fixed exchange rate system, when inflation rates were similar across currencies, it was primarily real interest rate risk that could be diversified. However, with more divergent inflation rates under the flexible system borrowers as well as lenders have the opportunity to diversify away some inflation risk as well by holding an international basket of currencies. Especially on long-term fixed interest loans for which real exchange risk may be less of a concern than inflation risk, the opportunity to hold long-term debt in several currencies can be risk reducing. Since there are fixed costs associated with bond or debt issues, only very large firms are able to use this opportunity directly. There are currency baskets, however, in which bonds can be denominated. For example, the Special Drawing Right (SDR) as well as the European Currency Unit (ECU) has gained increasing acceptance in the 1980s as a denomination for corporate bond issues. If inflation rates underlying the different basket-currencies' values are very similar, then there is little value in this diversification, however.

Interest rate futures markets offer an alternative instrument for hedging against interest rate changes in the future. Like foreign exchange futures and forward contracts, interest rate futures are contracts to deliver or receive an interest bearing security at a price which is agreed upon when the contract is entered. Thus, if the interest rate increases above the agreed upon rate (implicit in the futures' price), the security will be cheaper in the spot market and the seller in the futures market makes a profit.

Consider a firm borrowing over two years and assume it has the choice among: (a) taking a two-year loan at a fixed interest rate, (b) taking two consecutive one-year loans with an uncertain second year interest rate, and (c) taking two consecutive one-year loans combined with an interest rate futures contract to deliver a security with a certain interest rate at the beginning of the second period. If the one-year interest rate increases unexpectedly before the beginning of the second year, the firm in case (b) suffers an increase in borrowing costs, while the firm in case (c) is compensated by an offsetting gain on the futures contract, since it can buy a security at a lower price than the futures price to fulfil the contract. Since the firm obtains the same protection by taking a two-year loan directly with a rate i_2, we would expect that the interest rate on the futures contract for the second year (i_1^2) would be such that firms are indifferent between cases (a) and (c). This indifference occurs when

$$(1 + i_2) = (1 + i_1)(1 + i_1^2) \qquad \text{(III.11)}$$

where i_1 is today's one-year interest rate. The expected interest rate for the second year $E(i_1^2)$ need not be equal to the rate on the futures contract (i_1^2), however, since risks associated with cases (a) and (c) on the one hand and (b) on the other are different.

The incentive to hedge against interest rate uncertainty by means of futures contracts would obviously depend on the source of the uncertainty. If the uncertainty consists primarily of real interest rate uncertainty, then the contract offers a hedge. On the other hand, if interest rate uncertainty reflects inflation uncertainty, then there is less uncertainty about real interest costs when the firm chooses case (b), i.e., two consecutive one-period loans.

The above discussion implies that if a firm is locked into a two-year fixed interest rate loan and inflation uncertainty is substantial, then the futures contract provides a (partial) hedge against unanticipated inflation in the second year. For example, if after one period there is an decrease in expected inflation for the second year then the associated higher real interest cost on the fixed interest loan will be offset if the firm has purchased a one-year security in the future market. The lowering of the expected inflation rate leads to a decrease in the one-period interest rate in the second year and therefore the price of the one-year security increases. Thus, the buyer of the security in the futures market makes a gain when the security is sold in the spot market.

A serious disadvantage of futures markets is that contracts are limited to short maturities as well as size. In the market for interest rate swaps, on the other hand, contracts can be tailor-made to the long-term needs of firms provided there is an interested swap-partner. In analogy with swaps in the foreign exchange market, an interest rate swap implies the simultaneous purchase and sale of liabilities with different payment conditions. For example, a firm borrowing at a fixed rate may 'trade' or swap loans with another firm borrowing at a floating rate. The reason for such a swap is, as for foreign currency swaps, that the two firms are unable in their local markets to obtain loans with desired payment conditions at reasonable costs. One firm may desire a fixed rate loan when its cash inflows are contracted in monetary terms for a long period, while another firm may desire a floating rate loan when its cash inflows are inflation sensitive. If, at the same time, both firms have relatively cheap credit in the undesirable type of loan, then these are grounds for a swap. Each firm could obviously change the characteristics of its payments by buying or selling interest rate futures contracts as well, but in the case of swaps the two firms can match the account and timing of loans, interest payments, and repayments exactly. Both firms may also obtain an interest rate advantage in their desired type of loan through the swap, if each firm lacks access to a market in which the desired loan type is in relatively large supply.

A disadvantage of the swap is that the firms should match each other well in terms of loan size and maturity. As a result, large banks have started to act as intermediaries in the market for swaps. The market is developing rapidly and a few large banks even act as market makers in swaps. This enables the bank to match one firm on one side of the swap with a number of firms on the other side with approximately offsetting needs. In the process the bank may be temporarily or permanently exposed to interest risk for a part of the swap-amount.

The increased involvement of banks as intermediaries and market makers has made it possible for a secondary market in swaps to develop. Thus, one party to the swap can reverse the transaction before the loans mature. Options in swaps have also developed. This means that a firm may borrow in, for example, Swiss francs and simultaneously obtain an option with a bank to swap to a dollar denominated loan before or at a specific future date.

Table III.9 Different kinds of swaps

Firm 1 borrows at	Firm 2 borrows at	Currency denominations
Currency swaps		
1. Fixed interest (CHF)	Fixed interest ($)	Different
2. Floating interest (CHF)	Floating interest ($)	Different
Interest rate swaps		
3. Fixed interest	Floating interest	Same
4. Floating interest	Floating interest	Same
Currency and interest rate swaps		
5. Fixed interest (CHF)	Floating interest ($)	Different

Examples
1. Firm 1 (2) obtains through swap a dollar (CHF) loan.
2. Same as 1.
3. Firm 1 (2) obtains a floating (fixed) interest loan in the same currency.
4. Firm 1 (2) borrows at Libor* (US commercial paper) rate and swaps to obtain loan at US commercial paper (Libor) rate.
5. Firm 1 (2) obtains floating rate dollar (fixed CHF) loan through swap after borrowing in local market at fixed CHF (floating dollar) interest.

* London Interbank Offered Rate.

Table III.9 shows major types of swap transactions in international financial markets. Types 1 and 2 are pure currency swaps, types 3 and 4 are pure interest swaps, and type 5 is both a currency and an interest swap.

III.5 COUNTRY RISK ANALYSIS

Country risk analysis has received widespread attention during the last decade (see, for example, Frank and Cline, 1971; Feder and Just, 1977; Korth, 1979; Edwards, 1984; Oxelheim, 1984b; and Dufey and Giddy, 1984). It has, nevertheless, avoided attempts at being defined operationally. In other words, there is no clear definition of country risk exposure and, therefore, little guidance for managing such exposure. Instead, the concept of country risk seems to capture the exposure to uncertainty about a large number of factors affecting the political and the economic environment of a country. In this subsection we review and discuss a few attempts to come to grips with the concept of country risk.

One type of country risk evaluation is performed by banks when lending for purposes of balance-of-payments deficit financing or for financing development projects. This kind of analysis mixes economic considerations of ability to repay and political consider-ations of willingness to repay (see, e.g., Sachs, 1982; Glick, 1986).

A second type of country risk evaluation with which we are concerned, is performed as part of the capital budgeting analysis of capital investment in foreign countries (or domestically). In this connection, country risk refers to uncertainty about a large number of political and regulatory factors and about general economic conditions influencing the return on investment.

Oxelheim (1984b) divides country risk into *political risk* and *risk related to economic developments* in the investment country. It is also argued that these two risks are interrelated, since bad prospects for the economic growth and external balances for a country will increase the risk for political interventions. Risk related to economic development may overlap with the macroeconomic risks we discuss in this book, though we will analyse them from the ongoing firm's perspective while in country risk analysis these risks are analysed from the perspective of whether physical investments should or should not be located in a country.

The possibility of changes in legislation and regulation that may influence the return on investment is often called political risk. It involves uncertainty about ownership rights in a particular country, i.e., rights of operational control, use of funds, disbursement of funds, and remittances. The possibility that exchange controls may be imposed in a country is then a political risk which may depend on the choice of exchange rate regime, the conduct of monetary policy, political pressures, etc. The most extreme political risk is the risk of expropriation (see, e.g., Kobrin, 1979).

The risk of suspended payments is an extreme form of exchange controls. Suspended payments occur when remittances are completely blocked, in which case shareholders lose the ability to obtain cash flows from a foreign project for the foreseeable future. Though political risk is considered a vague and multidimensional concept, it can still be defined with a reasonable degree of intuitive clarity. Country risk related to economic developments in a country is even more vague, however, since it is hard to relate to specific factors underlying economic development.

At the present time, country risk estimates are often based on macroeconomic measures, such as GNP growth, balance of payments, foreign exchange reserves, debt-service ratios, and savings ratios. In the long run, however, a country's economic development would be determined by productivity development in different industries.

The longer the time horizon to which country risk refers, the more difficult the forecasting problem. In the absence of an international, dynamic model of economic and political development, ambitions with respect to forecasting must be modest.

In Oxelheim (1984b) it is argued that there is a need for leading indicators concerning the productivity development or 'the growth perspective' over the long term. Two groups of factors are identified in addition to purely technological progress. The first group is 'production-centered' and comprises factors expressing the readiness to face changes in the international demand situation for firms and industries. The second is 'organizational' and involves indicators expressing the ability to exploit various types of scale advantages and the utilization of human resources.

'Production centered' factors that may help forecast economic development can, according to Oxelheim, be divided into those describing size and content relative to demand, and those describing diversification on the production side. Organizational factors may be subdivided into those describing ownership structure, degree of concentration, and internationalization such as diversification of purchases across countries. These factors change only slowly and by obtaining proxies for them one should be able to obtain a reasonable forecast for the medium term—say five years—of economic development in a country *relative to* a potential path determined by the rate of technological progress. Table III.10 summarizes the factors as given in Oxelheim (1984b) and lists plausible proxies.

Table III.10 Factors and proxies used in analysing medium-term economic development and country risk

Production centered factors			Organization factors		
Size	Contents	Diversification	Ownership	Concentration	Internationalization
Industrial base capacity	Research and development expenditure	Market-diversification (geographical and product diversification)	Cooperatives	Concentration ratios*	Foreign ownership
Rate of investment	Product technology	Sector shares in production and exports	State-ownership		Foreign direct investments
Growth of manufacturing	Kind of investment		Wage-earner funds		Export share in total sales
	Raw material share in production		Concentration of private stockholding		Diversification of purchases
	Specific industrial concentration				
	Industrial subsidies				
	Share of services in production and exports				

* E.g., large companies relative contribution to value added in manufacturing industries.
Source: Oxelheim (1984b).

III.6   LIMITATIONS OF CURRENT APPROACHES

Much of the discussion in this book is motivated by limitations in the approaches to macroeconomic risk management presented in this chapter. The purpose of this subsection is, therefore, only to describe briefly the problems which we will encounter in other chapters and try to deal with there.

As mentioned before, the major objection to the approaches discussed in previous subsections is that the different risks are *not independent* since the sources of different kinds of risk, such as exchange rate risk and interest rate risk, may be one and the same. Fiscal policy shifts, for example, influence both exchange and interest rates. Similarly country risk and political risk in the form of, for example, interest rate and foreign exchange regulations are closely related to interest rate and exchange rate uncertainty. If the risks are not independent, the procedure of managing them independently can be seriously questioned. Chapter IV will derive measures of exposures in such a way as to recognize explicitly the relationships among various risks.

Another problem we have mentioned is that several exposure measures may be *unstable* over time. For example, the actual economic relevance of translation exposure depends on whether exchange rate changes correspond to inflation or real exchange rate changes, and whether exchange rate changes are expected to be temporary or permanent. However, all exchange rate changes are not alike in these respects. Therefore, fixed rules for dealing with translation exposure may be inappropriate. Stability of exposure measures are also discussed in Chapter IV.

When talking about exposure it must always be remembered that it refers to the firm's sensitivity to unforeseen or *unanticipated* changes in relevant variables. Thus, analysis of the impact of exchange rate and other variables on the firm should distinguish between anticipated and unanticipated changes. *Anticipated* changes are captured by forecasting and, to some extent, production, marketing, and financial plans can be adjusted accordingly.

Unanticipated changes may impact in a different way since they are not foreseen, and commitments are based primarily on anticipations. Unanticipated changes can be measured by the variance of the probability distribution of possible outcomes as was discussed in Chapter II. By exposure management we emphasize the firm's handling of unanticipated exchange rate changes, inflation, and interest rate changes, as well as government policy actions. We presume in general that anticipated changes are already incorporated in the firm's budget and planning procedures. It is important to recognize, however, that accounting procedures do not distinguish between the two types of changes, and that budgets have a tendency to become relatively optimistic targets rather than forecasts.

To a large extent, the above exposure measures neglect non-contractual exposures, i.e., exposure to changes in future cash flows that are not contracted at the time of the exposure analysis. Cash flows from future sales of products are mostly non-contractual. Thus, the exposure of a firm's physical assets are primarily of this nature. This exposure consists of uncertainty about *volume* as well as prices. The cash flow exposure measure discussed in Section III.2.e takes volume exposure into account while traditional transaction and translation exposures neglect it almost entirely. Nevertheless, non-contractual exposure may over time prove to be the most important. Traditional exposure measures seem to be geared towards exposures that can be measured with available accounting information rather than towards those of particular importance for the firm.

Availability of accounting data limits exposure analysis both in time and scope. Firms tend to focus on relatively short-term well-defined exposures such as transaction exposure of current account receivables and payables rather than the possible longer-term impact of the exposure of future cash flows that do not yet appear as explicit assets and liabilities on the balance sheet. In Chapter V we emphasize the importance of having the firm's overall objective with respect to return, risk, and time-horizon in mind when choosing an exposure management strategy. For most reasonable objectives it is necessary to free the exposure analysis from the constraints of accounting rules.

MEASURING TRANSLATION EXPOSURE UNDER FASB 8 AND FASB 52: AN EXAMPLE

The following table shows the balance sheets of two subsidiaries of MNC USA, a holding company, at the end of year 0. All foreign currency (FC) denominated accounts are translated at the rate $1/FC, which has been the exchange rate since the firm started its foreign operations.

			MNC Home conv. rate	dollars	MNC Foreign conv. rate	dollars
Cash	$	100	–	100	FC 50 1	50
A/R	$	200	–	200	$ 100 –	100
	FC	150	1	150	FC 100 1	100
Inv.	$	300	–	300	FC 200 1	200
P/E	$	1000	–	1000	FC 600 1	600
				1750		1050
A/P	$	150	–	150	$ 100 –	100
	FC	100	1	100	FC 50 1	50
L.t.Debt	$	800	–	800	FC 400 1	400
Owner's eq. (residual)				700 (residual)		500
				1750		1050

Note: A/R = Accounts Receivable   P/E = Plant and Equipment
       A/P = Accounts Payable   L.t. Debt = Long-term Debt

Under *FASB 8* the translation exposure at the end of year 0 is the sum of all monetary items translated at the current rate:

$$FC[Cash + A/R] - FC[A/P + L.t.D.],$$

which for MNC Home is FC 150 − FC 100 = FC 50 and for MNC Foreign it is FC[50 + 100] − FC[50 + 400] = −FC 300. Thus total FASB 8 exposure is −FC 250.

Under *FASB 52* the translation exposure at the end of year 0 is:

$$FC[Cash+A/R+Inv+P/E] - FC[A/P+L.t.D.]$$

which for MNC Home is FC 150 − FC 100 = FC 50 and for MNC Foreign it is FC[50+100+200+600] − FC[50+400] = FC 500. Thus, total FASB 52 exposure is FC 550. The two methods result in accounting exposures with opposite signs!

We turn next to the balance sheets at the end of year 1. Over the year the foreign currency has appreciated to $1.10/FC.

MNC Home's balance sheet remains unchanged:
Only monetary items are FC denominated for MNC Home. Therefore, the two methods lead to the same result. Since MNC Home's balance sheet has remained unchanged before translation, net income for MNC Home must have been zero. The translation

			FASB 8		FASB 52	
			conv. rate	dollars	conv. rate	dollars
Cash	$	100	−	100	−	100
A/R	$	200	−	200	−	200
	FC	150	1.10	165	1.10	165
Inv.	$	300	−	300	−	300
P/E	$	1000	−	1000	−	1000
				1765		1765
A/P	$	150	−	150	−	150
	FC	100	1.10	110	1.10	110
L.t.D.	$	800	−	800	−	800
Owner's						
eq. (residual)				705		705
				1765		1765

exposures similarly remain constant over the year. We can then explain the $5 increase in owners' equity as:

Translation gain = average FC exposure over the year × exchange rate change

$$= 50 \cdot (1.10 - 1.00) = \$5$$

under both FASB 8 and FASB 52.

During the year more substantial changes occurred in MNC Foreign. We present first the balance sheet at the end of year 1 for this subsidiary:

Cash	FC 75	
A/R	$ 100	
	FC 125	(bought evenly over year 1)
Inv.	FC 200	(additional non-depreciated P/E bought
P/E	FC 650	evenly over year 1)
A/P	$ 100	
	FC 50	
L.t.D.	FC 400	

Before translation with FASB 8 it is necessary to determine depreciation over the year in order to translate all P/E bought at historical cost. MNC Foreign's year 1 income statement is:

Revenues	FC 600 (evenly over year)
Cost of goods sold (COGS)	FC 200 (FIFO)
Depreciation	FC 125 (on P/E bought before year 1)
Other expenses	FC 75 (evenly over the year)
Profits before tax	FC 200
Tax 50%	FC 100 (paid evenly over the year)
Profit after tax	FC 100

We are now in a position to translate MNC Foreign's balance sheet at the end of year 1, as well as the income statement of this subsidiary. The following two tables describe these translations under FASB 8 and FASB 52, respectively.

	FASB 8		FASB 52	
	Conv. rate	dollars	Conv. rate	dollars
Cash	1.10	82.50	1.10	82.50
A/R	–	100.00	–	100.00
	1.10	137.50	1.10	137.50
Inv.	1.05	210.00	1.10	220.00
	(year average)			
P/E	1.00	658.75	1.10	715.00
	(600–125),			
	1.05 on			
	(650–475)			
		1188.75		1255.00
A/P	–	100.00	–	100.00
	1.10	55.00	1.10	55.00
L.t.D.	1.10	440.00	1.10	440.00
Owners' eq.	residual	593.75	residual	660.00
		1188.75		1255.00

Finally, we translate the income statement:

	FASB 8		FASB 52	
	Conv. rate	dollars	Conv. rate	dollars
Revenues	1.05	630.00	1.05	630
COGS	1.00	200.00	1.05	210
	(inv. held			
	1 year)			
Dep.	1.00	125.00	1.05	131.25
	(P/E bought			
	before			
	year 1)			
Other expenses	1.05	78.75	1.05	78.75
Profits before tax	–	226.75	–	210.00
Tax 50%	1.05	105.00	1.05	105.00
Profits after tax	–	121.25	–	105.00

We can now summarize information and show how net income, translation gains, and changes in owners' equity are related in dollar terms. Under FASB 8 the change in owners' equity for MNC Foreign is 593.75 − 500 = 93.75. Out of this amount, net income explains 121.25. The translation gain (loss) must be the difference, i.e., a loss equal to 27.50. We check this:

Translation exposure at the beginning of the year under FASB 8 = -300.
Translation exposure at the end of the year under FASB 8 = FC[75 + 125] − FC[50 + 400] = −FC 250.
Average exposure under FASB 8 = −FC 275.
Exchange rate change = 1.10 − 1.00 = .10
Translation gain = 0.1·(−275) = −$27.50 (loss).

Under FASB 52, similar calculations can be made.

Change in owners' equity under FASB 52 = +160
Of this amount net income explains 105
The translation gain must be +55

We check this by noting that exposure at the beginning of the year is FC 500 while the transaction exposure at the end of the year is:

FC[75+125+200+650] − FC[50+400] = FC 600.

Thus, average translation exposure is FC 550 and the translation gain is .10 · 550 = $55. In both cases the translation gain (loss) plus net income is the change in owners' equity.

APPENDIX III.2 _____

THE PURCHASING POWER PARITY THEORY AND REAL EXCHANGE RATE THEORIES

The concept of Purchasing Power Parity (PPP) has long held a central position in economic theory. According to Einzig (1962), it can be traced back to the Spanish economists of the Salamanca school in the sixteenth century. According to one school, equilibrium between prices for traded goods in different countries is maintained by variations in exchange rates, while the prices in themselves are determined internally. Another school argues that PPP should hold in the long run for average price levels. According to Frenkel (1981), much of the controversy concerning the usefulness of the PPP doctrine is due to the fact that it does not specify the precise mechanism by which exchange rates are linked to prices nor does it specify the precise conditions that must be satisfied for the doctrine to be correct. Rather the PPP doctrine may be viewed as a short-cut; it specifies a relationship between two variables without providing the details of the process which brings about a relationship and, according to Frenkel, it should not be viewed as a theory of exchange rate determination. Rather, prices and exchange rates are determined simultaneously.

Officer (1982, p. 289) is more positive in his extensive work about the PPP theory when he concludes:

> ... the PPP theory has three interrelated properties that put it in the forefront of exchange-rate theories. First, it is a simple

and intuitively appealing theory. Second, there is an inherent concreteness to the PPP approach. The ingredients of the theory are minimal and basic: price levels and exchange rates (for absolute PPP), inflation and exchange-rate changes (for relative PPP). Third, whether or not the strict PPP theory holds, the theory is of interest. It is useful to know to what extent the PPP theory is valid, for example, what proportion of relative-price changes between countries is likely to be offset by exchange-rate changes.

As mentioned in the quotation, the theory or the doctrine exists in two forms, one relative and one absolute. As a special case we also have a third version, 'the law of one price'. PPP in its absolute version, as described by Boyd (1801), for example, the exchange rate is in equilibrium when a buyer at a random point in time receives the same amount of goods for his money, regardless of which country he buys them from. This can be written:

$$e^{12} = \frac{P_1}{P_2} \qquad \qquad \text{(AIII.1)}$$

where e^{12} = spot rate (currency in country 1/currency in country 2)

P_1 = price level in country 1

P_2 = price level in country 2

The revival of interest in this theory during the twentieth century has generally been ascribed to Gustav Cassel. According to Cassel (1922) the Purchasing Power Parity theory means that:

When two currencies have undergone inflation...the normal rate of exchange will be equal to the old rate multiplied by the quotient of the degree of inflation in the one country and in the other.

Keynes (1923) made comparisons for the period 1919–21 and found that the method functioned satisfactorily. In his view the Purchasing Power Parity theory tells us that

...the movements in the rate of exchange between two countries tend, subject to adjustments in the 'equation of exchange', to correspond pretty closely to movements in the internal price levels of the two countries, each expressed in their own currencies.

Both Cassel and Keynes refer to relative PPP. Movements in internal price levels correspond to movements in the exchange rate. The relative version can be written as:

$$\hat{e}^{12} = \hat{P}_1 - \hat{P}_2, \qquad\qquad (AIII.2)$$

or more exactly:

$$\frac{e_t^{12}}{e_{t-1}^{12}} = \frac{P_{1,t}/P_{1,t-1}}{P_{2,t}/P_{2,t-1}} \qquad\qquad (AIII.3)$$

The rate of change in the equilibrium exchange rate ($\hat{e}_{12}$) is proportional to the difference between the rate of change in the price levels ($\hat{P}_1 - \hat{P}_2$) in the two countries concerned. The principle is simply that if goods or services of the same kind do not cost the same in all countries after adjustment for taxes, transport costs, and transaction costs, there will be a flow of products and production factors which will force prices back to a state of equilibrium. Starting from a base year when the exchange rate between two countries reflects prices *and costs* correctly, this means that if prices rise x percent faster in country 1 than in country 2, country 1's exchange rate can be expected to be depreciated by x percent (floating exchange rates) or to have a potential for devaluation of x percent (pegged exchange rates).

This theory holds in the short run only if commodity arbitrage is perfect. In the long run, it should hold even without this condition, and it can then be regarded as a characteristic of the equilibrium in trade between two countries with money economies.

Does the theory hold for countries with high inflation? Huang (1984) concludes that for an exchange rate between two countries with hyperinflation (Germany and Poland during the 1920s hyperinflationary periods) and subjected to predominantly monetary shocks, Purchasing Power Parity holds as expected.

Those who criticize the Purchasing Power Parity (PPP) theory in its relative form for the long run do so mainly because if the theory is to hold, according to these critics, important real economic factors influencing relative prices between traded and non-traded goods and the terms of trade should remain constant. PPP theory is, nevertheless, an essential ingredient in the analysis of long-term exchange rate changes. As Dornbusch and Krugman (1976) put it:

Under the skin of any international economist lies a deep-seated belief in some variant of the Purchasing Power Parity theory of the exchange rate.

There is now widespread agreement that PPP does not hold in the short run, or even for periods as long as two or three years. Substantial real exchange rate fluctuations occur. The debate around short-run PPP focuses instead on whether deviations follow a random process or whether the deviation or its rate of change is mean-reverting. Most researchers believe in a mean-reverting process, but, on the other hand, Roll (1979) and Pigott and Sweeney (1985) present empirical evidence that the rate of change of deviations from PPP is a random walk.

Before embarking on an empirical illustration of the PPP theory, three fundamental technical problems have to be discussed:

- Choice of index for describing relative price movements.
- Choice of base period.
- Choice between bilateral and multilateral measurements.

Choice of Index

A problem that has long occupied economists concerns the choice of an index to describe changes in relative inflation. A summary of the various arguments can be found in Thygesen (1977).

The index numbers should be easily accessible, they should be frequently reported, and they should measure the relative movements in inflation for goods and services in foreign trade. The problem is complicated by the variety of consumption patterns. Choosing an index can be regarded as a problem of representativeness in the statistical sense. It should be noted that there is no index which is perfect for the purpose of PPP. When the structure of internal relative prices is stable the choice among price indexes seems to be less important. According to Frenkel (1981), internal relative prices—as measured by the relationship between the cost of living and the wholesale price indices—have not changed much in the US and the UK. They have changed dramatically for France, however, which may account for more severe problems with the PPP-equation for the French franc.

An index can be chosen among the GNP deflator, the consumer price index, the wholesale price index, the producer price index, the export price index, and the index for relative unit labour costs. The choice of index will depend on the intended use of the PPP-result. The requirements are different when the PPP-relation is used for managing the exchange rate compared, for instance, to a situation when it is used for comparison of living standards.

The *GNP deflator* is recommended by many as providing the broadest coverage of goods and services. But it is difficult to obtain figures more frequently than once a year. This implicit index contains a high proportion of non-traded goods, which may or may not be an advantage for PPP comparisons. It is a disadvantage if PPP is viewed as a commodity arbitrage relationship but it is an advantage if PPP is seen as a monetary equilibrium condition.

The *wholesale price index* has a broad coverage, and the OPTICA group used it in their calculations for the major OECD countries (OPTICA, 1977), pointing out that empirically it had proved to be a good compromise choice. However, comparisons were complicated by statistical problems, since national index numbers differed in coverage and in the weights employed.

The *export price index* is criticized mainly on the grounds that it is narrow. The OPTICA group rejected it on both statistical and conceptual grounds, claiming that it covered too limited a range of goods and services and lacked direct information about prices.

Compared with the wholesale price index the *consumer price index* includes many more goods and services which do not form part of the trade between countries. PPP based on this index is, therefore, sensitive to price changes on non-traded goods. Furthermore, it refers to an index for expenditures rather than total production like the GNP deflator. The preference for either index would depend on whether expenditures or production is the most immediate determinant of real money demand.

The *producer price index* is similar to the wholesale price index. It has a smaller coverage than the consumer price index. *Unit labour cost measures* suffer from their limitation to one factor of production, and from the difficulty of measuring production volume.

There is little general agreement in the literature when it comes to recommending any one of these index categories. As mentioned before, the choice is dependent on the intended use. As a basis for the analysis in our present context different index choices have been tried. However, the differences proved to be very small when the validity of the PPP theory was tested for the different indexes.

Figure A.III.1 shows real bilateral exchange rates based on wholesale prices of finished goods. The index value 100 corresponds

Figure A.III.1 Real bilateral dollar exchange rates and the US current-account balance 1972–85

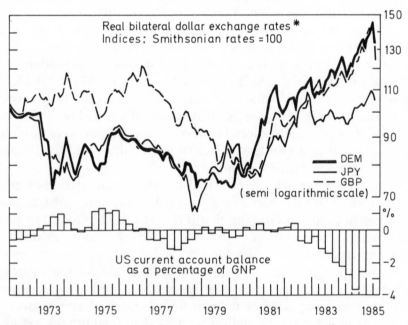

* Adjusted on the basis of movements in relative wholesale prices of finished goods.
Source: Bank for International Settlements, 1985

to an assumed PPP rate. The figure shows the pattern of deviations quite clearly. Values under 100 mean that the US dollar is 'undervalued' in relation to the other currency. Such deviations constitute potentials for appreciation, if PPP is expected to hold over the longer term. Similarly a value over 100 can be regarded as a potential for depreciation. In general deviations can potentially be exploited for profit by firms in international trade.

In a longer-term perspective the cumulative rise in the US dollar has been no less than extraordinary. Between its 1978 low point and late February 1985 the dollar had appreciated by 80 per cent in nominal terms on the average while in real terms the dollar had appreciated against the Deutche Mark and the yen by 95 and 65 percent, respectively. In a still longer perspective, at their recent peaks the dollar's real exchange rates against the Deutche Mark and the sterling stood 40 percent above their Smithsonian (December 1971) levels. Even against the Japanese yen the US dollar had appreciated in real terms by about 10 percent over this entire period. In 1986 the bilateral PPP relations were almost restored by the sharp fall in the value of the dollar. Nevertheless the increase in the real US value of the dollar in the early 1980s was historic. There is no parallel for the phenomenon of an ever strengthening currency with continuous capital inflows, and with the current external account steadily deteriorating for such a long period of time.

Choice of Base Period

In order to provide a meaningful picture of developments, it is important to find an appropriate base period when the exchange rate is assumed to be at PPP and satisfactorily reflects an equilibrium based on the relative competitive positions of two countries. A starting point or an equilibrium point can be identified by analysing the behaviour of a country's competitiveness, its trade balance and the exchange market. Price competitiveness is often measured in terms of relative international market shares. Therefore, a possible hypothesis is that when the exchange rate is in equilibrium the country will not gain or lose market shares, and firms profit margins are constant.

There are other ways in which a base period for PPP can be chosen and it is difficult to say whether a certain choice is the best for all purposes. However, it is possible to obtain important information about the variability of deviations over time even if the *level* of deviations cannot be assessed with certainty.

Choice between Bilateral and Multilateral Measurements

A multilateral calculation of relative purchasing power parity calls for the weighting of a number of bilateral real exchange rates. In Figures A.III.2 and A.III.3 we have chosen to use the weighted averages of the various bilateral purchasing power parity indexes for two groups of countries, i.e. real effective exchange rates. The weights in each index are bilateral trade weights. A PPP index can also be derived with more sophisticated weighting schemes allowing for non-zero export and import price elasticities and considering trade with third country. Test of PPP with such weights have been shown to give similar results, but require much more work on analyses and estimations (see, for example, Artus and McGuire, 1982).

Bilateral and multilateral measures are both interesting in their own way. Thus, if we want to assess the likelihood of a devaluation in the near future, it could be a good idea to analyse changes in the PPP index for a whole currency basket. On the other hand, if, for example, we are trying to find principles for evaluating claims and debts in various currencies, we need to make bilateral comparisons.

Figure A.III.2 shows the development of the real effective exchange rate for major OECD countries; 1980–82 is base period and the wholesale price index has been used. This data covers the period 1976–86. It is quite obvious that the deviations from PPP have been substantial for this group of countries. We can also see that the deviations have been long lasting for at least the US dollar and the pound. The amplitudes in the deviations and the time it takes to restore PPP differ among the four countries. These differences can be explained by differences in degree of openness to international trade and in trade elasticities. For the period covered in Figure A.III.2, trade in Japan and the USA accounted for 10–15 percent of a GDP, while the corresponding figure for West Germany and the United

Figure A.III.2   Real effective exchange rates – major OECD countries 1976–86

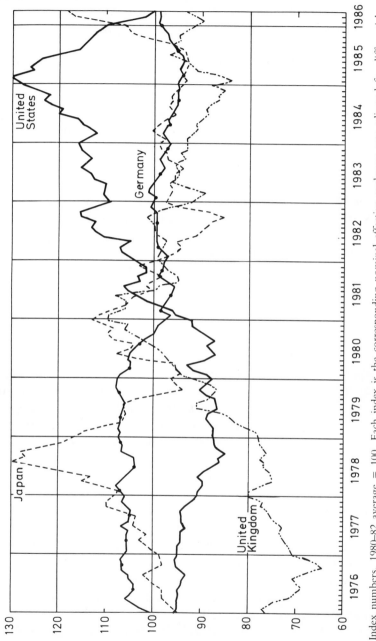

Index numbers, 1980–82 average = 100. Each index is the corresponding nominal effective exchange rate adjusted for differential inflation in wholesale prices of non-food manufactures.

Kingdom was 25–30 percent. In addition, the US dollar has a special role in the world economy, which may add further explanation why the behaviour of this currency deviates from that of other currencies in the figure.

The United Kingdom also deserves special mention since the discovery of North Sea Oil might have caused a change in the PPP-equilibrium level.

From 1976 the real effective exchange rate index shows a powerful rise for the UK. From its lowest value of just around 65, the index had reached 110 by 1979. Thygesen (1977) noted this tendency for the period up to 1977 and commented:

> The sterling and lira depreciations in 1976 are the most obvious examples that exchange rates may move quite a bit further than observation of past and current inflation differentials would suggest. Temporary departures from PPP will tend to justify themselves, as depreciation feeds into domestic costs and prices. It is possible to check some of these defects by a subsequent tightening of policy, only at considerable short-run cost in terms of employment.

The sharp turn in the index in December 1976 was partly the result of a policy; in December 1976 the British government was granted a loan of 3.9 billion USD from the International Monetary Fund, and undertook at the same time a more restrictive economic policy. The sharp swing can be ascribed to expectations in connection with the new policy as well as the prospects associated with North Sea oil.

Figure A.III.3 exhibits the development of real exchange rates in some small and relatively open economies representing three different exchange rate regimes. The pattern of deviations is different as compared to that presented for the major OECD countries. We can see smaller amplitudes and shorter times for restoring PPP. The development for the Swiss franc 1977–78 reminds us about the development of the US dollar 1979–86, i.e., it is characterized by a dramatic increase in the real effective exchange rate. However, the measures taken to restore PPP differ in the two countries. The restoring of PPP for the US dollar has taken very long time and international policy cooperation has been attempted. The fast return

Figure A.III.3. **Real effective exchange rates – small and relatively open economies 1976–86**

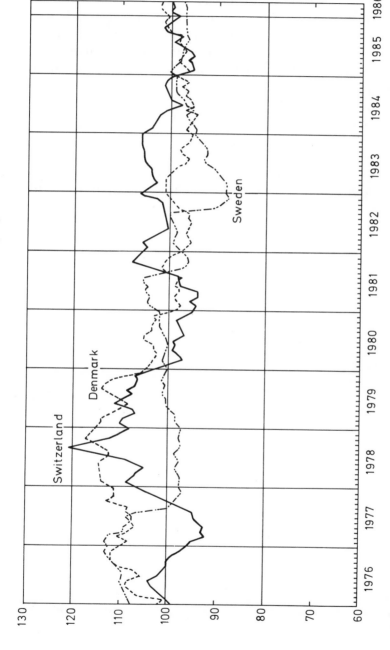

Index numbers, 1980–82 average = 100. Each index is the corresponding nominal effective exchange rate adjusted for differential inflation in wholesale prices of non-food manufactures.

to equilibrium for the Swiss franc was effected with the help of negative interest rates on deposits in Switzerland for foreigners.

For many pegged currencies, especially currencies in LDCs, there is a tendency for the deviations from PPP always to be in the same direction. Thus even if a mean-reverting process might prevail the expected value of the deviations may differ from zero. In this case there are excess profit opportunities in international trade. Though, their duration may be hard to forecast.

The PPP theory seems to command greater validity as the length of the period increases. Large deviations can persist over periods of several years as a result of political measures and interventions. We have noticed substantial deviations in short-term and medium-term perspectives, but at least a tendency towards a return to PPP over the long run even for countries with a pegged exchange rate.

APPENDIX III.3 _____

FISHER OPEN: INTEREST RATES AND EXPECTED EXCHANGE RATE CHANGES

The Fisher Open Relationship (FO) refers to the equilibrium in international interest rates after adjustment for expected exchange rate movements. The relationship, which is also known as Fisher's International Effect (after Irving Fisher, whose results were published in 1896 in an essay entitled 'Appreciation and Interest'), or International Fisher Parity can be written:

$$\frac{e^*_{t+1} - e_t}{e_t} = \frac{i^D_t - i^F_t}{1 + i^F_t} \qquad (AIII.4)$$

where

e = spot rate at time t,

e^*_{t+1} = market expectations at time t regarding future spot rate at time $t + 1$,

i^D_t = domestic interest rate for one period at time t,

i^F_t = foreign interest rate for one period at time t.

According to FO the expected exchange rate change is reflected in the interest differential for assets under equal financial risk in two countries. Tests of FO include a hypothesis about expectation formation and are therefore never conclusive. The main debate surrounding FO is whether there is a systematic deviation that could reflect a risk-premium on holding a particular currency. We cannot review the masssive amount of tests that have been performed. We note, however, that there is increasing evidence of systematic deviations but there is little agreeement on whether the deviations represent risk-premia, market inefficiency, or a learning mechanism.

FO is sometimes tested by an analysis of the ability of the forward exchange rate to serve as a predictor of the future spot exchange rate. The equivalence between this test and direct FO-tests depends on interest rate parity (IRP), i.e., the forward premium on a currency relative to another reflects the interest differential between the currencies or

$$\frac{f_t - e_t}{e_t} = \frac{i_t^D - i_t^F}{1 + i_t^F} \qquad \text{(AIII.5)}$$

where f_t is the forward rate at time t for delivery of currency at time $t+1$.

Comparing equation AIII.5 for IRP with equation AIII.4 for FO shows that if both hold, then $f_t = e_{t+1}^\star$, i.e., the forward rate is the expected future spot rate. IRP holds if covered arbitrage between currencies is feasible without large transaction costs and exchange controls. This arbitrage operation is between currency positions with identical risk. Therefore, we would expect IRP to hold, and there is overwhelming empirical evidence that it does within the euro-markets, but to a lesser extent between, say, T-bills issued in different countries. The tests of FO which compare forward premia with exchange rate changes is therefore equivalent to comparing interest differentials in euro-markets with exchange rate changes.

One simple way of illustrating FO is to analyse *ex post* data for exchange rate changes and substitute these for expectations in the FO relationship (AIII.5). It may be assumed that on the average over time expectations should be correct, and *ex post* deviations from FO should represent surprises and occur randomly. We want to illustrate the validity of the FO relationship by using SEK as a representative small open economy currency. The use of the Swedish krona is also interesting since it has been surrounded by a severe exchange control. However, it seems to have been eroded during the early 1980s. Unfortunately, a problem with SEK is that there is no formal euro-interest rate for a longer period. As an

Figure A.III.4   Deviations from Fisher Open Relationship – Eurorates

Weekly data, per cent/quarter
—— Actual changes in exchange rate, per cent/quarter
---- Differences in Eurorates (three-month)

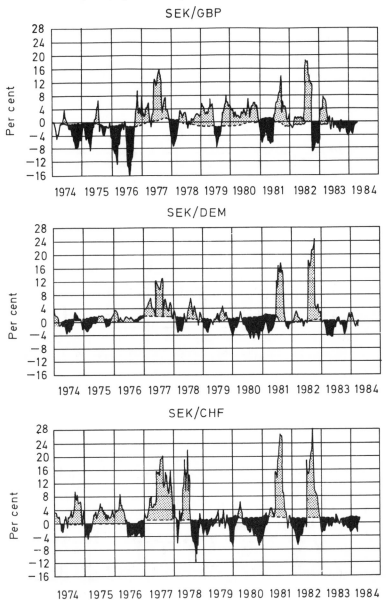

Source: Oxelheim (1985).

alternative, for illustrative purposes, we may 'create' a 'euro-SEK' rate by adding the premium on the SEK/USD to the euro-dollar rate.

Figures A.III.4 shows interest differentials, exchange rate changes and deviations from FO on a weekly *ex post* basis between the three-month 'euro-SEK' rate and the euro-pound (GBP), the euro-

Figure A.III.5　Deviations from Fisher Open Relationship – Treasury bill rates

Monthly data
—— Actual changes in exchange rate, per cent/quarter
---- Differences in treasury bill rates (three-month)

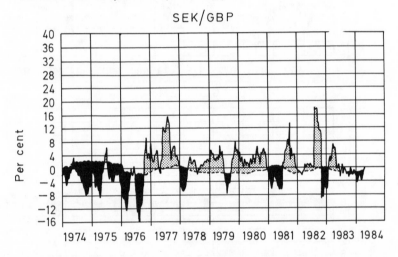

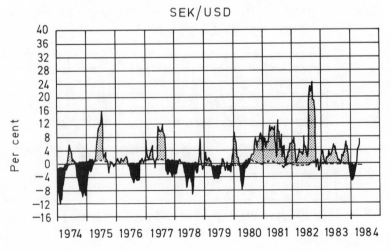

mark (DEM), and the euro-swiss franc (CHF) rates, respectively. The figures reveal large short-term deviations from FO on an *ex post* basis. In other words, interest differentials predict only a small share of exchange rate changes. The shaded areas above and below the dotted lines should be equal for FO to hold, i.e., if expectations on the average are correct. Furthermore, the deviations should be

Figure A.III.5   (cont'd)

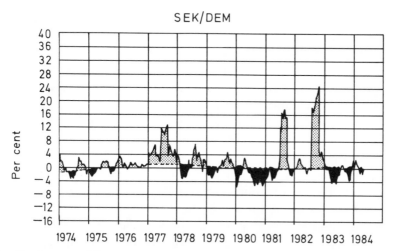

SEK/DEM

Note: For Germany differences in treasury bill/Frankfurt rates (three month).

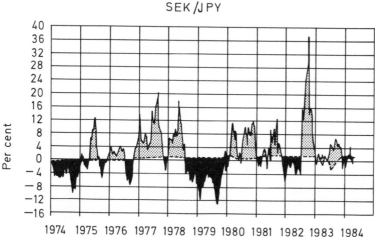

SEK/JPY

Source: Oxelheim (1985).

randomly distributed to strongly support FO. Just by eyeing the figure it seems there is substantial positive serial correlation among deviations. This is an indication of risk-premia, market-inefficiencies or learning processes. In the latter case FO may hold, but it takes time for agents to learn a new pattern of exchange rate changes.

Figures A.III.5 show on a monthly basis the FO relationship for Treasury-bill rates between Sweden on the one hand and the UK, the US, Germany, and Japan on the other. Again, we compare differences in three-month T-bill rates with actual exchange rate changes. The securities for which these rates are quoted need not be identical in terms of political and default risks. However, the differences are most likely small and influence rates only slowly. Deviations for the UK are consistently negative for 1974–1976 and, thereafter, mainly positive. For the US, there are consistently positive deviations after 1980, and for Japan there are also long periods with non-random deviations. In summary, it seems as if FO does not necessarily hold on the average for T-bill rates, but we noted above that due to political risk, this result can be expected when the comparison refers to securities issued in different countries. Furthermore, on an *ex post* basis, deviations seem non-randomly distributed. This result contradicts much work on FO for countries with floating exchange rates. Sweden, however, has a pegged rate and the central bank often pursues a policy of pegging interest rates as well. In markets with perfect mobility of financial capital we would still expect FO to hold and only risk-premia to cause deviations. We are unable to determine with these simple illustrations whether the strong serial correlation in *ex post* deviations from FO actually captures *ex ante* deviation and, in that case, whether deviations depend on risk premia, market inefficiencies or learning processes. One can expect a large amount of research into these issues in the near future.

IV

A COMPREHENSIVE APPROACH TO MEASURING AND HEDGING MACROECONOMIC EXPOSURE

IV.1 INTRODUCTION

In Chapter III we reviewed several approaches to measuring and managing exchange rate and other risks related to the macroeconomic environment of the firm. It was noted that all these approaches were partial in the sense that the interdependences among different risk sources were not recognized. Furthermore, most were partial in the additional sense that the exposure measures included only a proportion of the firm's cash flows.

In this chapter we show how exposure to different macroeconomic risks can be measured taking into consideration interdependences among exchange rates, inflation rates, interest rates, and the relative prices of the firm's outputs and inputs. The exposure measure we suggest expresses the sensitivity of either cash flows or the firm's market value to changes in relevant variables. We demonstrate how such measures can be obtained using regression analysis of historical data. In Chapter V we discuss how managerial judgment may be used to complement the analysis of past periods.

A measure of the firm's exposure to changes in exchange rates and other variables should be *operational* in the sense that it provides relevant guidelines for hedging and cover decisions, if so desired.

Two problems arise in this connection. The first problem concerns the stability of exposure measures. The second problem is one of relating exposure measures to hedging instruments.

Stability of measures is important since exposure based on regression analysis is estimated from historical data, while hedging and cover actions are forward looking. We discuss and compare from the point of view of stability alternative ways of measuring exposure to *either* market-price variables such as exchange rates and interest rates *or* to policy disturbances and other international economic events, such as money supply changes and oil prices changes. *Political risk* in this connection is identified as uncertainty about the exposure coefficients in the regression equation that describes the firm's exposure.

Problems with relating exposure measures to specific hedging instruments occur when the variable for which exposure is identified is not directly related to a variable for which a hedging instrument exists. For example, forward foreign exchange contracts provide hedging against variability in the exchange rate, but exposure may be more closely related to money supply and budget deficit variability.

In Section 2 we analyse and compare different methods of measuring exposure. This discussion is based on Oxelheim and Wihlborg (1986). Section 3 discusses how increased stability of exposure measures may be obtained by decomposing cash flows. Thereafter, in Section 4, we turn to the problem of using the exposure measures in hedging transactions.

Finally, in Section 5 the role of the firm's time-perspective for exposure measures and hedging is discussed. Appendix IV.1 uses data on Swedish manufacturing to illustrate the practical application of the chapter's more theoretical discussion.

IV.2 EXPOSURE MEASURES

IV.2.a Problems of Defining Cash Flow Exposure

Exposure often has the connotation of concern about risk and it may therefore seem that only risk-averse firms would worry about exposure. However, even a risk-neutral firm concerned primarily with expected returns needs to understand the sensitivity of its value and cash flows to changes in exchange rates and other macroeconomic variables in order to measure the impact of expected changes in these variables. Therefore, most of the analysis below has validity for both risk-neutral and risk-averse firms. Only risk-averse firms in the sense described in Chapter II would be concerned about hedging, however.

We assume that the firm has an economic objective. Such an objective may be defined in terms of the net present value of future expected cash flows as in Lessard (1979), or in terms of near-term cash flows, or profits. Exposure measures would be defined correspondingly as the sensitivity of net present value, cash flows or profits with respect to, for example, exchange rate changes. According to Oxelheim (1984a), many firms desire an exposure measure closely related to sensitivities of this kind. For example, some firms worry about fluctuations in market value, caused by exchange rates, others about fluctuations in profits or cash flows.

Here we define exposure as the sensitivity of cash flows to changes in different macroeconomic variables. Since the net present value depends on future expected cash flows, it is simple—at least conceptually—to take the additional step of defining exposure in terms of the net present value. We return to this issue in Section 4 of this chapter.

In Chapter III, Section 2.e we presented a measure of exchange rate exposure in terms of cash flow (X) sensitivity:

$$\frac{\text{cov}[e_t, X_t]}{\text{var}[X_t]}$$

This measure is the covariance between cash flows and the exchange rate relative to the variance of all cash flows and tells us the contribution of the exchange rate to the variance of all cash flows. It could be obtained by regressing cash flows on the exchange rate. This exposure measure has serious drawbacks:

1. It is not separate from exposures to variables related to the exchange rate, such as interest rates and the inflation rate, and by disregarding the influence of these variables, the above exposure measure may provide a strongly misleading impression of exchange rate exposure.

2. It may not be stable over time, and exposure coefficients obtained from historical data may not provide good guidance for the future.

The first point can be seen by considering a firm's other exposures. For example, if exchange rate exposure is defined as above, the firm would consistently measure interest rate exposure by estimating

$$\frac{\text{cov}[i_t, X_t]}{\text{var}[X_t]}$$

where i_t is the interest rate in period t. Since the exchange rate and the interest rate are correlated, according to most macroeconomic models, the two exposures would be partly overlapping. Similarly, if the firm measures inflation risk, and inflation and exchange rates are correlated, inflation exposure and exchange rate exposure would be overlapping. To resolve this overlap problem the exposure coefficients should be *partial* correlation coefficients such that covariances are estimated holding all other variables constant. A *multiple regression* of the cash flows on the exchange rate and variables suspected of correlation with this variable in a general equilibrium system would accordingly resolve the problem of overlap.

An important reason for instability in a simple exchange rate exposure measure is that an exchange rate change may be real or nominal, and its cause may be a real or a monetary disturbance. In our terminology a real exchange rate change is a deviation from relative purchasing power parity. Relative purchasing power parity holds when the rate of change of the exchange rate offsets the inflation differential between two countries. Therefore, a real exchange rate change implies that there is a change in the relative price between countries of a bundle of goods. Formally,

$$e_t/e_{t-1} \equiv [P_t^{US}/P_{t-1}^{US})/(P_t^{F}/P_{t-1}^{F})]\cdot(u_t/u_{t-1}),$$

where e_t is dollars per unit of foreign currency, P_t^{US} and P_t^{F} are the US and the foreign price levels, respectively, and u_t is the deviation from PPP—the real exchange rate.

The above identity for the relationship between the nominal and the real exchange rate does not reveal that, depending on the underlying disturbance, changes in the relative prices of goods and demand changes may accompany nominal and real exchange rate changes, as well as inflation and interest rate changes. The complexity of the relationship among these variables provides a strong reason for using multiple regression analysis to measure exposures. There are econometric problems associated with multiple regression analysis as well. We discuss them briefly in the Appendix to this chapter. If regression analysis cannot be conducted, then it becomes necessary to form judgment based on an understanding of macroeconomic relationships and the cash flow effects of changes in different variables. In Chapter V we will look in more detail at information requirements for forming such judgments, and in Chapter VI a scenario approach to measuring exposure is presented as an alternative to the regression approach.

We suggest now two ways in which improved exposure measures can be obtained from historical data by means of regression analysis. In the first—presented in Section IV.2.b—we clarify better the distinction between real and nominal variables while in IV.2.c the exposures are defined as functions of underlying macroeconomic disturbances. Thereafter, in III.2.d, we argue that the advantage of one measure over the other depends largely on uncertainty about the behaviour of government authorities, i.e., on political risk.

IV.2.b Exposure in Terms of Market Price Variables

The firm trying to evaluate its exposure could run the following regression using, for example, quarterly data on cash flows and market price variables:

$$
\begin{aligned}
\frac{X_t^\$}{P_t^{US}} = E_{t-1}&\left[\frac{X_t^\$}{P_t^{US}}\right] + a_1(P_t^{US} - E_{t-1}\,[P_t^{US}]) \\
&+ a_2\,(P_t^F - E_{t-1}\,[P_t^F]) + a_3(e_t - E_{t-1}[e_t]) \qquad (IV.1)\\
&+ a_4(i_t^{US} - E_{t-1}[i_t^{US}]) + a_5(i_t^F - E_{t-1}[i_t^F])\\
&+ a_6(r_t - E_{t-1}[r_t]) + \epsilon_t
\end{aligned}
$$

where:

$X_t^\$$ = total cash flows in dollars
P_t^{US} = price level in the USA (shareholders' habitat)
E_{t-1} = expectations operator in period $t-1$
P_t^F = foreign price level

e_t = exchange rate
i_t^{US} = interest rate in the US
i_t^F = foreign interest rate
r_t = relative price(s) of relevance for firm's profitability
ϵ_t = error term

Equation IV.1 has the shareholders' real value of cash flows as the dependent variable. Thus, nominal accounting data should be deflated with a price index. The independent variables are separated into *expected* cash flows as of period $t-1$ and cash flow effects of *unanticipated* changes in the domestic price level, the foreign price level(s), the exchange rate(s), the domestic and the foreign interest rate(s), and relative prices in the firm's commodity markets. Expected cash flows would depend on the expected levels of the different variables and the cash flow sensitivity to expected changes in the variables in the following way:

$$E_{t-1}\left[\frac{X_t^{\$}}{P_t^{US}}\right] = a_0' + a_1' E_{t-1}[P_t^{US}] + a_2' E_{t-1}[P_t^F]$$

$$+ a_3' E_{t-1}[e_t] + a_4' E_{t-1}[i_t^{US}] + a_5' E_{t-1}[i_t^F] \qquad \text{(IV.2)}$$

$$+ a_6' E_{t-1}[r_t]$$

where the primed parameter $a_1' - a_6'$ shows the sensitivity of cash flows to expected changes in variables. The expected values of different variables are forecasts.

The sensitivities $a_1' - a_6'$ may or may not differ from coefficients $a_1 - a_6$ for unanticipated changes. The former may be obtained by regression analysis, or total expected cash flows could be obtained from the firm's budget, to the extent that this represents a carefully developed forecast. In the remainder we focus on exposure to unanticipated changes.

The length of one period over which cash flow effects are estimated would depend on the length of time over which the firm forms its expectations of cash flows and the speed with which it may wish to take action in the form of hedging, etc. For realism we may envision all data as quarterly averages.

We have here taken the position that exchange rate changes may correspond to either country's inflation rate or to deviations from PPP, in which case there are *real* exchange rate changes. The coefficient a_3 captures effects of *real* changes, i.e., of nominal exchange rate changes at constant price levels. The cash flow effects of the two kinds of exchange rate changes are bound to be different, since a real exchange rate change implies a change in relative prices between countries. The cash flow effect would depend on which relative prices and which demand and cost effects are associated with domestic inflation, foreign inflation, and real exchange rate changes, respectively (see e.g., Cornell, 1980; Shapiro, 1983). It is important also to distinguish between the impact of those relative price changes which are *independent* of exchange rates and inflation, and relative price changes which occur in the macroeconomic adjustment process. The former impact is captured by coefficient a_6 and the latter by a_1, a_2, and a_3, since the cash flow effects of inflation and exchange rate changes would depend on the relative price effects that occur in the macroeconomic adjustment process. Without using this kind of approach to measuring exposure, a firm could easily be misled by relative price changes, believing their source is a fundamental change in business conditions rather than a temporary effect of macroeconomic disturbances.

Each a coefficient is an exposure measure, i.e., a sensitivity measure in the form of a covariance between real cash flows and each variable *holding other variables constant*, relative to the total variance of real cash flows. The coefficient in front of expected cash flows should be equal to one and the error term should be randomly distributed. If not, additional variables may have to be introduced into the equation, for example, by distinguishing between several foreign currencies.

IV.2.c Exposure in Terms of Macroeconomic Disturbances

Real exchange rate changes may occur for a number of reasons. An unanticipated monetary disturbance such as a money supply increase would, according to many macroeconomic models, lead to an immediate real depreciation, a fall in the interest rate, and an increase in the demand for goods. A fiscal contraction—an aggregate real disturbance—on the other hand, could lead to a real depreciation, a fall in the interest rate, and a decrease in the demand for goods. Clearly, the magnitude of the demand effect associated with a particular real exchange rate change would depend on the source of the disturbance. Accordingly, the coefficient a_3 in equation IV.1 may not be stable over time but depend on the relative frequency and magnitude of monetary and fiscal policy changes.

These considerations suggest that exposure could be defined in terms of underlying macroeconomic disturbances. We may, for example, define exposure based on coefficients in the following expression:

$$\frac{X_t^\$}{P_t^{US}} = E_{t-1}\left[\frac{X_t^\$}{P_t^{US}}\right] + b_1(M_t^{US} - E_{t-1}[M_t^{US}])$$

$$+ b_2(M_t^F - E_{t-1}[M_t^F]) + b_3(D_t^{US} - E_{t-1}[D_t^{US}]) \quad \text{(IV.3)}$$

$$+ b_4(D_t^F - E_{t-1}[D_t^F]) + b_5(r_t - E_{t-1}[r_t]) + \pi_t$$

where:

M^{US}, M^F = the money supplies of the United States and foreign country(ies), respectively

D^{US}, D^F = the budget deficit of the United States and foreign country(ies), respectively

π_t = error term.

Equation IV.3 can naturally be extended to include other macroeconomic variables such as productivity growth and oil price shocks until the error term obtains desired properties. Econometric problems may arise as a result of multicollinearity—high correlation among independent variables—when the number of independent variables increases. As we argue in the Appendix to this chapter, such multicollinearity forces the analyst to reduce the number of variables in order to capture the most essential relationships.

The sensitivity coefficients represent the covariances between real cash flows and each exogenous disturbance holding other variables constant relative to the total cash flow variance as in the previous case. Estimating cash flow as a function of a set of exogenous variables as in equation IV.3 can be seen as an alternative to the APT (Arbitrage Pricing Theory) for analysing the contribution of risk factors to the rate of return on assets (see e.g., Ross, 1976). APT refers to equilibrium asset pricing, however, while our exposure analysis does not require a stable relationship between cash flows and equilibrium asset prices.

IV.2.d   Comparing the Exposure Measures and Political Risk

We argued above that the a coefficients in equation IV.1 may not be stable over time since their magnitudes depend on the source of underlying disturbances. Can we expect the b coefficients in equation IV.3 to be stable? As Lucas (1976) has pointed out, shifts in the behaviour of policy authorities influence coefficients in regressions like equation IV.3. Assume, for example, that the central bank first behaves according to a rule like $M_t = \bar{M} + v_t$, where $\bar{M}$ is a constant and v_t is a random disturbance. The authority then shifts to another rule like $M_t = cM_{t-1} + v'_t$ where c is a correlation coefficient and v'_t is the new random disturbance term. If cash flows in period t depend on the expected future money supply for period $t+1$, then the relationship between cash flows and the money supply in period t in a reduced form like equation IV.3 would be influenced by the above policy-rule shift. In other words, the coefficient b_1 in the reduced form equation is influenced by policy rules. Similar arguments can be made for coefficients b_2, b_3, and b_4. The stability of each of these coefficients depends on the stability of policy rules for domestic and foreign fiscal policy, and foreign monetary policy, respectively.

Uncertainty about policy rules is an element of *political risk*. The above analysis implies that political risk causes *uncertainty about the coefficients* of sensitivity of cash flows to macroeconomic disturbances. Another source of political risk is the potential imposition of exchange controls and credit controls. Such controls could influence structural relationships among, for example, real exchange rates, interest rates, and money supplies. Direct regulatory policy measures may have direct cash flow effects as well (see Dooley and Isard, 1980), but to the extent they are not forecast, their most important effects would be structural, i.e., they would influence sensitivity coefficients like policy rule shifts do (see, e.g., Wihlborg, 1982).

An important effect of uncertainty about policy rules is that it creates uncertainty for each economic agent about the expectation formation of other agents. Rational expectations models generally presume that each agent knows how other agents form expectations based on known structural relationships and policy rules. However, after each policy rule shift it takes time for all agents to learn the new rule. In the meantime, the relationship between the current level of a policy variable and average expectations of future levels will be changing. During this learning process the exchange rate and other price variables are changing or fluctuating even at constant money supplies and fiscal policies (see, e.g., Frydman, 1982).

This discussion indicates that when there is uncertainty about policy rules and average perceptions of these rules are changing, there occur exchange rate changes, and inflation and interest rate changes that cannot be explained by exogenous disturbances in a simple regression like equation IV.3. Another way of expressing the same phenomenon is that the b coefficients in regression (IV.3) are changing during the learning process. Meese and Rogoff (1983) confirm this discussion by showing, using alternative models of the exchange rate, that a large share of the exchange rate variance cannot be explained by 'fundamental' variables and that coefficients tend to be unstable.

We would expect that periods of learning are characterized by a large amount of speculative activity since individual and average expectations differ. Therefore, periods of substantial speculative activity should be characterized by relatively large exchange rate changes without simultaneous changes in 'fundamental' factors like the money supply or the budget deficit.

This discussion indicates that, in a comparison of equations IV.1 and IV.3 as ways of measuring exposure, equation IV.1 is relatively more stable when there is substantial political risk. The reason is that with higher political risk, the instability of the coefficients in equation IV.3 increases, and the exchange rate and other price variables tend to change and fluctuate even at constant levels of policy variables. The larger the proportion of the variance in the price variables in equation IV.1 that cannot be explained by shifts in policy variables, the more likely it is that the a coefficients in equation IV.1 are stable. In other words, exchange rate changes, interest rate changes, and other price changes may be viewed as purely exogenous disturbances in themselves. On the other hand, with relative certainty about policy rules, the coefficients in equation IV.1 could be unstable since they depend on the nature of underlying disturbances. The most appropriate way of measuring exposure can be selected by. running regressions over subperiods. Thereby, the stability of coefficients can be evaluated, if data exists for a sufficiently long period.

IV.3   DECOMPOSING CASH FLOWS

Coefficients of the type described in equations IV.1 and IV.3 are economic measures of exposure, and they provide a guide for hedging or adjusting business activity. Their estimation enables the manager to judge how sensitive the firm is to macroeconomic disturbances without having to estimate a complete macroeconomic model. Thus, the estimation of such coefficients would be an important objective of exposure analysis. We turn now to a discussion of the difficulties associated with the implementation of this kind of exposure analysis.

We mentioned that it is desirable to distinguish between anticipated and unanticipated changes in variables influencing cash flows. Anticipated changes are obtained by forecasting. The firm's budget ideally can be seen as a forecast of cash flows based on forecasts of exchange rates, prices, etc. To fulfil this role, the budget must, of course, truly reflect market price forecasts rather than being based on current prices or being an optimistic 'best case' target. We return in Chapter VII to a discussion of the role of the budget in exposure analysis.

When implementing the exposure analysis a decision must be made regarding the *level of aggregation* of cash flows on which the analysis should be performed. Total cash flows (X in equations IV.1 and IV.3) evaluated *after tax* may consist of flows from a number of products as well as from several subsidiaries in different countries. The total real after-tax value of cash flows for product i in country j in dollar terms ($X^{ij\$}/P^{US}$) can be written as:

$$\frac{X^{ij\$}}{P^{US}} = \frac{X^{ij} \cdot e^j}{P^{US}} \tag{IV.4}$$

where X^{ij} is after-tax cash flows in j-currency and e^j is dollars per j-currency unit. These cash flows can be decomposed further. After defining

$$e^j \equiv \frac{P^{US}}{P^j} \cdot u^j$$

we can express cash flows for product i in subsidiary j in the following way:

$$\frac{X^{ij}\cdot u^j}{P^j} = u^j \cdot q^{ij}\left(\frac{OP^{ij}}{P^j} - \frac{IP^{ij}}{P^j} - \frac{W^{ij}}{P^j}\right)\cdot(1-T^j) \qquad \text{(IV.5)}$$

$$+ \frac{T^j\cdot DEP^{ij}\cdot u^j}{P^j} - \frac{u^j}{P^j}[(1-T^j)\cdot i^j\cdot L^{ij} - (1-\beta^j)\cdot \hat{P}^j\cdot L^{ij}]$$

where

$$u^j/P^j \equiv e^j/P^{US},$$

and

u^j	= the real exchange rate between the dollar and j's currency,
q^{ij}	= quantity sold of product i in country j,
OP^{ij}	= i-output price in country j,
IP^{ij}	= input price per unit of i-output in country j,
W^{ij}	= wages per unit of i-output in country j,
T^j	= tax rate for subsidiary in country j,
DEP^{ij}	= depreciation in country j for product i,
i^j	= interest rate for subsidiary in j,
L^{ij}	= nominal debt in j-currency associated with production of product i,
β^j	= degree of indexation of debt in country j,
$P^j(\hat{P}^j)$	= price level (inflation) in country j.

Equation IV.5 decomposes cash flows for a particular product in a particular country into a 'business operation component' (a function of relative prices), a depreciation tax shield component, and a financial cost component. In Chapter V we discuss in more detail how different cash flows are influenced by different types of disturbances. Here it is sufficient to note that the impact of market price variables and macroeconomic disturbances on total cash flows depends on the composition of cash flows.

All terms on the right-hand side are expressed as *real* cash flows in terms of country j's currency multiplied by the real exchange rate between the home currency (dollars) and country j's currency. We can see in the first term on the right-hand side how real cash flows from business operations are influenced by volume and relative price effects. The second term is the depreciation tax shield evaluated in real foreign currency terms and multiplied by the real exchange rate.

The third term captures financial costs after taxes. We include this term under the assumption that the firm is concerned with cash flows available for distribution to shareholders. L^{ij} refers to the debt capacity from the project and is expressed in the foreign currency. Financial costs consist of tax-deductible interest costs and non-taxable real capital gains from inflation. The inflation gain is a positive cash flow under the assumption that the firm's debt-equity ratio is held constant. This assumption allows us to keep the real discount rate independent of the inflation rate. If $\beta = 1$, there is perfect indexation of foreign currency debt and the inflation gain is zero. Alternatively, inflation gains (losses) could have been viewed as decreases (increases) in the real value of debt. The discount rate should then be considered exposed to inflation, however. Our approach is expositionally more simple.

Equation IV.5 shows the main categories of cash flows on which exchange rates, interest rates, and price levels have an impact. Clearly, these variables may influence each category in a different way. Equation IV.5 also demonstrates how exposure may depend on capital intensity (through depreciation) and capital structure (through debt capacity).

Total cash flow for a firm is the summation of cash flows as in equation IV.5 over products (i) and countries (j). Thus, the estimation of a cash flow exposure by means of equations IV.1 or IV.3 on an aggregate level presumes that the share of product i and country j in cash flows is constant, and that depreciation tax shields as well as financial cash flows remain constant shares of each subsidiary's cash flows.

Recognizing the possible variability in the structure of cash flows in equation IV.5 as well as in the macroeconomic relationships underlying the exposure coefficients in equation IV.1 and equation IV.3, there are substantial informational advantages to be gained from decomposing cash flows for purposes of exposure analysis. Cash flows may be broken down by:

i. country,
ii. product,
iii. variable cash flows from business operations as opposed to depreciation and financial cash flows.

After decomposition, exposure coefficients of the type described in equation IV.1 and equation IV.3 may be estimated for each cash flow component. Further decomposition into cash flows that are *adjustable* and *non-adjustable* in terms of currency denomination is desirable, if there are opportunities to influence exposure by adjusting the currency denomination of loans, currency of invoice, etc.

After decomposition of cash flows, dispersed judgmental information can be used to complement regression analysis of exposure coefficients for different parts of the firm. In times of political uncertainty and uncertainty about the validity of regression coefficients, this kind of judgment may be particularly valuable.

In the next chapter we discuss in more detail how to operationalize the principles for exposure management when regression analysis on historical data provides unreliable exposure measures. In this chapter we continue to analyse how hedging can be accomplished, assuming that we have obtained the relevant coefficients for different kinds of exposure.

IV.4   HEDGING MACROECONOMIC EXPOSURES

IV.4.a   An Example of Exposures to Market Price Variables

In this section we illustrate how cash-flow exposures measured by regression equations can be hedged. We prefer the term hedge to cover since there need not be a one to one correspondence between the position in a currency and the offsetting contract.

The first issue is the form in which regression equations should be estimated. In equations IV.1 and IV.3 all variables are levels, but we could equally well express all variables as rates of change (see Appendix IV.1). Assume this is done for equation IV.5 and that we have obtained the following result for the percentage rate of change of a firm's real cash flow in terms of market price variables.

$$\hat{X}_t^\$ - \hat{P}_t^{US} = E_{t-1}\left[\hat{X}_t^\$ - \hat{P}_t^{US}\right]$$

$$- .1(\hat{P}_t^{US} - E_{t-1}[\hat{P}_t^{US}]) + 0(\hat{P}_t^F - E_{t-1}[\hat{P}_t^F]) \quad \text{(IV.5')}$$

$$- .5(e_t - E_{t-1}[\hat{e}_t]) - .005\,(\hat{i}_t^{US} - E_{t-1}[\hat{i}_t^{US}])$$

$$+ 0(\hat{i}_t^F - E_{t-1}[\hat{i}_t]) + .6(\hat{r}_t - E_{t-1}[\hat{r}_t])$$

This equation shows the percentage change ($^\wedge$) in the US purchasing power of cash flows from a one percent unanticipated change in each of the right-hand side variables holding other variables constant. Note that an individual's price index may differ from the index of the representative shareholder, in which case the individual's exposure may differ as well. With knowledge of such consumption differences, individuals may wish to take additional hedge contracts, which are not discussed here.

The first term on the right-hand side indicates the expected change in cash flows. The figure for this term must be obtained from forecasting as demonstrated in equation IV.2. Next, we see that a one percent unanticipated change in the US price level (inflation) leads to a .1 percent fall in real cash flows. Real cash flows are insensitive to changes in the foreign price level and the foreign interest rate, while a one percent unanticipated change in the exchange rate causes a .5 percent drop in real cash flows, holding other variables constant. A one percent unanticipated interest rate change (i.e., from 10 percent to 10.1 percent) causes a .005 percent fall in real cash flows. The relative price r can be seen as the firm's output price relative to a price index. A one percent increase in this ratio induces an increase of .6 percent in real cash flows.

To obtain the magnitude in dollar terms we need to know the level of expected cash flows. Assume this is $30 million. Then we can calculate cash flow effects in dollars as in Table IV.1. Examples of changes that would cause effects of the described kind are given in the right-hand column. It is important to note that all exposure coefficients are partial, i.e., they refer to the sensitivity of real cash flows to changes in each variable, while other variables are held constant. For example, the exchange rate coefficient indicates the effect of an exchange rate change at a constant price level and a constant interest rate. The relative price coefficient is the sensitivity of cash flows to purely commercial disturbances in the relative price. The firm can now decide whether it wishes to hedge all kinds of macroeconomic exposure or only, say, exchange rate exposure.

Assume that there is a forward market for foreign exchange (pounds in this case) and a futures market for T-bills. Thus, there are two types of hedging contracts but four types of exposure. It is in this case impossible to hedge completely unless two types of exposure can be hedged by internal means. For example, inflation exposure could be hedged by indexation of contracts. We assume first that the firm chooses this route for inflation risk and decides not to hedge purely commercial risk. It remains then to hedge the real exchange rate risk and the interest rate risk, which is also *real* in the sense that it is the risk of changes in interest rates at a constant inflation rate. In a second example, we will assume that the firm chooses to hedge the real interest rate risk internally and the inflation risk through the T-bill futures markets, while remaining exposed to commercial risk. As a third possibility we consider how the firm could partially hedge a combination of inflation and interest rate risk in the T-bill futures market.

IV.4.b Hedging Real Exchange Risk and Real Interest Rate Risk

We use the data in Table IV.1. In addition we know that the forward rate (three months) is $2/£. We know that, if there is a one percent depreciation of the dollar from $2 to $2.02, then there is a real cash flow loss of $.15 million. Thus, in order to hedge, the firm should buy in the forward market a number of pounds such that if the future spot dollar rate depreciates by one percent more than expected, then there would be a cash gain on the forward contract equal to $.15 million. Set the contract size equal to C_F. Then,

$$150\ 000 = C_F\ (2.02 - 2.00) \qquad (IV.6)$$

On the left-hand side is the desired gain on the forward contract in dollars from a one percent change in the exchange rate. On the right-hand side is the contract size in pounds, C_F, times the gain per pound if the exchange rate changes one percent relative to the forward rate, i.e., if pounds are bought at $2.00, and then sold at $2.02. The contract size C_F is £7.5 millions. Buying this amount of pounds for delivery in three months implies that, if there is a depreciation of the dollar equal to one percent, then the firm obtains a cash gain of .15 million, offsetting the cash flow loss of the same amount.

A similar operation can be performed in the futures market for T-bills. We know that a one percent change from 10 to 10.1 percent causes a real cash flow loss of $.0015 millions or $1500. Assume that the three-month T-bill rate is 10 percent, or 2.5 percent on a

Table IV.1 Cash flow effects in million $ of a one percent (unanticipated) change in a market price variable
Assuming other variables constant and expected real cash flows are $30 million

	Exposure coefficient	Real dollar effect (million)	Example
Domestic price level	−.1	−.03	Consumer price index (CPI) goes from 100 to 101 (unanticipated) or a rise in inflation from 10% to 11%
Foreign price level	0	0	
Exchange rate	−.5	−.15	$/£ from $2 to $2.02
Domestic interest rate	−.005	−.0015	Interest rate from 10% to 10.1%
Foreign interest rate	0	0	
Relative price	.6	.18	Output price index relative to CPI increases from 1 to 1.01

quarterly basis, today as well as in the futures market. Then, the spot and future price of a $1000 three-month T-bill is $975.61 (1000/1.025). *How many such T-bills for delivery in three months should be bought in order to gain $.015 million if the interest rate goes to 10.1?* Such an interest rate change would cause a fall in the three-month T-bill price to $975.37 (1000/1.02525). The number of contracts to obtain an offsetting gain for a one percent increase in the interest rate is C_T in:

$$1500 = C_T(975.37 - 975.61) \qquad (IV.7)$$

C_T is −6250. In other words, 6250 T-bills should be *sold* in the futures market. Then if the interest rate goes up from 10 to 10.1 percent, the price on T-bills falls in three months. Accordingly, to fulfil the contract the firm buys 6250 T-bills in the future spot market and fulfils the contract to deliver, receiving a $0.24 gain on each contract or $1500. This gain offsets the $1500 loss in the firm's cash flow, due to the same interest rate change. Also there will be an offsetting gain for any percentage change in interest rates.

In this case only the risks due to changes in the inflation rate and relative prices remain, but by indexing wage contracts, loan contracts, etc., inflation exposure can be avoided. Therefore, all macroeconomic exponents have been hedged and the firm can focus on dealing with uncertainty in its commercial operations, i.e., its exposure to changes in demand and cost conditions.

IV.4.c Hedging Real Exchange Risk and Inflation Risk

In this subsection we assume that real interest rate risk is of no concern. The manager may consider the real interest rate stable. Instead, inflation is uncertain and fluctuations in the inflation rate may cause fluctuations in the nominal interest rate, as well as uncertainty about the profitability of the firm's commercial operations. Both effects are captured by the inflation sensitivity coefficient in equation IV.5. Thus, the firm wishes to hedge exposure to inflation risk as well as real exchange rate exposure. The latter exposure is hedged as in the previous example. Since real interest rate risk is negligible, the T-bill futures market can be used to hedge inflation risk.

In this case the first task is to obtain a measure of the sensitivity of the T-bill interest rate to inflation, since T-bill futures are used to hedge inflation risk. Assume a regression for the T-bill interest rate on unanticipated inflation shows that:

$$i = 10 + .5(\hat{P}_t^{US} - E_{t-1}[\hat{P}_t^{US}]) \qquad (IV.8)$$

where 10 is the anticipated T-bill rate and .5 is the change in the T-bill rate from a one percent change in the inflation rate. For example, a one percentage point increase in the interest rate would lead to a change from 10 to 10.5 percentage points in the interest rate.

We know from Table IV.1 that a one percentage point unanticipated increase in the inflation rate causes a loss of $30 000. Thus, we ask *how many T-bill futures should be bought in order to gain $30 000 when the inflation rate increases one percentage point*. First, we observe that the increase in the inflation rate causes an increase in the interest rate from 10 to 10.5 percent. Then, the three-month T-bill price falls from 975.61 to 974.42 (= 1000/1.02625). Accordingly, to obtain an offsetting gain the number of T-bills to buy in the futures market, C_1, should be

$$30\ 000 = C_1(974.42 - 975.61) \qquad \text{(IV.9)}$$

Thus $C_1 = -25\ 210$. The firm *sells* T-bills in the futures market, and if the inflation rate goes up by one percentage point, the interest rate would go up by half a percentage point, the spot price of T-bills would fall by $1.19 per contract, and the firm would make this gain on each T-bill it must deliver.

IV.4.d Hedging a Combination of Inflation and Interest Rate Risk in the Market for T-bills

In the above examples, one macroeconomic risk—either inflation risk or real interest rate risk—had to remain unhedged since there were only two hedging contracts for three types of macroeconomic risk (in addition to the commercial relative price risk). If the lack of contracts is known to begin with, the exposure of the firm could be measured in terms of those variables for which hedging contracts exist. In our case, these contracts are forward contracts, on which prices are linked to the exchange rate, and T-bill futures, on which prices are linked to the nominal interest rate in each country. Thus, by estimating exposure or sensitivity coefficients for cash flows on exchange rates and nominal interest rates alone, the firm could obtain coefficients that can be used for hedging, as in the example in Subsection IV.4.b above. In other words, the regression would be:

$$(\hat{X}_t^\$ - \hat{P}_t^{US}) = E_{t-1}\left[\hat{X}_t^\$ - \hat{P}_t^{US}\right] + c_3\,(\hat{e}_t - E_{t-1}[\hat{e}_t])$$

$$+\ c_4(\hat{i}_t^{US} - E_{t-1}[\hat{i}_t^{US}]) + c_5(\hat{i}_t^F - E_{t-1}[\hat{i}_t^F])$$

$$+\ c_6(\hat{r}_t - E_{t-1}[\hat{r}_t]) + \pi_t \qquad \text{(IV.10)}$$

In equation IV.10 inflation rates are neglected. Instead, the other coefficients c_3 through c_6 would be influenced by inflation effects and differ from the coefficients for these variables in the previous regressions. Therefore, equation IV.10 is misspecified unless inflation covaries perfectly with one of the other variables. Coefficients are not necessarily stable over time, and the error term could be non-random. Nevertheless, the advantage here is that hedging contracts exist for remaining specific variables in the regression and the coefficients c_3 through c_5 can be used immediately to estimate the hedging contract. In this case, it is possible that the T-bill hedge will be a combination of real interest rate and inflation hedges, and the forward contract will be a combination of real exchange rates and inflation hedges. No hedge will be perfect as in the previous case. The larger remaining variance of cash flows after hedging shows up in the (larger and perhaps serially correlated) error term in equation IV.10 as compared to equation IV.5.

IV.4.e Hedging for Macroeconomic Disturbances: A General Approach

We suggested in Section IV.2 that exposure should be measured by running the regression for cash flows on policy disturbances and possibly other disturbances of a macroeconomic nature as in equation IV.3. This regression can also be formulated with all variables as percentage rates of change in the following way:

$$(\hat{X}_t^\$ - \hat{P}_t^{US}) = \cdot E_{t-1} \left[\hat{X}_t^\$ - \hat{P}_t^{US} \right]$$

$$+ d_1 (\hat{M}_t^{US} - E_{t-1} [\hat{M}_t^{US}]) + d_2 (\hat{M}_t^F - E_{t-1} [\hat{M}_t^F])$$

$$+ d_3 (\hat{D}_t^{US} - E_{t-1}[\hat{D}_t^{US}]) + d_4 (\hat{D}_t^F - E_{t-1} [\hat{D}_t^F]) \qquad \text{(IV.11)}$$

$$+ d_5 (\hat{r}_t - E_{t-1}[\hat{r}_t]) + \epsilon_t$$

As we noted, it is most desirable to use this type of equation for exposure measurement when each policy authority follows a reasonably stable rule of behaviour. From a hedging point of view the firm is now faced with the problem that there are no hedging contracts directly corresponding to money supply uncertainty and budget deficit uncertainty, respectively, in each country. This problem is easily solved, however, by running regressions for the variables that determine profits and losses on hedging contracts on the same macroeconomic disturbances that determine the firm's real cash flows in equation IV.11. Accordingly, in addition to running a regression determining the sensitivity of cash flows to disturbances, the firm runs the following regression for exchange rate changes:

$$\hat{e}_t = E_{t-1}[\hat{e}_t] + g_1(\hat{M}_t^{US} - E_{t-1}[\hat{M}_t^{US}])$$

$$+ g_2 (\hat{M}_t^F - E_{t-1}[\hat{M}_t^F]) + g_3(\hat{D}_t^{US} - E_{t-1}[\hat{D}_t^{US}]) \qquad (IV.12)$$

$$+ g_4 (\hat{D}_t^F - E_{t-1}[\hat{D}_t^F]) + g_5(\hat{r}_t - E_{t-1}[\hat{r}_t]) + \epsilon_t$$

where $E_{t-1}[\hat{e}_t]$ is also the forward premium. This regression shows how the value of a forward contract in foreign currency depends on changes in the money supply, budget deficits, and relative prices. Similar regressions can be run for changes in the domestic interest rate ($\hat{i}^{US}$) with coefficients h_1 through h_5 and changes in the foreign interest rate ($\hat{i}^F$), with coefficients k_1 through k_5 which determine gains or losses on future contracts in T-bills in US dollars and foreign currency, respectively.

Assume now that there is considerable uncertainty about the US money supply for a three-month period and the firm wishes to hedge against the real cash-flow effects of an unanticipated change in the money supply. From equation IV.11 it is known that a one percent unanticipated increase in the US money supply causes a d_1 percent increase in real cash flows. Thus, in order to hedge, the firm should take contracts in the forward market and the T-bill futures markets such that the total effect of a one percent increase in the money supply will be a loss of d_1 percent.

We can solve the hedging problem by considering the matrix in Table IV.2. Real cash flow effects are described in the first line, while the sensitivity of hedging contracts are described in the next three lines. In order to hedge against US money supply uncertainty we take contracts C_F in forward markets, C_T in domestic T-bill futures, and C_{FT} in foreign T-bill futures such that:

$$-E_{t-1}\left[\frac{X_t^\$}{P_t^{US}}\right] d_1 = C_F g_1 + C_T h_1 + C_{FT} k_1 \qquad (IV.13)$$

The left-hand side shows the real dollar loss of a one percent increase in the US money supply. The right-hand side shows the sum of the gains on hedging contracts of sizes C_F, C_T, and C_{FT}, respectively, of a one percent change in the US money supply.

Table IV.2 Sensitivity coefficients
Percentage change

	$\hat{M}_t^{US} - E_{t-1}[\hat{M}_t^{US}]$	$\hat{M}^F - E_{t-1}[\hat{M}_t^F]$	$\hat{D}^{US} - E_{t-1}[\hat{D}_t^{US}]$	$\hat{D}^F - E_{t-1}[\hat{D}_t^F]$
$\hat{X}_t^s - \hat{p}_t^{US}$ real cash flows	d_1	d_2	d_3	d_4
$\hat{e}_t$ forward contract	g_1	g_2	g_3	g_4
$\hat{i}^{US}$ domestic T-bills future	h_1	h_2	h_3	h_4
$\hat{i}^F$ foreign T-bills future	k_1	k_2	k_3	k_4

It can be seen that if the firm is interested in hedging only US money supply risk, then there are many possible combinations of contracts that may constitute a hedge. In fact, only one type of contract is needed. On the other hand, if the firm wishes to hedge all four macroeconomic risks, then three types of hedging contracts are insufficient. The firm may then select one of the risks, say foreign budget deficit risk, as relatively unimportant, and focus on hedging the other three by solving for C_F, C_T, and C_{FT} in a system of three equations consisting of equation IV.13 and the following two:

$$-E_{t-1}\left[\frac{X_t^\$}{P_t^{US}}\right] d_2 = C_F g_2 + C_T h_2 + C_{FT} k_2 \qquad (IV.14)$$

$$-E_{t-1}\left[\frac{X_t^\$}{P_t^{US}}\right] d_3 = C_F g_3 + C_T h_3 + C_{FT} k_3 \qquad (IV.15)$$

In this case, the optimal hedge can be obtained from a combination of contracts. The remaining variance of the firm's real cash flows would depend on the variances of foreign budget deficits, relative price changes due to factors other than policy disturbances, and the pure unsystematic error term ϵ_t in equation IV.11.

IV.5 EXPOSURE, HEDGING, AND THE FIRM'S TIME PERSPECTIVE

In the previous section we assumed that the firm was concerned with cash flows in a certain period. However, we have mentioned that the stockholders' concern is with the net present value of future cash flows. Whether exposure of cash flows as expressed in equations IV.1 and IV.3 actually affects stockholders' valuation of a firm depends on four factors. *First*, intertemporal covariances among macroeconomic variables causing exposure in specific periods influence the degree to which cash flow exposure translates into net present value exposure (see, for example, Lessard, 1979). *Second*, the cost of capital at which future cash flows are discounted influences the relative weights of near term and distant cash flows in the net present value. *Third*, the extent to which stockholders can diversify macroeconomic risk influences the firm's response to exposure.

When macroeconomic risk is diversifiable, stockholders will not claim compensation for absorbing such risk. *Fourth*, if cash flow variability causes outright costs in terms of an increased probability of costly default or costs of adjustment in output and sales, then high cash flow variability reduces the stockholders' valuation of the firm (see Chapter II).

In this section we focus on the first and the second factors. The time perspective of the firm is directly reflected in the second factor—the discount rate. The importance of the first factor—the intertemporal pattern of cash flows—increases with the length of the firm's perspective. As an illustration of the role of the discount rate for the firm's exposure management strategy, we may consider a firm with quarterly cash flows of X units of foreign currency. Assume that the firm has the choice of always leaving these X units uncovered, or of covering *in every quarter* next quarter's cash flow by selling X units of foreign currency in the three-month forward market. Under what conditions for the discount rate is it meaningful to cover cash flows in the next quarter?

The present value of a stream of X units of foreign currency uncovered is:

$$PV_{uc} = E\left[\frac{X \cdot e_1}{(1+d'/4)} + \ldots + \frac{X \cdot e_n}{(1+d'/4)^n}\right] \qquad \text{(IV.16)}$$

where d' is the nominal discount rate and e_1 through e_n are exchange rates.

If the firm consecutively covers on a quarterly basis its present value becomes:

$$PV_c = E\left[\frac{X \cdot f_0}{(1+d'/4)} + \ldots + \frac{X \cdot f_{n-1}}{(1+d'/4)^n}\right] \qquad \text{(IV.17)}$$

where f_0 is *today's* forward rate for three months delivery, and f_{n-1} is the forward rate in period $n-1$ for delivery in the following quarter, period n.

Variances of PV_{uc} and PV_c can be written in the following way:

$$V[PV_{uc}] = X^2 \cdot V\left[\frac{e_1}{(1+d'/4)} + \ldots + \frac{e_n}{(1+d'/4)^n}\right] \qquad \text{(IV.18)}$$

$$V[PV_c] = \frac{X^2}{(1+d'/4)^2} \cdot V\left[\frac{f_1}{(1+d'/4)} + \ldots + \frac{f_{n-1}}{(1+d'/4)^{n-1}}\right] \qquad \text{(IV.19)}$$

where $V[\cdot]$ is a variance of the expression within brackets.

If n is large, the last term in equation IV.18 is negligible, in which case the relative variance of equations IV.18 and IV.19 depends on the discount rate, d', and the variance of spot and forward rates, respectively. (We assume that conditions for obtaining finite variances are fulfilled.) It has been noted by Levich (1979), Mussa (1982), Shapiro (1983), and Oxelheim (1985) that the forward rate tends to change with changes in the spot rate, such that $V[e_t] \approx V[f_t]$ (see also Chapter V for empirical evidence). Then, the gain from consecutive covering depends only on the discount rate, d', or more properly on $(1+d'/4)^2$, which for most firms is not likely to differ much from one. The 'ineffectiveness' in terms of variance reduction of consecutive covering (noted also by Clarke, 1973) arises due to the *discrepancy between the firm's long time perspective as reflected in the discount rate and its short 'action horizon'*.

Naturally, if the firm's planning horizon is only say one year, and cash flows beyond one year are not considered, then the variance of cash flows within this year can be reduced by covering in forward markets all flows within the year. (Remaining uncertainty would depend on the credit risk and payment discipline of customers.) It does not seem to be a rational objective of the firm, however, to give zero weight to flows beyond a specific cutoff date unless this date is distant.

The importance of intertemporal covariances can also be seen in equations IV.18 and IV.19. If the exchange rate in equation IV.18 is mean reverting, the variance of PV_{uc} tends to *decrease* with a longer time perspective (a lower discount rate). In the theoretical macroeconomic literature, the *real* exchange rate has this property, although there has been some contradictory evidence in recent empirical literature (see, e.g., Roll, 1979; Pigott and Sweeney, 1985). The price level certainly does not have this property, however, with the consequence that inflation uncertainty tends to become the dominate cause of exchange rate uncertainty in the long run. Since the forward rate, f, tends to follow the nominal exchange rate, which depends on both inflation and real exchange rate changes, the forward market becomes a more inefficient hedge of real exchange rate risk the more distant are cash flows.

Without going further into hedging policy, we conclude that although exposure of cash flows is an essential component of measuring the exposure of present values, a hedging policy for present value should take into consideration complementary judgment about intertemporal relationships as well.

IV.6 SUMMARY OF THE COMPREHENSIVE APPROACH

Traditional exposure measures are either partial, accounting based, or both. Partiality reveals itself in two ways. First, exposure measures are often restricted to a limited share of cash flows (e.g., transactions exposure). Second, they usually refer to exposure to exchange rate changes neglecting variables that may be related to these exchange rates in a general equilibrium system. Since changes in these related variables also cause exposure, management of exchange rate and related exposures should be coordinated.

Exposure may be defined in terms of market price variables or in terms of underlying macroeconomic disturbances. The advantage of one approach over the other would depend on the relative stability over time of estimated exposure coefficients. We argue that in times of high uncertainty about the behaviour pattern of policy authorities exposure should be defined in terms of market price variables. Then, a large share of the exchange rate variability will be independent of variability in exogenous macroeconomic variables.

We suggest that before estimating exposure coefficients, cash flows should be disaggregated by, for example, product, subsidiary, and type of cash flow (e.g., commercial versus financial). The advantage of such disaggregation is that changes in the composition of the firm's cash flows are easily recognized.

The analysis at a comprehensive level has strong implications for firm's exposure management strategies. One implication is that the relevant exposure to, for example, an exchange rate, should take into account that it may be overlapping with exposures to interest rates, inflation rates, and the commercial exposure of the firm. We showed how the firm can hedge cash flow exposures based on coefficients from regression equations that isolate the influence of different macroeconomic variables or disturbances from each other and from pure business conditions for the firm.

Finally, we discussed the link between cash flow exposure and net present value exposure. Intertemporal covariances between different variables and the firm's discount rate determine whether cash flow exposures tend to cancel over time. If a variable is mean reverting, as is often assumed for the real exchange rate, then the exposure of the firm's value may be negligible in comparison with the cash flow exposure for one period.

APPENDIX IV.1 ─────────────

THE EXPOSURE OF MANUFACTURING INDUSTRIES: ECONOMETRICS

In this Appendix we present as an example results from regression analysis of cash flows of Swedish manufacturing firms. We compare simple exposure measures for the exchange rate alone with more elaborate formulations as suggested in the chapter. We finally discuss some econometric problems arising in the process of measuring exposure.

Exposure analysis should be performed on the firm level with actual cash flow data. Since firms are unwilling to have their basic cash flow figures presented publicly, we have chosen to use publicly available but highly imperfect aggregate accounting data to measure cash flows. Total cash flows consist of commercial flows (gross profits before deduction of depreciation) and financial flows (net interest payments including exchange rate gains or losses). The extent to which firms have covered or hedged different kinds of exposure cannot be determined in aggregate data. The results illustrate, nevertheless, that measures of, say, exchange rate exposure are sensitive to the specification of the regression equation. All data are annual from 1970 through 1983, and all variables are defined as percentage rate of change as suggested in the main text of this chapter. Thus, coefficients indicate the percentage change in real or nominal cash flows from a one percent change in each variable, holding other variables constant.

Table A.IV.1(a)   Exposure measures 1971–83 – All manufacturing
Sample of 40 firms; billions SEK.
Dependent and independent variables in % rate of change.

Dependent	Constant	P^{SWE}	P^{WORLD}	e	i^{SWE}	i^{WORLD}	r
Commercial cash flows							
(1) X_t^{SEK}	12.3 [1.64]	–	–	.97 [.89]	–	–	–
e is trade weighted							
R^2 (adj) = –.02; D.W. = 1.5							
(2) X_t^{SEK}/P_t^{SEK}	5.5 [1.18]	–	–	–.27 [–.21]	–	–	–
e is real trade weighted							
(prod. price index)							
cash flows trade weighted							
R^2 (adj) = –.08; D.W. = 1.4							
(3) X_t^{SEK}/P_t^{SEK}	13.20 [1.77]	2.36 [1.49]	–3.83 [–1.80]	–.18 [–.21]	–1.62 [–2.68]	1.48 [3.67]	–
(prod. price index)							
T-bill interest rate							
R^2 (adj) = .71; D.W. = 2.12							
(4) X_t^{SEK}/P_t^{SEK}	31.40 [1.88]	–3.44 [–2.40]	.35 [.14]	.91 [1.36]	–.81 [–.88]	1.22 [3.06]	1.02 [.87]
(cons. price index)							
r = producer prices manufacturing/consumer prices							
R^2 (adj) = .88; D.W. = 2.17							
Total cash flows							
(5) X_t^{SEK}/P_t^{SEK}	40.90 [.70]	–4.70 [–.94]	.93 [.11]	1.34 [.57]	–1.65 [–.49]	1.3 [.80]	1.58 [.39]
R^2 (adj) = .39; D.W. = 1.84							

Figures in [ ] are *t*-statistics.

Tables A.IV.1(a) through A.IV.1(c) show regression equations for a sample of all kinds of manufacturing firms, for the mechanical engineering industries, and for the paper, pulp, and wood products industries, respectively. We assume implicitly that all changes in independent variables are unanticipated, since we lack measures of anticipated changes. At least for the exchange rate the assumption is not unrealistic.

Equation (1) in each table is a regression of *nominal* commercial cash flows on the nominal (trade weighted effective) exchange rate.

Table A.IV(b) Exposure measures 1971–83 – Mechanical engineering industry

Variables defined as in A.IV.1(a)
Dependent and independent variables in % rate of change.

Dependent	Constant	p^{SWE}	p^{WORLD}	e	i^{SWE}	i^{WORLD}	r
Commercial cash flows							
(1) X_t^{SEK}	16.20	–	–	.05	–	–	–
	[4.00]			[.08]			
R^2(adj) = −.09; D.W. = 1.10							
(2) X_t^{SEK}/P_t^{SEK}	6.18	–	–	−.23	–	–	–
	[2.10]			[−.29]			
R^2 (adj) = −.08; D.W. = 1.20							
(3) X_t^{SEK}/P_t^{SEK}	19.36	3.29	−6.10	−.82	−.02	.89	–
	[3.38]	[2.70]	[−3.74]	[−1.29]	[−.05]	[2.87]	
R^2 (adj) = .57; D.W. = 2.25							
(4) X_t^{SEK}/P_t^{SEK}	23.53	−4.18	2.11	.87	−.06	.66	−1.57
	[1.33]	[−2.70]	[.90]	[1.23]	[−.05]	[2.11]	[−.96]
R^2(adj) = .48; D.W. = 1.10							
Total cash flows							
(5) X_t^{SEK}/P_t^{SEK}	16.80	−4.85	4.32	.95	−1.41	.47	−1.14
	[.49]	[−1.61]	[.94]	[.69]	[−.71]	[.77]	[−.49]
R^2 (adj) = .16; D.W. = 1.81							

Figures in [ ] are *t*-statistics.

Thus, the coefficient for the exchange rate is the exchange rate exposure measure—$\mathrm{cov}(e_t, X_t)/\mathrm{var}\ X_t$—which does not take into account the interdependence between the exchange rate and other market price variables. The coefficient is insignificant in all tables but not small for the paper, pulp, and wood-products industries. The coefficient 1.61 indicates that a one unit appreciation— approximately a one percent change—causes a gain of SEK 1.61 billion. The low significance level indicates that a negligible proportion of the industry's cash flow variation is explained by the exchange rate, however.

Equations numbered (2) are regressions of *real* cash flows—deflated by a producer price index—on the real exchange rate (deviations from PPP for a producer price index). The real exchange rate proves to be of even less explanatory value than the nominal rate.

Table A.IV.1(c) Exposure measures 1971–83—Paper, pulp, wood-products
Variables defined as in A.IV.1(a)
Dependent and independent variables in % rate of change

Dependent	Constant	p^{SWE}	p^{WORLD}	e	i^{SWE}	i^{WORLD}	r
Commercial cash flows							
(1) X_t^{SEK}	11.17	–	–	1.61	–	–	–
	[.85]			[.84]			
R^2 (adj) = –.02; D.W. = 1.73							
(2) X_t^{SEK}/P_t^{SEK}	5.83	–	–	–.36	–	–	–
	[.73]			[–.17]			
R^2 (adj) = –0.09; D. W. = 1.81							
(3) X_t^{SEK}/P_t^{SEK}	9.59	3.05	–3.98	.15	–2.93	2.14	–
	[.67]	[1.01]	[–.98]	[.09]	[–2.54]	[2.79]	
R^2 (adj) = .64; D.W. = 1.91							
(4) X_t^{SEK}/P_t^{SEK}	51.42	–4.66	–1.22	1.92	–1.10	1.86	1.70
	[1.19]	[–1.97]	[–.21]	[1.56]	[–.48]	[2.44]	[1.25]
R^2 (adj) = .82; D.W. = 2.04							
Total cash flows							
(5) X_t^{SEK}/P_t^{SEK}	96.68	–7.65	–4.17	2.91	–.02	2.01	2.71
	[.94]	[–1.35]	[–.30]	[1.04]	[–.01]	[1.10]	[.82]
R^2 (adj) = .51; D.W. = 1.63							

Figures in [ ] are *t*-statistics.

Equations numbered (3) regress real cash flows, defined as in the previous case, on a number of macroeconomic market price variables. We use the Swedish price level, the (trade-weighted) foreign price level, the (trade-weighted) exchange rate, the Swedish bond interest rate, and the (trade-weighted) world bond rate. The relative price for each industry is not included in (3)-equations, however. Price indexes refer again to producer prices. We notice that the explanatory values of the equations are high in all tables. The exchange rate coefficient is not significant in any of the three (3)-regressions. However, both the Swedish and the world interest rate are strongly significant for all manufacturing, though with opposite signs. The significance level of coefficients for price levels is also high enough for exposure coefficients to be taken seriously for all manufacturing in the Table (a). For example, real cash flows rise with an increase in the Swedish price level but fall with a rise in the foreign price level. On the other hand, a rise in the Swedish interest rate causes a fall in cash flows, while an increase in the foreign interest rate causes an increase in real cash flows. The pattern is similar for the two industries in Tables (b) and (c), though exposure coefficients as well as significance levels differ among industries. Simultaneous increases in the Swedish interest rate and price level would have offsetting effects.

Equations numbered (4) and (5) are different from the (3)-equations in several ways. In the (4)- and (5)-equations, we use *consumer price indexes* to deflate cash flows and to measure price levels. Thus, cash flows in the (4)- and (5)-equations are closer to shareholders' concerns. In addition, we include a relative price term (r) in the form of a ratio between the industry's producer price index and the consumer price index in Sweden as suggested in equations IV.1 and IV.3. The difference between (4)- and (5)-equations is that in the (4)-equations we study commercial cash flows while in eg. (5) financial cash flows are included. Surprisingly, few exposure coefficients are significant for changes in total cash flows, while for commercial cash flows, changes in the Swedish price level and the foreign interest rate again are significant in most cases. It is also noteworthy, that for commercial cash flows, the significance level for the exchange rate should not be neglected though it does not reach a significance at a 10 percent level. For all manufacturing, as well as for the two industries, a depreciation of the Swedish currency leads to increasing real commercial cash flows.

We can observe that the explanatory value, R^2, for commercial cash flows increases substantially for all manufacturing, and paper-pulp industries when the relative price term is included in (4)–equations. Note that signs of coefficients for inflation rates change in several cases in (4)- and (5)-equations when consumer prices are used instead of producer prices and the relative prices term is included separately. It is possible that the absence of the relative price term in (3) lends excessive weight to macroeconomic variables. Equations numbered (4) and (5) are our preferred specification on theoretical grounds, though in our limited sample few degrees of freedom remain. Relative to the (3)-equations, one degree of freedom has been lost. This loss may also explain why some macroeconomic variables' significance level has dropped. The results in the (4)-

equations demonstrating significant exposures to price levels and interest rates should therefore be taken seriously.

A comparison of the (4)-equations that include only commercial cash flows with the (5)-equations for all cash flows, reveals that exposure coefficients for changes in the Swedish price level, the exchange rate, and the foreign interest rate are more significant when financial cash flows are excluded. Thus, it seems as if financial cash flow exposures have tended to offset non-financial cash-flow exposures for these variables. We do not know whether conscious exposure management explains this result. As noted above, the results of the (3)-equations indicate substantial macroeconomic exposure for total cash flows as well. It is clear, however, that pure exchange rate exposure is insignificant for total cash flows in all industries, though active exchange rate exposure management could explain this result.

For reasons indicated above the results here are only indicative and cannot be used as a basis for exposure-management. The most important reasons for this are that our cash flows are crude accounting proxies for cash flows and that substantial exposure management may influence cash-flow figures. A firm with access to better cash flow data on the firm level will obtain more reliable results for management guidance in the firm. Furthermore, at the firm level a differentiation between anticipated and unanticipated changes could be made with internal data on the firm's actual forecast in each period.

Some Econometric Considerations

There are a number of techniques for generating proxies for previous years' forecasts of each variable in order to distinguish between anticipated and unanticipated changes. One method is to use so-called ARIMA models with the purpose of generating the best possible forecast for a variable in period t from observations of the same variable in previous periods. Another more sophisticated method is to use the so-called VAR technique. A set of variables are regressed on current and historical observations of the same variables. The error terms can be used as proxies for unanticipated changes in the variables. The VAR technique enables the observer to decompose the variance of, for example, real cash flows, into percentages of the total variance which are explained by different factors. These econometric techniques are explained in econometric textbooks, and existing software packages allow implementation of the techniques once data has been collected.

A number of econometric problems are encountered when measuring exposures by means of regression-analysis. First, when using *rates of change* for a dependent variable, which varies around zero there is a possibility that a non-linear relationship is introduced. Therefore, care should be taken when deciding whether to run regressions on levels, rates of change or simply on changes.

A second problem, which arises when there are several independent variables (or exposures), is *multicollinearity*. This implies that independent variables, for example, exchange rates and interest rates are strongly correlated. It is then desirable to reduce the number of variables to which exposure is measured. If there is strong multicollinearity, the explanatory value of the regression should be reduced by very little when a variable is excluded. The remaining measured exposure coefficients would be equally useful for hedging purposes, since effects of the excluded variable are captured by remaining variables. It might be the case that policy variables such as interest rates are adjusted by central banks in response to, for example, exchange rate changes. Interest rate exposure can then be captured by the coefficients for exchange rates, and, provided policy authorities' behaviour is consistent over time, interest rate exposure would be hedged in conjunction with the hedging of exchange rate exposure in forward markets.

Our experimentation with exposure measures has indicated that the explanatory value of regressions increases significantly when cash flow data is *seasonally adjusted*. The reason is that in many industries cash flows have strong seasonal patterns, which for the firm is predictable. Thus, if a distinction is made between anticipated and unanticipated changes, the seasonal adjustment may make little difference. If this distinction is not clearly made then seasonal is often important.

Another problem is related to firms' *acquisitions* and *mergers*. Unless such changes in the nature and scale of the firm are not reflected in the decomposition of cash flows, they can be dealt with in regressions by means of dummy variables. For example, if in the middle of an estimation period, a firm has acquired another firm, then exposure coefficients as well as the average level of cash flows may have changed. Therefore, dummy variables should be applied to both coefficients and intercepts in the regression.

There are naturally a number of potential pitfalls in applying regression analysis. It would take too long to enumerate all possible problems here and we refer simply to any elementary econometric textbook for further reading. The problems should not be exaggerated, though. They can most often be discovered by experimentation with alternative formulations. We want to emphasize, however, that without good data as input, no sophisticated econometric technique will enable the analyst to obtain reliable results. On the other hand, with good data even simple techniques tend to give meaningful results if not the final answer.

V

A FRAMEWORK FOR DETERMINATION OF EXPOSURE MANAGEMENT STRATEGY AND INFORMATION NEEDS

V.1   INTRODUCTION

In Chapter III we mentioned that most firms seem to use a measure of translation and/or transaction exposure to determine exchange rate exposure. Hedging and cover decisions are then made by means of a rule such as 'cover always', 'never cover', or 'cover selectively' in currencies if the exposure is 'too large' or the exchange rate is 'to volatile'. In this chapter we call such rules exposure management strategies. They are systematic rules determined at a relatively high level in the firm and provide guidance for operational decisions. The strategy may be more or less explicitly formulated.

Few firms seem to have a clear concept of the relationship between the rule or strategy for exposure management, on the one hand, and the firm's overall objectives and the potential opportunity costs in financial and goods markets of specific strategies. It seems rather as if the relatively easy access to some kinds of accounting-based data determines the exposure concept, while operational decisions with respect to hedging and cover tend to be based on managers' personal risk-attitudes. These attitudes depend strongly on how managers are evaluated when there are gains and losses due to exchange rate changes, inflation gains and losses, interest rate changes, etc.

Given the firm's objective with respect to shareholders and other stakeholders, as discussed in Chapter II, it is naturally desirable that an exposure management program is made consistent with the objective. This consideration implies that an exposure management strategy should refer to some concept of *economic exposure* rather than being accounting-based. Furthermore, once a strategy is determined, it is important that managers are evaluated in such a way that their incentives are consistent with the firm's objective. For such an evaluation to be possible an explicitly formulated strategy is needed. In this chapter we discuss the necessary elements to determine an 'economic' exposure management strategy, while problems of evaluation are discussed in Chapter VII.

We discuss several dimensions of the firm's objective that determine an exposure management strategy. First the objective may be stated in terms of economic value, economic cash flows, economic profits, or in terms of accounting measures of these target variables. Second, the time-perspective of the firm is important. Third, the risk-attitude—the willingness to incur costs to reduce uncertainty about the target variable—influences strategy in important ways, as we shall see.

If exposure coefficients, as described in Chapter IV, are accepted as current estimates of exposure, then these coefficients plus a strategy or a rule that specifies the acceptable opportunity cost for reducing exposure, plus cash flow forecasts would be sufficient to implement an exposure management program. However, exposure coefficients in regression equations are based on historical data, while up to date measures are needed. If there are reasons to suspect that exposure measures are unstable over time, then additional information may be needed to form judgments on the current macroeconomic exposures. Because of this it is necessary to understand in more detail the sensitivity of cash flows to changes in macroeconomic variables as well as causes of potential changes in sensitivities. The sensitivities—the exposure coefficients—and their stability depend on the type of cash flows the firm is expecting and on the nature and stability of the relationship among price-levels, exchange rates and interest rates, i.e., on the duration and stability of the adjustment processes in goods and financial markets. Management's view on these processes is, as we shall see, an important input for determining an exposure management strategy.

There are two aspects to the choice of exposure management strategy that we want to particularly emphasize in this chapter. The first is that a strategy for exchange rate management cannot be selected independently of strategies for dealing with other kinds of exposure since exchange rates, interest rates, and other prices are interdependent. Other authors have also emphasized that the exchange rate's correlation with other variables should be taken into account when measuring exchange rate exposure (see, for example, Adler and Dumas, 1983; Cornell, 1980; Glick, 1986; Hekman, 1985; Oxelheim, 1984a; Shapiro, 1984; Wihlborg, 1980a), but none of these authors have emphasized the problem of how to simultaneously determine strategies for different kinds of macroeconomic exposure.

The second aspect we emphasize is that choosing a strategy is, to a large extent, an information problem. Information with respect to the firm's overall objective, and goods and financial market price-relationships are needed to determine a *desired* strategy, but the operational information requirement may constrain the choice of the *feasible* strategy.

We discuss first in this chapter the elements that determine a desired strategy and then the information requirements associated with each strategy are derived. In Section 2 we describe in more detail how cash flows may be influenced by different macroeconomic price variables. Cash flow forecasts provide the basic element in the exposure management program and in the identification of profit opportunities. Thereafter, in Section 3, we discuss how international goods market and financial market price relationships determine the nature of exposure, i.e., the exposure coefficients, and what kind of profit opportunities may arise as a result of macroeconomic disturbances. The existence of such opportunities depends on the degree of market efficiency.

In Section 4, the firm's choice of target variable, its time perspective, and the risk-attitude in its statement of objective are discussed. These elements jointly determine a strategy, and the information needed to implement each strategy can be derived, as we do in Section 5. It is possible that the firm's objective and its view of market price relationships are such that the information needs are overwhelming. Our analysis can then be used to ask what strategy is feasible with a certain amount of information and what is potentially lost by using simplified strategies. These issues are discussed in Section 6. For example, we can ask whether it is worthwhile to try to manage only transaction exposures in the short-time perspective given the firm's view of market relationships and its objective. In Section 7 the discussion concludes by pointing to relatively innocuous assumptions that may simplify exposure management drastically.

V.2   ANALYSING CASH FLOW AND VALUE EFFECTS OF CHANGES IN PRICE VARIABLES

In order to understand sources of exposure and profit opportunities arising as a result of macroeconomic disturbances, it is necessary to analyse in more detail how cash flow and value depend on exchange rates, price levels, interest rates, and relative prices. In this analysis we face the problem of choosing the proper level of aggregation and the time period over which cash flows are forecast. Cash flows can be broken down in many dimensions. There are, for example, cash flows from operations (commercial flows) versus financial flows, domestic versus foreign, contractual versus non-contractual, adjustable versus non-adjustable. We discuss these distinctions in more detail in Section 6 in connection with other operational considerations in exposure management.

The purpose of our analysis of cash flow is to provide a framework within which sources of change in the corporate cash flows on, for example, a quarterly basis can be identified. A multinational corporation's flows originate in a number of subsidiaries in different countries. It is probably meaningful to analyse each subsidiary's cash flows separately, since, as we mentioned in Chapter III, the flexibility of remittances implies that shareholder's cash flows do not correspond to *cash flows available for remittance*. We are concerned here with this latter cash flow and will therefore discuss the cash flows of a subsidiary in a host-country using local currency (LC). The parent company may be assumed to reside in the US without loss of generality.

The problem is now to explain *real* cash flows in local currency (X_t^{LC}/P_t^{LC}) as a function of macroeconomic disturbances and other factors influencing the firm. We may, for simplicity, use the expression for cash flows in Chapter IV and rewrite it for the subsidiary in the LC-country. The real cash flow for period t is:

$$\frac{X_t^{LC}}{P_t^{LC}} = E_{t-1}\left[\frac{X_t^{LC}}{P_t^{LC}}\right] + a_1(P_t^{LC} - E_{t-1}[P_t^{LC}])$$

$$+ a_2(P_t^F - E_{t-1}[P_t^F]) + a_3(e_t - E_{t-1}[e_t])$$

$$+ a_4(i_t^{LC} - E_{t-1}[i_t^{LC}]) + a_5(i_t^F - E_{t-1}[i_t^F]) \qquad (V.1)$$

$$+ a_6(r_t - E_{t-1}[r_t]) + \epsilon_t$$

where X_t^{LC} = local currency cash flows
r_t = relative price of firms outputs (inputs)
P^{LC} = local currency price level
P^F = foreign price level
e_t = exchange rate
i^{LC} = domestic interest rate
i^F = foreign interest rate
E = denotes expectations
ϵ_t = error term (unexplainable random cash flows).

In equation V.1 we have limited ourselves to one foreign country but the analysis could easily be extended to include several countries. In general, variables (countries) may be added until the error term obtains desired properties. We also present the equation in levels though it may also be expressed in rates of change.

We discussed in Chapter IV the coefficients a_1 through a_6 in equation V.1. These coefficients describe the sensitivity of cash flows to unanticipated disturbances, that is, the relative covariance between real cash flows and unanticipated changes in each variable holding other variables constant. For example, coefficient a_3 for the nominal exchange rate refers to unanticipated *real* exchange rate changes, since it is defined at constant price levels. Coefficient a_6 describes a pure commercial exposure, while exposure to relative price changes associated with inflation, exchange rate changes, and other macroeconomic disturbances are captured by the other coefficients.

The first term is *expected cash flows* which as in equation IV.2 depends on forecasts of each price variable, sales, repayments on loans, expected borrowing, etc. As mentioned in Chapter IV it is desirable to distinguish between expected (anticipated) and unanticipated changes in price variables, since risk refers specifically to unanticpated changes. The cash flow sensitivity to anticipated and unanticipated price changes, respectively, may or may not be different.

The value of the subsidiary to the shareholders in the US depends on the discounted value of expected local currency (LC) cash flows in the following way *if* all (net) cash flows are remitted immediately to the parent:

$$\frac{\text{NPV}_0^{\text{US}}}{P_0^{\text{US}}} = E_0 \left[\sum_{t=0}^{n} = \frac{X_t^{\text{LC}} \cdot (e_t/e_0)}{(1 + d)^t \cdot (P_t^{\text{US}}/P_0^{\text{US}})} \right] \qquad (V.2)$$

$$= E_0 \left[\sum_{t=0}^{n} \frac{X_t^{\text{LC}} \cdot (u_t/u_0)}{(1 + d)^t \cdot (P_t^{\text{LC}}/P_0^{\text{LC}})} \right] \qquad (V.3)$$

where we utilize that (e_t/e_0) is identically equal to $[(P_t^{\text{US}}/P_0^{\text{US}})/(P_t^{\text{LC}}/P_0^{\text{LC}})] \cdot (u_t/u_0)$. When u_t is greater or smaller than one, there is a deviation from PPP (purchasing power parity). d is the *real* discount rate of the firm.

Dividend remittance adjustability may reduce the shareholders' exposure, as weargued in Chapter III, since in reality firms may be able to avoid remitting at unfavourable real exchange rates. Then the time subscript for the real exchange rates (u_t) need not be the same as the time subscript for the cash flows in local currency (X_t^{LC}). This consideration illustrates the importance of *adjustability* in time and currency denomination of cash flows. Cash flows may be divided into *adjustable* and *non-adjustable* flows, respectively. It could be argued that equation V.1 should be restricted to non-adjustable flows. Adjustable flows, on the other hand, can be used to obtain the desired exposure. We return to this issue in Section 6.

In order to demonstrate how different flows depend on market price variables and what determines the exposure coefficients in equation V.1, we construct a simple example in the form of a cash flow table for the local subsidiary. Table V.1 shows the subsidiary's cash flows in period 0. In the current period 0, all cash flows may be contracted in magnitude and currency-denomination. Assume as in Table V.1, that sales revenues will be received in the form of

Table V.1 Cash flows in period 0

IN_0	X_0^{LC} (in US dollar equivalents*)	OUT_0
$(1 - T)$ FC $20 \cdot e_0^{LC-FC}$ (sales)	$(1 - T)$ USD $40 \cdot e_0^{LC-USD}$ (inputs)	
$(1 - T)$ USD $30 \cdot e_0^{LC-USD}$ (sales)	$(1 - T)$ LC 30 (wages)	
$(1 - T)$ LC 50 (sales)	$(1 - T)$ LC 2.5 (interest costs =	
$T \cdot$ Depreciation in LC	$L_0^{LC} \cdot i_0^{LC}$)	
LC 100	$X_0^{LC} = (1 - T)$ [LC $17.5 -$ USD $10 \cdot$ $e_0^{LC-USD} +$ FC $20 \cdot e_0^{LC-FC}$] $+$ T·Depr. $=$ to cash or shareholders in LC	

*Translation rate $= 1$.
$T =$ tax rate.

FC 20, USD 30, and LC 50. Payments for inputs from the US parent are USD 40 while wages amount to LC 30. Interest costs are 10 percent of a LC debt equal to LC 25. The tax shield on depreciation in local currency is also a positive cash flow. For simplicity we set the exchange rate at time 0 equal to one so that figures are dollar equivalents.

For any future period t most expected cash flows are not contracted for in every respect (non-contractual flows). Sales may respond to different factors, while currency denomination may or may not be adjustable. We describe in Table V.2 after tax cash flows from sales in each currency (country) in period t as the cash flows in period 0 (Table V.1) adjusted for changes in price levels (P_t/P_0), and adjusted for relative price changes on output (OP_t/P_t), inputs (IP_t/P_t) and wages (W_t/P_t), respectively. Relative price changes may be associated with sales volume effects as well. In Table V.2, γ_1 refers to quantity adjustment as a result of an intra-country relative price change for output. γ_2 refers to the quantity adjustment due to a relative price change between countries (deviations from the 'Law of One Price', LOP). The table footnotes show that volume effects depend on the size of the relative price change and a sales elasticity. Depreciation cash flows may be considered a contractual transaction exposure, since in most countries depreciation allowances depend on costs at the time of acquisition.

We turn now to financial cash flows which may be contracted to a smaller or larger extent. Coefficients of exposure for financial flows—particularly those for interest rates and price levels—would depend on the degree to which financial flows are contracted over shorter or longer periods.

Table V.2 shows how financial flows may be expressed for period t in local currency when all loans are denominated in this currency. These flows may vary over time depending on the variability of the interest rate and the covariance between the current interest rate and current inflation and exchange rate changes. In some cases, loans may be indexed to a price level. If not, inflation causes real gains or losses.

In Table V.2, L_0^{LC} represents the original net-financial liability position. We assume as in Chapter IV that the firm holds a fixed share (L/V) of its total liabilities in the form of financial liabilities. Then we my treat the capital structure and the discount rate as a constant, which simplifies the analysis. If there is inflation and the firm's value increases proportionately, its borrowing capacity (L_t) at a fixed discount rate increases proportionately. We assume that

Table V.2　After tax cash flows in period t

IN_t	X_t^{LC}	OUT_t
$(1-T)FC\ 20 \cdot P_t^{FC}(OP^{FC}/P^{FC})_t \cdot$ $e_t^{LC-FC} \cdot [1 + \gamma_1^{FC} + \gamma_2^{FC}]\star$		$(1-T)USD\ 40 \cdot P_t^{US}(IP^{US}/P^{US})_t \cdot$ $e_t^{LC-USD} [1 + \gamma_1^A + \gamma_2^A]\dagger$
$(1-T)USD\ 30 \cdot P_t^{US}(OP^{US}/P^{US})_t \cdot$ $e_t^{LC-USD} \cdot [1 + \gamma_1^{US} + \gamma_2^{US}]$		$(1-T)LC\ 30 \cdot P_t^{LC}(WP^{LC}/P^{LC})_t \cdot$ $[1 + \gamma_1^A + \gamma_2^A]$
$(1-T)LC\ 50 \cdot P_t^{LC}(OP^{LC}/P^{LC})_t \cdot$ $[1 + \gamma_1^{LC}]$		$(1-T)LC\ L_0 \cdot P_t^{LC} \cdot i_t^{LC} = LC(1-T)$ $OP_t^{LC} \{E_t[i_t^{RLC}] + E_t[\hat{P}_t^{LC}]$
$T \cdot$Depreciation in LC in period t $L_0^{LC} \cdot P_t^{LC} \cdot \hat{P}_t^{LC}$		$+ \beta(\hat{P}_t^{LC} - E_t[P_t^{LC}]\}$
		Residual to cash or to shareholders in LC

$\star$ γ_1^{FC} refers to the increase in sales due to a relative price change and equals $(\dfrac{OP_t^{FC}}{P_t^{FC}} - 1)\epsilon_1^{FC}$, where ϵ_1^{FC} is the elasticity of sales with respect to the relative price; γ_2^{FC} refers to the increase in export sales due to a deviation from LOP and equals $(\dfrac{OP_t^{FC} \cdot e^{LC-FC}}{OP_t^{LC}} - 1) \cdot \epsilon_2^{FC}$, where ϵ_2^{FC} is the elasticity of sales in the FC-country with respect to a deviation from LOP.

$\dagger$ γ_1^A and γ_2^A refer to average volume effects over all countries.

such inflation gains are available for distribution to shareholders. These (untaxed) gains appear on the left-hand side in Table V.2 and are equal to the inflation rate in period t multiplied by the debt position. In Chapter VI we will see in an example that the treatment of these inflation gains are very important for the cash flow effects of macroeconomic disturbances.

On the right-hand side we have the tax-deductable pure interest costs on the firm's financial position ($L_0 \cdot \hat{P}_t^{LC}$). These costs consist of three components—the expected real interest rate at the beginning of period t, $E_t[i_t^{RLC}]$, the expected inflation rate, $E_t[\hat{P}_t^{LC}]$, and the adjustment due to partial or complete indexation. When $\beta = 1$, indexation is complete, while if $\beta = 0$ there is no indexation for the period. In the latter case, nominal interest costs correspond to the nominal interest rate which can be contracted for at varying intervals. This nominal interest cost for the non-indexed loan is defined as:

$$i_t^{LC} \equiv E_t[i_t^{RLC}] + E_t[\hat{P}_t^{LC}] \qquad (V.4)$$

To obtain total LC financial cash flows we deduct from the tax-deductible interest costs on the right-hand side in Table V.2 the non-taxable gain—the increase in debt-capacity—on the left-hand side. Thus in the absence of indexation:

LC-financial flows ($\beta = 0$) =

$$-L_0^{LC} P_t^{LC} \{(1 - T)(E_t[i_t^{RLC}] + E_t[\hat{P}_t^{LC}] - \hat{P}_t^{LC})\} \qquad (V.5)$$

while with complete indexation:

LC-financial flows ($\beta = 1$) =

$$-L_0^{LC} P_t^{LC} \{(1 - T)(i_t^{RLC} + \hat{P}_t^{LC}) - \hat{P}_t^{LC}\} \qquad (V.6)$$

The degree of indexation depends on the length of period t, and the frequency with which interest rates on loans are renegotiated. The more flexible the interest rate is, the closer $E_t(\hat{P}_t)$ in equation V.5 is to $\hat{P}_t$ and the more certain is $E_t[i_t^{RLC}]$. In equation V.6 we can also note that even in the case of perfect indexation, inflation is not neutral, since taxes in most countries apply to nominal interest payments. Before discussing exposure in greater detail we must discuss important relationships among prices, exchange rates, and interest rates. In this chapter the discussion is general, while in Chapter VI scenarios with specific data are developed.

V.3   MARKET PRICE RELATIONSHIPS AND EXPOSURE

It is well-known that the degree of efficiency of international financial markets and the adjustment speed in international goods markets are important for the exposure of firms. (See, for example, Wihlborg, 1978; Lessard, 1979; Cornell, 1980; Shapiro, 1984.) We will summarize important relationships and apply them within the above cash flow framework.

We turn first to *goods market* relationships and commercial cash flows. Exchange rates and inflation are irrelevant to a firm's commercial operations if the 'law of one price' (LOP) holds for all goods and if relative prices among goods are independent of exchange rate changes and inflation. Such assumptions are unrealistic but provide a point of reference. We mean by PPP that LOP holds for all goods. This is convenient in order to distinguish between intersectoral and intercountry price changes. For example, a 10 percent inflation rate in the host country of a subsidiary and a 5 percent inflation rate in the US would, under PPP, lead to a 5 percent appreciation of the dollar versus LC (see also Appendix III.2).

One may nevertheless observe deviations from PPP as a result of relative price changes when consumption bundles differ among nations. However, from a firm's perspective it is often the deviations from PPP in terms of a particular bundle of goods that matters. For such a bundle, PPP must hold if LOP holds for all commodities and services. Exchange rate changes may also be correlated with relative price changes with the implication that coefficient a_3 in equation V.1, the coefficient for the exchange rate, can be non-zero even when LOP holds for all goods. It is, for example, commonly observed that prices of exportables are relatively stable in the producing country but change with the exchange rate in the importing country. Prices of some products like oil are determined in world markets in US dollars, while local currency prices fluctuate with the exchange rate. Then exchange rate changes cause relative price changes in local currency between oil and other products.

We define the relationship between the exchange rate and inflation rates in a foreign country (FC) and the host country of a firm (LC) as in Section II:

$$e_t/e_0 \equiv [(P_t^{LC}/P_0^{LC})/(P_t^{FC}/P_0^{FC})]\,(u_t/u_0) \qquad (V.7)$$

where u_t is the average deviation from LOP, i.e., deviations from PPP. It may also be called the real exchange rate. The magnitude and duration of real exchange rate changes are important for the exposure of cash flows in Table V.2, since they influence the competitiveness of firms located in different countries. Thus, the path of u_t is an important component of coefficient a_3.

Suppose price level P in any country is determined by two goods, y and z, in the following way:

$$P_t = aP_{y,t} + (1 - a)P_{z,t} \qquad (V.8)$$

Deviations from LOP for good y are denoted by u_y in the following expression between local and foreign currencies,

$$e_t/e_0 \equiv [(P_{y,t}^{LC}/P_{y,0}^{LC})/(P_{y,t}^{FC}/P_{y,0}^{FC})] \cdot (u_{y,t}/u_{y,0}). \qquad (V.9)$$

where LOP holds in a relative sense if $(u_{y,t}/u_{y,0}) = 1$.

If there are deviations from LOP in varying degrees among sectors during the adjustment to macroeconomic disturbances, then relative prices among sectors, as well as among countries, will change during both an inflation and an exchange rate adjustment process. The effects of such relative price changes appear particularly in coefficients a_1, a_2, and a_3 in the cash flow equation V.1 depending on whether specific relative price changes are correlated with price level changes or real exchange rate changes. Their magnitudes depend on the nature of the macroeconomic adjustment process, as well as on γ_1 and γ_2 in Table V.2, the volume sensitivities to relative price changes. For some products, like oil, LOP holds well and $(u_{\text{oil},t}/u_{\text{oil},o})$ tends to be close to one. For other more differentiated products, like cars, LC prices as well as FC prices are determined by market conditions in each country. Therefore, $(u_{\text{cars},t}/u_{\text{cars},o})$ depends strongly on exchange rate changes over quarters or even for periods as long as a year.

To illustrate how market relationships affect cash flows, we may take the cash-flow FC 20 in Table V.1 for period 0. In period t the LC-value of this cash flow is expressed in Table V.2 as $20 \cdot P_t^{FC} \cdot (OP_t^{FC}/P_t^{FC}) \cdot e_t^{LL-FC} \cdot [1 + \gamma_1^{FC} + \gamma_2^{FC}]$. Then using equation V.9, for the output commodity (OP), the local LC value in period t for the subsidiary's exports to the foreign country may be expressed as:

$$20 \cdot P_t^{FC}(OP_t^{FC}/P_t^{FC})(OP_t^{LC}/OP_t^{FC}) \cdot u_{OP,t} \cdot [1 + \gamma_1^{FC} + \gamma_2^{FC}]$$

assuming all prices are one in period zero. In *real* (time 0) local currency terms the first part of this expression reduces to $20 \cdot (OP_t^{LC}/P_t^{LC}) \cdot u_{OP,t}$. Thus, if the exported product is a car, then the LC real cash flows from export sales depend on LC car prices relative to the LC-price level (OP^{LC}/P^{LC})—the domestic relative price—multiplied by the deviation from LOP for cars (u_{OP}). In addition, volume effects (γ_1, γ_2) occur in conjunction with these two relative price changes. Thus, the sensitivity of non-financial (commercial) cash flows to changes in macroeconomic price variables in equation V.1 depends on the relationship between each price variable and domestic relative prices, deviations from LOP, and volume effects in the adjustment. Any one firm may have to be concerned with a number of relative prices for outputs, inputs, and wages. From an information gathering point of view it is therefore advantageous if a regression equation like equation V.1 can be estimated.

We turn now to *financial markets* and financial cash flows. The degree to which the Fisher Open (FO) relationship holds is particularly important for the choice of the currency denomination of the firm's debt. (See also Appendix III.3.) FO is often referred to as the highest level of international financial market efficiency. It holds if information and transaction costs are negligible and there are risk-neutral speculators in the market, who consider assets denominated in different currencies perfect substitutes. In its approximate form, FO at the beginning of period t can be written as:

$$i_t^{LC} = i_t^{FC} + E_t[\hat{e}_t] \qquad (V.10)$$

When this relationship holds, a firm's expected borrowing costs are independent of the currency denomination of debt provided exchange gains and losses are treated like interest costs for tax purposes. Equation V.10 holds for one period loans. For longer loans the timing of interest payments and debt service influences the exact form of the relationship between interest rates and exchange rate changes over the maturity period. In general, equation V.10 indicates that the interest rate differential equals the expected average annualized rate of change of the exchange rate.

In order to evaluate the exposure of financial cash flows in different currency denominations, we compare these cash flows of the subsidiary, when it borrows in local currency and in foreign currency, respectively. The first case has already been discussed in Section V.2 where we saw how the real value of financial cash flows depends on the expected real interest rate, the expected inflation rate in local currency, and the degree of indexation. The case of borrowing in foreign currency is described in Table V.3. On the right-hand side we have the LC-value in period t of interest costs in foreign currency. On the left-hand side we have the gain or loss in debt capacity as a result of changes in asset values with LC inflation. As before, the firm borrowed the equivalent of LC25 in period 0 and initial prices and exchange rates are one.

Our treatment of exchange gains and losses on the right-hand side in Table V.3 implies that we consider such gains (or losses) taxable (or tax-deductable). To form an expression for total financial cash flows with and without indexation, we make use of an approximate relationship between exchange rate changes, inflation rates, and real exchange rate changes — $\hat{e} = \hat{P}^{LC} - \hat{P}^{FC} + \hat{u}$. The exposure of financial flows related to FC-loans is best understood by inserting this exchange rate expression in Table V.3 and adding the two sides. In the absence of indexation we obtain:

LC-value of financial flows (FC loan, $\beta = 0$)

$$= -L_0 P_t^{LC} \{(1 - T) \cdot E_t[i_t^{RFC}] +$$

$$(1 - T)(E_t[\hat{P}_t^{FC}] - \hat{P}_t^{FC} + \hat{u}) - T \cdot \hat{P}^{LC}\} \qquad (V.11)$$

In the case of indexation we obtain:

LC-value of financial flows (FC loan, $\beta = 1$)

$$= -L_0 P_t^{LC} \{(1 - T) i_t^{RFC} + (1 - T)\hat{u} - T \hat{P}^{LC}\} \qquad (V.12)$$

Table V.3 Financial cash flows: FC-loan

IN	in LC	OUT
LC $L_0 P_t^{LC} \cdot \hat{P}_t^{LC}$	LC$(1-T)L_0 P_t^{LC}\{E_t[i_t^{RFC}] + E_t[\hat{P}_t^{FC}] + \beta(\hat{P}_t^{FC} - E_t[\hat{P}_t^{FC}]) + \hat{e}_t\}$	

Comparing equations V.11 and V.12, we note again that as the time period over which interest rates are fixed shortens, the non-indexed expression V.11 approaches the indexed expression V.12 since the difference between $E[\hat{P}_t^{FC}]$ and $\hat{P}_t^{FC}$ approaches zero.

Comparing the indexed FC loans in equation V.12 to the indexed LC loan in equation V.6, we observe that they differ in exposure to real exchange rate changes, $\hat{u}$, but both loans are exposed to LC-inflation in spite of indexation. The reason for this exposure is that the firm's debt capacity increases with LC-inflation and this gain is not taxed.

Comparing the non-indexed FC-loan in equation V.11 to the non-indexed LC loan in equation V.5, we find there is a difference in their inflation exposures over the contract period. The FC loan is exposed to foreign inflation and to local inflation over this period, while the LC loan is exposed only to local inflation. The asymmetry depends again on non-taxation of the increase in debt capacity with local inflation.

The above expressions show that coefficients for inflation rates and exchange rate changes in a regression equation like V.1 for the real value of financial cash flows, will depend on the currency denomination of loans and on the degree of indexation, i.e., the interest rate flexibility of the loan. Note that there is exposure to local inflation in all cases. Therefore, the coefficient a_1 for local inflation should always be non-zero. However only the non-indexed FC loan is exposed to foreign inflation. Therefore the coefficient a_2 in equation V.1 could be zero for other kinds of loans.

Interest rate exposure, i.e., the coefficients for interest rates in equation V.1, depends obviously on the effect of real interest rates on cash flows. Furthermore, interest-rate coefficients depend on the relationship between inflation expectations, actual inflation at the time contracts are entered, and the real interest rate. Assume, for example, that inflation expectations covary perfectly with current inflation, and that real interest rates are constant. Then, coefficients a_4 and a_5 for interest rate exposures are zero, while coefficients a_1 and a_2 for inflation capture the total financial exposure in each currency denomination. In most cases we would expect at least one interest rate and one inflation exposure coefficient to be non-zero. The relative magnitude of different effects will become clearer in the scenario analysis in Chapter VI.

Note finally that risk related to contractual cash flows may depend on the consumption bundle of investors and borrowers. Specifically, when the real exchange rate is correlated with relative prices among commodities as described above, the purchasing power of an investment (a loan) in a particular currency varies with the exchange rate even when LOP holds for all goods and services (see Wihlborg 1978). An example may illustrate this case. Assume that an American investor plans to purchase a Jaguar in the US in three months and is facing the question of whether to hold dollars or pounds for those months. The payment is going to be made in dollars to the US dealer. The Jaguar price in the US follows LOP so that the US price is the constant list price in pounds times the dollar/pound exchange rate. In this case, the investor would avoid exchange risk by holding pounds since, if the pound appreciates, both the dollar value of the investment *and* the dollar price of the Jaguar will increase.

V.4 STATEMENT OF THE FIRM'S OBJECTIVE

In the previous section we demonstrated how cash flows can be analysed in order to determine exposure. Before a decision is made on how to deal with exposures, the firm's objective must be considered. As mentioned in the introduction to this chapter, there are three dimensions to this objective of relevance for exposure management. These are: (a) the choice of target variable, (b) the firm's risk-attitude, and (c) the firm's time perspective.

V.4.a The Choice of Target Variable

A target variable may be defined in terms of accounting or economic principles, and in real or nominal terms. Since our objective here is to determine how a rational exposure management strategy can be determined with stakeholders' interest in mind, we neglect accounting based and nominal definitions. As noted in Chapter III, firms use accounting based concepts of exchange rate exposure, perhaps due to lack of knowledge of economic exposure. Firms concerned with their stockmarket value may also consider accounting measures of income and net worth important, since published statements are accounting based. Nevertheless, it is hard to argue that pure accounting gains and losses without tax effects should matter to the firm. Stock market analysts learn over time the relationship between accounting income and economic income. Furthermore, even when there are specific rules for dealing with exchange rate changes and inflation in accounting, there is nothing that prevents firms from informing stockholders about their managers' views of the economic relevance of specific accounting rules.

Assuming now that an economic objective is chosen, the target variable could be profits, cash flows, economic value, or market value. In the study of Swedish corporations reported in Oxelheim (1984a), many firms referred to market value as their target variable, though many failed to distinguish between real and nominal values. Market value depends on market participants' subjective expectations about the prospects of the firm. In the long run one would expect market value to coincide with economic value. The reason is that firms have the incentive to inform the market when management perceives that economic value exceeds market value. Another reason to use economic value as opposed to market value is that the former cannot be manipulated by management's information release. Thus, it makes more sense to use economic value as the target variable for our discussion, even when shareholders' wealth maximization constitutes the ultimate objective.

The choice between cash flows or profits in the near term as opposed to economic value, is to a large extent a question of time-perspective since the economic value is the discounted value of expected future cash flows. A high discount rate implies that near-term cash flows dominate the economic valuation, while with a low discount rate cash flows into the distant future are relevant. Thus, cash flows in the near future may be considered the relevant target variable for the firm that chooses a high discount rate, for example, because the business is considered very risky by shareholders. Profits are often referred to as a target variable. However, cash flows seem more appropriate, since funds available for remittance to shareholders depend on cash flows. Profit is obviously the most important component of cash flows and may sometimes serve as an approximation, since it is easily available and serves as a basis for taxation. It is preferable, however, to work with cash flows, since economic value depends on flows.

Another aspect of the target variable is the distinction between real and nominal values. Real values refer to purchasing power while nominal values refer to monetary terms. If the objective of the firm is to maximize cash flows or economic value, it does not make any difference whether real or nominal terms are used in the analysis. Maximizing a nominal value will also maximize a real value. However, if the variance of the target variable is part of the firm's objective, then it is necessary to distinguish between real and nominal magnitudes. The reason is, as we have seen, that nominal values may vary with the price level at a constant real value. Thus, fixing nominal values may cause inflation exposure and variability in the purchasing power of cash flows or economic value. When a distinction needs to be made real values will be emphasized, as we already have in Section 2 of this chapter.

Other stakeholders than shareholders may be of management concern, and the firm's objective could be adjusted accordingly. In Chapter II we emphasized in particular employees and their job security. We argued that output variability may be costly and, therefore, optimizing economic value implies a willingness to incur costs to reduce output variability. From the point of view of exposure management, this consideration could imply that not only total cash flows but cash flows from commercial operations become a target variable in the sense that the latter cash flows should be managed to reduce their variability. Output variability could be reduced by inventory adjustment in many industries, but a cost minimizing strategy for decreasing output variability would most often include both inventory adjustment and a reduction of the variability of sales (cash). These considerations are related to the firm's risk-attitude, which is discussed next.

V.4.b THE FIRM'S RISK ATTITUDE

In Chapter II we distinguished between different stakeholders in the firm and the role of each in forming the risk-attitude of management. We distinguished between *risk-aversion* and *risk-neutrality*. The risk-neutral firm maximizes the value of its target variable, while the risk-averse firm is willing to incur a cost in order to reduce the variance of the target variable, i.e., cash flows or economic value.

Finance theory tells us if risk-averse shareholders can reduce their portfolio variance by diversifying, then the firm need not be concerned with the variance of its cash flow or value. However, once other stakeholders are considered, there is a strong case for a degree of risk-aversion in the firms. We mentioned that bond-holders and other lenders can induce risk-aversion with respect to cash flows or economic value, and employees can induce risk-aversion with respect to the optimal output/employment level. This kind of risk-aversion would be consistent with stockholder wealth-maximization as well. There is no unanimity of opinion about the importance of these concerns for bondholders and employees in shaping firms' objectives. For our purposes it is sufficient to note that management must consider its risk-attitudes in its objective and that there are arguments in favour of both a risk-neutral and a risk-averse stand.

In the case of risk-aversion a decision must be made about which target variable risk-aversion refers to. Without a conscious decision of this kind on a top management level, it is easy for subordinate managers' own risk-attitudes to shape the exposure management strategy. The internal evaluation system is, as we mentioned before and will come back to, also important for shaping internal risk-attitudes.

Risk-aversion may be well motivated with respect to economic value as noted in Chapter II. For the firm with a shorter time perspective, the variance of cash flows, instead of economic value, may be of concern. The importance of variance of commercial cash flows depends on the employees' attitude towards job security, the ease with which employees can be shifted among different activities, the cost of holding inventories, and the sensitivity of the optimal output level to changes in demand and cost conditions.

The practical problem of making a specific degree of risk-aversion an operational concept should ideally be solved by deciding how much a certain decrease in cash flow—or value—variance is worth in terms of lost return or increased cost. If the firm has estimated exposure-equations for cash flows of the type we have described above for different combinations of currency denominations of assets and liabilities, it is possible to make such specific trade-offs between return and risk. However, in the absence of well-formulated measures of exposure, risk-aversion will have to be translated into 'rules-of-thumb', for example, in terms of acceptable magnitudes of exposed positions in different currencies at different expected rates of return, borrowing costs, or profit margins on sales.

To form a judgment on the acceptable magnitude of exposure, information is needed about 'how risky' a particular position is. For example, positions in a particular currency could be particularly sensitive to real exchange rate risk, while other positions are sensitive to inflation risk or interest rate risk. The sensitivity would depend on factors discussed in Sections 2 and 3, i.e., whether the positions constitute contractual or non-contractual exposure, whether PPP holds and FO holds, etc. Non-contractual positions such as expected cash flows from sales may be relatively insensitive to inflation uncertainty but highly sensitive to real exchange rate uncertainty. A long-term contractual position in a specific currency, on the other hand, is often subject to inflation risk. Obviously, information requirements are substantial, except when the firm's objective can be translated into exposure management strategies of the simplest kind, such as cover/hedge everything or cover/hedge nothing. In Section 5 of this chapter we show that under certain conditions it is possible to specify such simple strategies.

V.4.c   The Firm's Time-Perspective

As we noted, the time perspective of the firm reveals itself in equation V.1 for the economic value of the real discount rate, d, by which expected cash flows are discounted. The firm using a high discount rate puts a relatively large weight on cash flows in the near future.

In order to determine the exposure of economic value, given information about the exposure of cash flows in each period, the firm with a long time perspective (a low discount rate) needs to consider the extent to which individual period cash flows may be negatively or positively correlated. If there is negative serial correlation, cash flow exposure for any period t need not translate into a value exposure at time 0. Real exchange rate changes tend to be negatively serially correlated or not correlated at all. Theory tells us that there should be negative correlation for PPP to hold. Inflation rates, on the other hand, tend to be strongly positively correlated, i.e., if inflation goes up it tends to remain at the new level. As mentioned in Chapter IV, these considerations would determine how simple cash flow exposure coefficients translate into value exposure coefficients.

The importance of having an exposure management strategy which is consistent with the firm's time perspective was illustrated in Chapter IV by considering the effect on the present value variance of the value of a specified foreign currency cash flow for a firm that covers these flows in different ways. We compared a strategy of never covering and one of covering consecutively the expected flow for the next quarter and found that the present value variance of following the latter strategy relative to the present value variance of the former, is $1/(1 + d/4)^2$, if changes in three-month forward rates are approximately equal to changes in spot rates. For example, if the real discount rate is 10 percent, the reduction in the present value variance of always covering is only about 5 percent.

We mentioned in Chapter IV that several studies demonstrate that as an empirical regularity, changes in forward rates are closely related to changes in spot rates. In Table V.4 we exemplify this regularity with data from the Swedish spot and forward exchange markets. The table indicates that the variances of the forward rates are nearly identical to the variances in the spot rates. We conclude, therefore, that a firm concerned with present value variance has little to gain from traditional transaction exposure-covering of near term cash flows. This example demonstrates that the time perspective over which exposures are managed must be consistent with the time perspective of the firm's objective. If the firm at time 0 covered all future cash flows within those periods that affect the present value substantially, then the value variance would naturally tend towards zero provided exchange rate risk is the only relevant risk.

Since economic value in general depends on expected flows into infinity, Adler and Dumas (1980) have argued that it is practical to determine a *cut-off point* in time after which the cash flows obtain zero weight in value. The higher the discount rate, the closer in time this cut-off date would lie. If the real discount rate is 10 percent the weight of cash flows in five years is 62 percent of current cash flows, while if the discount rate is 20 percent the corresponding

Table V.4 Standard deviations in three months relative changes in spot rates (σ_e) and in forward rates (σ_f) SEK/foreign currency. Percent per quarter. Tuesday closing market rates.

Foreign currency		GBP	USD	DEM	FRF	BEC	CHF	NLG	NOK	DKK	ITL	ATS	JPY	FIM*
1974–1984	σ_e	5.31	5.54	4.74	5.02	4.81	6.52	4.81	4.50	3.20	5.26	4.68	6.84	2.64
$n = 123$	σ_f	5.45	5.26	4.77	4.78	4.94	6.35	4.76	4.30	3.03	5.62	4.53	6.71	2.31
1974–1976	σ_e	4.87	5.34	1.51	3.66	1.06	3.43	1.23	1.39	0.96	5.48	1.16	4.92	2.04
$n = 36$	σ_f	5.24	4.82	2.03	3.47	1.22	3.46	1.57	1.42	0.79	6.56	1.52	4.59	2.04
1978–1984	σ_e	4.57	5.41	5.46	5.42	5.56	7.11	5.66	5.43	3.74	4.77	5.49	7.30	2.41
$n = 75$	σ_f	4.79	5.31	5.42	5.15	5.78	6.93	5.63	5.25	3.58	4.84	5.26	7.31	2.18

* The number of observations for FIM is 106 (1975–1984) and 19 (1975–1976).

weight is only 40 percent. Thus, the firm with a discount rate of 20 percent could decide to manage exposure with a five-year perspective, while the one with a 10 percent discount rate would extend the perspective to 10 years, at which time the weight of a cash flow is 40 percent of a current cash flow.

It is obvious that extremely high discount rates are needed in order to neglect cash flows beyond a few years. Conversely, one could say that the firm that manages cash flows within only one year uses an extremely high implicit discount rate. The reduction in value variance of reducing cash flow variance on an annual basis is relatively small for most realistic discount rates.

There are two ways in which economic value variance can be reduced by hedging and covering cash flow exposures. We touched upon these when discussing the relationship between transaction and translation exposure in Chapter III. One way is to enter hedging contracts for each type of exposure at time zero for expected cash flows in each period up to the cut-off date, using, for example, the hedging principles outlined in Chapter IV. As expectations about cash flows change over time, hedging contracts are adjusted accordingly. The problem with this method is that forward, futures, and options markets are limited in their maturities. Therefore, internal hedging methods may have to be used for longer time horizons.

The second way of hedging value using quarterly or annual cash flow exposure coefficients is to complement these coefficients with information regarding the relationships between cash flow effects in one period and economic value effects consisting of cash flow effects over several periods. For example, if it is expected that a real exchange rate change in one year will have no impact on cash flows in future periods (a temporary change), then hedging the cash flow exposure within the year is equivalent to hedging economic value against exchange rate changes within the year. On the other hand, if a real exchange rate change in one year is expected to result in a permanently higher rate, then a multiple of the one year cash flow-exposure should be hedged. In this case the exposure coefficient for the percentage change in cash flows due to a one per cent change in the exchange rate is equal to the coefficient for the percentage change in value.

V.5 EXPOSURE STRATEGIES AND INFORMATION NEED

In this section we combine the above elements to describe how a desired exposure management strategy and information needs can be determined by risk-attitude, time perspective, choice of target variable, market relationships, and the nature of cash flows.

First, management strategies and the nature of operational decisions will be determined by risk-attitude, and goods and financial market relationships. Then, information needs will be determined for each strategy by considering the risks to which a particular target variable is exposed. We limit the discussion here by using total real cash flows as the target variables. In principle, the analysis applies when economic value or commercial cash flows are the target variables. Actual hedging and cover policies will differ, however, depending on the target variable. We touch upon these differences only briefly.

In Table V.5(a) we list the risk-attitude of the firm in column (1) and financial market adjustment in terms of belief or non-belief in FO in column (2). Then, a strategy can be chosen for *financial* cash flows (including contractual commercial flows) in isolation in column (3), though we see later that it is usually not optimal to manage financial exposure independently of commercial exposure to macroeconomic variables.

The firm's view of goods market adjustment over the relevant time horizon is listed in column (4). Managers may believe in PPP, that there are real exchange rate changes between countries, or that exchange rate changes are correlated both with real exchange rate changes and relative price changes. Columns (5), (6), and (7) list the strategies for the operational decisions that would follow from the combination in previous columns for nominally contracted cash flows (5) (including depreciation), non-contractual commercial flows from sales and purchases (6), and non-contractual financial (flexible interest) cash flows (7). Thereafter, in Table V.5(b), we list in columns (8), (9), and (10) the information needs associated with the different strategies in order to implement operational decisions.

Certain interesting aspects of the table can be discussed without going into great detail. First, macroeconomic disturbances are completely irrelevant only in row 1. There are no financial profit opportunities and no commercial profit opportunities as a result of macro-disturbances, and the firm is not concerned with variances of cash flows. From this simple case the degree of complexity of the management task increases with the complexity of market adjustment and the degree of risk-aversion. Financial and commercial decisions are *separable* in lines (1–6) characterized by risk-neutrality.

The risk-neutral firm's exposure management strategy is always to maximize expected cash flows or economic value. However, with FO and PPP the 'laissez faire' strategy applies since there are no profit-opportunities in the macroeconomic adjustment process. All prices are equalized quickly among countries and the firm can focus its energies entirely on economic developments in its markets without concern for the macroeconomic environment.

Without FO there are potential profit-opportunities in selecting the currency with the highest expected rate of return, and without PPP there are profit opportunities in shifting sales from one country to another, or in adjusting production and sales as a result of relative price changes among sectors. These profit opportunities may arise as a result of macroeconomic disturbances such as monetary policy shifts. The *information need* in Table V.5(b) under risk-neutrality is limited to *forecasts* of real exchange rates, interest rates, and relative prices. Sensitivity coefficients to unanticipated changes in variables are not necessary since these potential changes are not considered when decisions are made. Sensitivity coefficients to anticipated changes in prices are, of course, valuable in order to forecast sales at expected prices. This kind of information is always needed to forecast cash flows and is not limited to exposure management decisions. Forecasting is nevertheless an extremely important and difficult task and it is an important decision to determine what kinds of forecasting deserve the firm's resources. For example, if managers believe that FO holds well, then publicly available interest rates and forward rates tend to be the best available forecast of exchange rates (see, e.g., Levich, 1980; Oxelheim, 1985).

With risk-averse attitudes the firm's information needs for exposure management increase and exposure management becomes more complex. On lines (7) through (10) in Table V.5(a), commercial decisions are still separable from financial decisions, however. On lines (7) and (10) for PPP, the reason for this separability is that the firm does not expect any price differentials among countries for its product. Thus, exposure management can be limited to financial cash flows while commercial cash flows need to be considered only if they are contracted at fixed prices. On line (7) with FO, the exposure management strategy becomes variance minimizing, i.e, hedge as much as possible since there are no profit opportunities in international goods and financial markets. On line (10) a trade-off decision must be made between acceptable financial exposure and the cost of decreasing this exposure since FO does not hold.

On lines (8) and (9) FO is assumed to hold while both commercial and financial flow exposure exist. Even here financial and commercial exposure decisions can be separated though the financial decision should be based on knowledge about commercial exposure. Specifically, commercial decisions can be made without considering risk. Commercial cash flows can simply be maximized. Then financial decisions are used to minimize the variance of *all* cash flows. The reason why financial positions may be adjusted in this way to whatever exposure arises on the commercial side, is that with FO expected returns and borrowing costs are equalized across currencies. Therefore, there are no market costs of hedging commercial exposure in financial markets.

The truly complex management strategy and information requirements arise with risk-aversion when real exchange rates and/or relative prices are sensitive to macro-disturbances *and* when FO does not hold on rows 11 and 12. All exposure coefficients could then differ from zero for financial as well as commercial cash flows. The strategy becomes one of trading-off risk and return over commercial as well as financial cash flows. The exposure of all cash flows should be estimated, and commercial as well as financial decisions should be evaluated in terms of both return and risk. If regression equations can be obtained for different kinds of flows using historical data, then the exposure coefficients for different kinds of cash flows can be revealed. These coefficients are useful for hedging decisions as demonstrated in Chapter IV.

If exposure coefficients cannot be obtained using historical data other methods for evaluating exposure are required. For example, expressions presented in Sections V.2 and V.3 for cash flows in terms of price levels, real and nominal exchange rates, and real and nominal interest rates, can be used as basis for judgment concerning the exposure of different cash flows. Thereafter, in order to evaluate

Table V.5(a) Strategies for exposure management

				Strategies for Operational Decisions		
(1) Risk-attitude	(2) Financial market adjustment	(3) Financial cash flow strategy	(4) Goods market adjustment	(5) Nominally contracted flows	(6) Non-contractual Commercial	(7) Non-contractual Financial
1	FO	Laissez faire	PPP		Laissez faire	Laissez faire
2			Real exchange rate changes		Int'l trade opportunities	
3			Rel. price + real exch. rate changes	Laissez faire	Int'l and intersectoral opportunities	Laissez faire
Risk neutral 4		Expected value maximization	PPP	Select highest expected value currency	Laissez faire	
5			Real exchange rate changes		Int'l trade opportunities	Select highest expected value currency
6	Non-FO		Rel. price + real exch. rate changes		Int'l and intersectoral opportunities	

				Strategies for Operational Decisions		
(1) Risk-attitude	(2) Financial market adjustment	(3) Financial cash flow strategy	(4) Goods market adjustment	(5) Nominally contracted flows	(6) Non-contractual Commercial	(7) Non-contractual Financial
7			PPP	Minimize infl. risk	Laissez faire	Minimize infl. and int. rate risk
8	FO	Variance minimization	Real exchange rate changes	Minimize variance for *all* cash flows	Int'l trade opportunities	See column (5)
9			Rel. price + real exch. rate changes		Int'l and intersectoral trade opport.	See column (5)
Risk averse 10	Non-FO	Expected value/ variance trade off	PPP	Trade off expected value/infl. risk	Laissez faire	Trade off expected value/ infl. and int. rate risk
11			Real exchange rate changes	Trade off int'l trade and financial opportunities/ variance of total cash flows		
12			Rel. price + real exch. rate changes	Trade off int'l, intersectoral and financial opportunities/ variance of total cash flows		

Table V.5(b)   Information needs related to macro-disturbances

Nominally contracted flows (8)	Non-contractual Commercial (9)	Financial (10)
1	None	
2 None	E[real exch. rates] volume adj. (γ_2)	None
3	E[real exch. rates] E[relative prices] volume adj. (γ_1, γ_2)	
4	None	E[int. rates] and E[exch. rate]
5 E[exchange rate]	E[real exch. rates] volume adj. (γ_1, γ_2)	
6	E[real exch. rates] E[relative prices] volume adj. (γ_1, γ_2)	
7 a_1, a_2 for contractual flows	None	
8 a_1, a_2, a_3, a_4, a_5 for contractual flows	E[real exch. rates] a_1, a_2, a_3, a_4, a_5 for com. flows	a_1, a_2, a_3 a_4, a_5 for financial flows
9 a_1, a_2, a_3, a_4, a_5 for contractual flows	E[real exch. rates], E[relative prices] a_1, a_2, a_3, a_4, a_5 for com. flows	
10 a_1, a_2 for contractual flows	None	E[exch. rates], E[int. rates] a_1, a_2, a_3, a_4, a_5 for financial flows

11 E[exch. rates], E[real exch. rates], E[int. rates], a_1, a_2, a_3, a_4, a_5 for total cash flows, volume adj. (γ_1, γ_2)

12 E[exch. rate], E[real exch. rate], E[relative prices], E[int. rates], a_1, a_2, a_3, a_4, a_5 for total cash flows, volume adj. (γ_1, γ_2)

the firm's total exposure to each price variable, it is necessary to evaluate the overlap among different kinds of exposure, i.e., to form estimates of the covariation among price levels, exchange rates, and interest rates. Without taking this interdependence among variables into account, partial hedging of, say, exchange rate exposure may increase another exposure, such as inflation exposure.

The proper definitions of exposure coefficients are listed in Table V.5(c). In addition to the coefficients of macroeconomic exposure presented in the Table, there is a coefficient a_6 for commercial exposure. This coefficient depends on the covariance between cash flows and relative prices after deducting the impact on cash flows of relative price changes due to macro economic disturbances. Econometric textbooks show how multiple regression coefficients such as $a_1 - a_6$ depend on simple regression coefficients, which are easier to evaluate if regression analysis is not feasible.

Obviously, it takes detailed knowledge of both the determinants of the firm's cash flows and the relationships among market price variables to evaluate exposure without regression analysis. The information may also be widely dispersed since, for example, the nature of the relationship between exchange rates and interest rates and the behaviour of policy authorities differ across countries.

Table V.5(c)   Notations and definitions

$E[\ ]$ = expected value

$$a_1 = \frac{\text{cov}\,[P_t^{LC}, (X_t^{LC}/P_t^{LC})]}{\text{Var}[X_t^{LC}/P_t^{LC}]} \quad \text{assuming other variables are constant}$$

$$a_2 = \frac{\text{cov}\,[P_t^{FC}, (X_t^{LC}/P_t^{LC})]}{\text{Var}[X_t^{LC}/P_t^{LC}]} \quad \text{assuming other variables are constant}$$

$$a_3 = \frac{\text{cov}\,[e_t, (X_t^{LC}/P_t^{LC})]}{\text{Var}[X_t^{LC}/P_t^{LC}]} \quad \text{assuming other variables are constant}$$

$$a_4 = \frac{\text{cov}\,[i_t^{LC}, (X_t^{LC}/P_t^{LC})]}{\text{Var}[X_t^{LC}/P_t^{LC}]} \quad \text{assuming other variables are constant}$$

$$a_5 = \frac{\text{cov}\,[i_t^{FC}, (X_t^{LC}/P_t^{LC})]}{\text{Var}[X_t^{LC}/P_t^{LC}]} \quad \text{assuming other variables are constant}$$

In principle, the above analysis is independent of the firm's time perspective. However, the longer the perspective, the more important it is to take into account the relationship between near-term adjustment of exchange rates and other price variables, and more distant changes in the same variables. Formally, the information requirements increase with the time horizon. On the other hand, many underlying price variables may over time follow a random or a mean-reverting process as mentioned in Section V.4. Then, based on such qualitative judgments, it may be determined that the firm need not be concerned with one or more kinds of exposure. It can then behave in a risk-neutral fashion with respect to these variables.

V.6 OPERATIONAL EXPOSURE MANAGEMENT

Most practitioners would argue that they do not believe financial market efficiency to be as strong as FO implies. They would also argue that goods markets adjust sluggishly, and that they are risk-averse. As a result, they place themselves in the difficult part of our Tables V.5(a) and V.5(b) on rows 11 and 12. Since most firms work primarily with short-term transaction exposure for contractual items and translation exposure, it would seem that their exposure management strategies, from an economic viewpoint, are highly inconsistent with their stated view of the world.

Assume that a firm's primary target variable is its market value, and that it is risk-averse so that some stabilization of value is desirable. Furthermore, assume that it believes in its own forecast ability, and more or less temporary deviations from LOP and PPP. Under these assumptions the information requirements to determine production, sales, and a financial position such that a desirable trade-off between level and variance of market value can be obtained, seem overwhelming. Before discussing how simplifying assumptions can be made in order to determine a *feasible strategy*, we show in more detail how the desired information would be obtained based on the regression/exposure coefficient approach we have outlined.

First of all, it is necessary to decide on the percentage decrease in market value (discounted cash flows) the firm is willing to sacrifice in order to decrease variance by a percentage point. Thereafter, market value and variance of market value must be determined for different combinations of sales in different countries and different financial positions. One of these combinations is then selected.

The applicability of historical data analysis to current exposure simplifies the evaluation of exposure by means of regression analysis. To implement such an analysis, the total cash flows must be decomposed into components that are *stable* in terms of their exposure. The components can then be added and weighted with their respective exposure coefficients to obtain a total exposure measure on which the firm can base its decisions to cover, hedge or adjust its cash flows.

In Section V.2 we decomposed cash flows for a subsidiary or a firm in a particular country. Table V.6 suggests a decomposition for a multinational firm with a number of products. In addition to the decomposition in Section V.2, we break down cash flows by subsidiary and product as in Chapter IV. Furthermore, for management purposes, all flows are divided into non-adjustable and adjustable flows in terms of financial or commercial exposure.

The adjustability of different flows depends on the nature and the time-horizon of the flows. Table V.7 lists a possible breakdown of flows related to one product in one subsidiary. Adjustability increases as we move towards the right and downward in the table. Near-term sales would normally be non-adjustable as would long-term debt amortization. Only short-term borrowing and lending and hedging flows would be adjustable within, say, a quarter. Over a longer time horizon the invoice currency for sales can be adjusted. The longer the time horizon, the more adjustable are cash flows. The profitability of different production and sales plans can be evaluated from real exchange rate and price forecasts, while exchange rates and interest rates determine expected borrowing costs in different currencies.

A suitable *point of reference* for exposure analysis is to determine adjustable and non-adjustable sales, production, and financial positions that *maximize* economic value. Similarly, the exposure of these positions, i.e., the variance of the value, is determined from knowledge of the exposure coefficients for different cash flows.

Given this point of reference, adjustable sales, production, and financial positions can be varied, and value and variance be determined for each combination.

Table V.6   Decomposition of cash flows

			Subsid. 1	Subsid. 2	Total
Non-contractual commercial	product group 1	adjustable*	‡		
		Non-adjustable			
	product group 2	adjustable*			
		non-adjustable			
Non-contractual financial (flexible interest rate)	currency denomination 1	adjustable†			
		non-adjustable			
	currency denomination 2	adjustable†			
		non-adjustable			
Nominally contracted (financial and depreciation tax shield)	currency denomination 1	adjustable†			
		non-adjustable			
	currency denomination 2	adjustable†			
		non-adjustable			

* Adjustable commercial flows may be subdivided further into terms of sale and invoice currency

† Financial flows could be subdivided further into maturities if these are adjustable.

‡ Empty spaces contain magnitudes and exposure coefficients as in equation V.1.

Cash flows may be variable in many directions, and the number of possible combinations may become extremely large as the time horizon increases. For example, invoice currency, trade credit conditions, and other methods listed in Table V.7 can be used to adjust the exposure of cash flows. Even if these measures are

Table V.7   Break-down of cash flows with different degrees of adjustability
Values based on forecast*. (In local currency)

				Quarter	
	1	2	3	. . . .	n
Commercial†					
External sales					
External purchases					
Net external					
Internal sales					
Internal purchases					
Net internal					
Total net commercial					
Financial‡					
Long-term debt service					
Long-term new loans					
Short-term debt service					
Short-term new loans					
Interest income					
Total net financial					
Hedging‡					
Forward purchases					
Forward sales					
Money market hedges (in)					
Money market hedges (out)					
Total net hedging flows					

* Commercial flows are adjusted for probability of non-payment.
† Can be subdivided by country and currency of invoice.
‡ Can be subdivided by currency.

grouped into fewer categories with similar exposure characteristics within each group, the search for an optimal exposure position becomes tedious, time-consuming, and costly, though computer programs similar to those used to determine optimal security portfolios could be used.

The information problem is further compounded by the potential unreliability of exposure-analysis based on historical data. By breaking down cash flows into components as suggested, internal judgmental information may be used to complement the analysis to determine exposure coefficients. Nevertheless, if simplifications of the strategy can be accomplished without substantially compromising the firm's objective, it is obviously desirable.

We turn next to a discussion of simplifying assumptions in order to determine a feasible strategy. The costs and benefits of the following simplifying assumptions will be discussed with the help of Table V.5(a) and V.5(b). We assume in order:

a. Commercial cash flows are non-adjustable to exposures.
b. LOP and PPP holds.
c. FO holds.
d. Risk-neutrality with respect to all or some cash flows.
e. Accounting based measures of exposure are valid.
f. All changes are either permanent or transitory.

These assumptions are not mutually exclusive as is obvious from Table V.5.

V.6.a   Treating Commercial Flows as Non-Adjustable to Exposure

Firms make substantial investments in product categories and in their commitments to customers in different countries. Therefore, once these investments (sunk costs) have been made, it is often prohibitively costly to shift sales among both countries and product groups. The magnitude of sunk costs depends naturally on the product. In the extreme case there is a commitment to a sales-volume per country and only extraordinary changes in the profitability picture are sufficient to motivate a shift in plans.

In firms with some adjustability, i.e., somewhat lower sunk costs, product and country sales plans may be adjusted only in response to *expected* real exchange rate changes and relative price changes above a certain magnitude. The sunk costs could be too large for it to be worthwhile to adjust sales plans to risk-considerations. Accordingly, exposure adjustment is left entirely to the financial side of the firm. The financial positions would then be determined with the *total* exposure in mind, but commercial exposure is by the financial managers treated as given.

The benefit and cost of this strategy with respect to commercial flows depend, as we noted, on the magnitude of sunk costs related to particular consumer groups, the time horizon over which investments are made, and on how rigid payment conditions are in terms of invoice currency and trade-credits.

It has been argued that payment conditions and invoice currency are of no importance to the firm (see, e.g., Rao and Magee, 1980), since in competitive markets, prices would adjust to reflect risk-bearing by sellers and buyers. In that case, a reduction in exposure can be achieved only by selling at a lower price. It would then seem as if exposure management for commercial flows were irrelevant. However, there are many firms with very different exposure characteristics and risk-preferences in any market. If contract terms are standardized it is highly unlikely that all firms can be compensated for risk-taking in prices in such a way that they are indifferent between actual contract terms and another sets of terms with lower exposure and lower price.

McKinnon (1979) argues also that invoice currency and trade credit terms are often determined in the market place with little choice for individual firms. He argues that for homogeneous goods, for which LOP holds, the dollar is the worldwide invoice currency, and firms are typically given credit for a *fixed term*. Thereby both exporters and importers can cover exposures. For differentiated goods, however, the exporter's home currency is often the invoice currency. The importer is then given an open account credit that enables the firm to adjust its exposure as it sees fit.

The costs to the risk-averse firm of viewing commercial cash flows as non-adjustable to exposure depends also on its risk-attitude, and on goods and financial market efficiency. Firms may be risk-averse primarily with respect to sales and output fluctuations, as we discussed in Chapter II, if it is costly to change the number of employees in production. For such a firm it is very costly to regard commercial flows as non-adjustable, since it is averse to the variance in these particular flows.

For firms that are risk-averse with respect to all cash flows or value, the costs are most likely smaller. Their magnitude depends on how large, long-lasting, and unpredictable deviations from LOP and PPP, and relative price changes in goods markets are after macroeconomic disturbances, since these variables determine the extent of exposure.

The FO relationship is relevant for the 'costs' of an exposure management strategy under which commercial flows are not adjusted for exposure, because when FO holds, the cheapest way to influence exposure is always through financial positions. The reason is, as we noted in Section V.5, that there is no market opportunity cost of changing the financial position among currencies. Therefore, when FO holds, it is rational for the risk-averse firm to minimize the variance of total cash flows solely by means of financial transactions, while maximizing commercial cash flows.

In general, the flows that can be adjusted to reduce exposure at the lowest opportunity cost should be adjusted first. Even when FO does not hold perfectly, it is not far-fetched to assume that the opportunity cost of adjusting financial flows is lower, in general, than the opportunity cost of adjusting commercial flows. The closer FO holds and the larger the sunk costs in sales commitments, the more validity this viewpoint has.

V.6.b Assuming LOP and PPP Hold

The advantage of a belief in strong goods market arbitrage, so that LOP holds for all goods and PPP holds, is that exposure and profit opportunities for commercial non-contractual exposure do not arise. Therefore, it is costless to focus entirely on financial exposure. This view seems unrealistic, however, based on, for example, observation of the large and long-lasting real appreciation of the dollar in the early 1980s. It is worth noting that even if LOP holds for a particular firm's product, such as for oil and other raw materials, large price changes occur relative to other products when there are large deviations from average PPP. These relative price changes among products are as important for exposure and profit opportunities as relative price changes among countries, i.e, deviations from LOP.

We conclude therefore that basing exposure management on the PPP assumption may be costly and expose the firm to considerable risk on commercial flows.

V.6.c Assuming FO Holds

We have already noticed that when FO holds, the value of commercial cash flows can be maximized and risk considerations need enter only financial decisions. We showed in Section V.5 that this argument holds even if commercial flows in principle are adjustable. A second drastic simplification as a result of FO which we also discussed is that financial positions can be used to *minimize* exposure. The difficult evaluation of the trade-off between risk and return is unnecessary. Thus, hedging for variance minimization as described in Chapter IV can be pursued.

The benefits of assuming FO are substantial. How large are the costs? The answer to this question depends on the firm's potential profits on financial positions from attempts to forecast exchange rates and interest rates. These potential profits can be realized only if the firm can beat future and forward rates of foreign exchange and T-bills. Evidence is gathering that it is not impossible for individuals to realize such profits for some time (see Appendix III.3), but the costs in terms of time spent on forecasting may be substantial. The mixed empirical evidence and lack of agreement on the biasedness of the forward rate as a predictor of future spot rates is an indication that the opportunity cost of behaving *as if* FO holds may be small for most firms.

V.6.d Risk-Neutrality With Respect to Some or All Cash Flows

The great simplification that results from taking a risk-neutral attitude is that variance is of no concern and, therefore, commercial and/or financial positions are determined entirely from forecasts and based on cash flow or value maximization.

As we have mentioned, risk-aversion versus risk neutrality may apply for total cash flows or only for commercial flows depending on the attitude of different stakeholders. Under risk-neutrality with respect to shareholders, but risk-aversion with respect to employees, it becomes the firm's objective to maximize expected return on financial positions but to trade off expected cash flows gains versus variance for commercial flows. In this case it is obviously not possible to use financial positions to offset commercial exposure. This kind of exposure management strategy is entirely production and sales oriented and, given the limited adjustability of commercial cash flows once investments are made, exposure consideration would enter primarily at the investment stage. Once investments are made, adjustment of sales and production to changes in the macroeconomic exposure are more costly, as we have noted.

V.6.e Accounting Data Are Used

This type of simplification is commonly used. As we noted in Chapter III, transaction and translation exposures are common measures based on which the firm hedges and covers. Transactions exposure may be seen as a near-term cash-flow exposure measure, while translation exposure could be viewed as a measure of value exposure. We have already noted that these measures are designed specifically to measure exchange rate exposure without consideration of macroeconomic exposures in general. Transaction exposure is partial in an additional sense in that it focuses on financial and other contractual flows.

Accounting based translation exposure measures are, as we noted in Chapter III, of little value in measuring economic value exposure to macroeconomic disturbances in general. Hedging translation exposure is, therefore, almost entirely a question of image.

Is it costly to hedge an irrelevant exposure? Since we expect that FO holds over time, the outright cost of hedging over time would be equal to transaction costs, which are relatively low. The cost would instead take the form of increasing confusion in the stock-market about the true exposure of the firm unless the firm announced exactly its hedging-transactions. In addition, by hedging an irrelevant exposure the firm actually exposes itself in economic terms. Thus, if economic exposure is of concern as well, then such hedging could be costly.

For similar reasons the outright costs of managing transaction exposure would be limited to the costs of taking actual covers and employee' time, which may be of considerable importance.

Transaction exposure has some relevance, however, since it refers to part of the cash flows of the firm. Without knowledge of the exposure of other flows, i.e., non-contractual flows, covering transaction exposure may increase, as well as decrease, the near-term cash flow exposure, even to exchange rate changes. Thus, it seems essential to expand conventional transaction exposure measures to include a wider variety of flows and periods beyond the next few quarters.

Transaction exposure also neglects other exposures than exchange rate exposure. This drawback may or may not be serious in the short run, however. The short-term variance of the real exchange rate tends to dominate exposure to the more stable price levels while interest rate variance may be high in the short run.

One may interpret the strategy of a firm hedging completely conventional measures of translation and transaction exposures as being based on:

i. A risk-averse attitude.
ii. The use of accounting net worth as the target variable.
iii. A belief in FO as a reasonable approximation.
iv. A belief that PPP and LOP do not hold, since all assets are considered exposed under current accounting rules.

Thus, the one, but very serious, problem with this strategy is the choice of an accounting target variable.

The firm covering only near-term *transaction* exposure consecutively would differ in its implicit assumptions, because: 1) its target variable is near-term cash flows rather than value and 2) implicitly commercial cash flows are considered not exposed since they are not part of the exposure (i.e., LOP and PPP are assumed). More distant transaction exposures are certainly a part of economic value and, therefore, from an economic point of view, it could be costly to neglect them in exposure analysis.

The firm choosing to *selectively hedge* or cover, is presumably also risk-averse but it does not believe in FO as a reasonable approximation. Its managers believe they can beat the market frequently or systematically. The burden of proof for this attitude should be laid rather heavily on the manager. Another problem faced with this strategy is that of determining a sensible and operational trade-off rule between an acceptable increase in risk and an increased rate of return.

V.6.f All Changes Are Either Permanent or Transitory

We have seen that the information required to manage exposure for a firm with a reasonable discount rate is very large. Even if the firm wishes to minimize exposure, there is a need to understand how a change in the exchange rate, a price level, or an interest rate in the near future affects the likelihood of additional changes or reversals in the variables. Assume, for example, that cash flow exposure on a quarterly basis has been estimated, but the concern of the firm is value exposure or market value stabilization. In this case it is necessary to translate cash flow exposures into value exposures, as we discussed in Section IV. We mentioned there that if the real exchange rate is expected to remain at the current level and to return to it if unanticipated changes occur, then real exchange rate changes are expected to be temporary. In this case, the cash flow exposure in real dollar terms to near-term real exchange rate changes amounts to the total exposure of economic value to these changes. In other words, cash flow exposures for different time horizons are independent. Hedging of value can then be accomplished by hedging a series of cash flow exposures. The analysis of hedging in Chapter IV, therefore, is applicable on cash flows in each future period.

There exists weak and highly controversial empirical evidence that the real exchange rate follows a 'random walk' as we noted in Chapter IV. If this is correct, real exchange rates are serially uncorrelated and the best guess of the future rate is the current rate. Therefore, any unanticipated real exchange rate change would be considered permanent, that is, *if* the rate changes, then the best guess is that the rate will remain at the new level. In such a case, coefficients of exposure of the *percent change* in cash flows (eg. IV.5) can be applied on value exposure, since the percentage change in value of an unanticipated change must be equal to the percentage change in cash flows during the same period. The reason is that expected cash flows in all periods would be influenced to the same degree as cash flows in the period the real exchange rate change occurred. Thus, the coefficient for cash flow exposure to unanticipated real exchange rate changes is also the coefficient for value exposure to these real exchange rate changes. The measurement of value exposure is, therefore, relatively simple when changes in macroeconomic variables are expected to be permanent.

The difficulty in obtaining an operational measure of value exposure increases when changes in variables are neither temporary nor permanent, and especially when changes vary in this respect over time. In the latter case, there is no fixed rule for translating between cash flow and value exposure. Even if a constant relationship exists, it would take time to obtain observations based on which a well-informed estimate of the degree of permanence can be formed.

V.7   SUMMARY: DETERMINATION OF A SIMPLIFIED STRATEGY AT LOW COSTS

We are now in a position to summarize our analysis and distinguish between the more or less innocuous assumptions that help the firm determine a strategy that is both feasible in its information requirements and does not lead to costly deviations from the firm's objective. We start with the often-stated view of firms that: 1) FO does not hold perfectly at all times, 2) there are substantial deviations from LOP and PPP, and 3) the firm will attempt to stabilize market (economic) value in consideration of shareholders' preferences, and/or stabilize commercial cash flows and employment, in consideration of the costs of adjusting employment. In Table V.8, we summarize potential simplifying assumptions and describe their associated strategies. We distinguish between those simplifying assumptions that would result in substantial opportunity costs (high-cost assumptions) and those that seem relatively innocuous (low-cost assumptions), given the above views of the world and the firm's objectives.

Starting from the end, we list among high-cost assumptions and strategies those based on traditional accounting measures of exposure (9) and (10), and those based on belief in LOP and PPP (8). Under these assumptions, measured exposure differs substantially from economic exposure. Taking a risk-neutral attitude with respect to commercial cash flows (7) and, therefore, limiting exposure considerations to financial cash flows causes the same neglect of a substantial part of macroeconomic impacts on the firm.

Table V.8 Simplifications of exposure management strategy by means of different assumptions

Cost assumption	Strategy
Low cost assumptions	
1. FO	Minimize variance of total cash flows by means of financial positions, while maximizing the value of commercial cash flows
2. Commercial cash flows are non-adjustable when target is to stabilize value of total cash flows	Use financial positions to achieve desired risk/return trade-off while maximizing the value of commercial cash flows
3. Risk-neutrality with respect to shareholders, when target is to stabilize employment	Maximize value of financial positions while adjusting sales and output decisions depending on their sensitivity to macroeconomic disturbances
High or low cost assumptions	
4. All changes in market price variables are temporary	Manage cash flow exposure
5. All changes in market price variables are permanent	Apply coefficients of sensitivity of percent change in cash flows on value and manage value exposure
High cost assumptions	
6. Commercial cash flows are non-adjustable when target is to stabilize employment	Exposure-considerations enter only at time of investment in production and sales capacity for different markets
7. Risk-neutrality with respect to commercial flows	Manage only exposure of value of financial flows
8. Law of one price (LOP) and purchasing power parity (PPP) hold	Manage only exposure of value of contractual flows
9. Use accounting measures of economic exposure	Manage translation exposure
10. Use conventional transaction exposure to estimate economic exposure	Manage transaction exposure

Assumption (6), treating commercial cash flows as non-adjustable, when employment and commercial cash flow stabilization is desirable, is almost tautologically costly, unless adjustment costs are so high that exposure considerations are feasible only at the time of investment decisions. However, if the firm's concern is to stabilize economic value, the non-adjustability of commercial cash flows (2) may be a very practical assumption, since financial positions can be used to obtain a desired exposure level for all cash flows. The cost of this assumption depends partly on how well FO holds, since, if it holds (1), the optimal strategy is to maximize the return on commercial flows while financial positions are used to minimize the variance of the value of all flows, given commercial exposure.

Taking a risk-neutral attitude with respect to shareholders in (3) is also tautologically costless when employment stabilization is the objective. Contractual exposure can then be neglected. The cost of assumptions (4) and (5), referring to specific time-patterns of market price variables, depends, naturally on the relevance of the assumption. Price level changes tend to be more permanent than real exchange rate and interest rate changes. Therefore, the firm may choose to consider changes in some variables as temporary and changes in other variables as permanent. However, the assumptions in this respect may have to vary over time.

VI

THE IMPACT OF MACROECONOMIC DISTURBANCES ON THE FIRM: A SCENARIO APPROACH

VI.1 INTRODUCTION

In the previous chapter we developed expressions for components of cash flows in order to demonstrate how macroeconomic disturbances impact on the firm through a variety of channels. In this chapter we utilize the same expressions in a number of constructed examples corresponding to different scenarios for the macroeconomic adjustment to policy disturbances. The magnitude of different cash flow effects can be observed in such examples. We illustrate how the cash flow effects depend on the extent to which the disturbance affects the price level, relative prices, exchange rates, and interest rates, respectively. The examples also show how exposure coefficients could be calculated with knowledge about firm specific factors, such as the effects of relative price changes on sales, and about the relationship between macroeconomic variables, such as exchange rates, price levels, and interest rates, on the one hand, and relative prices of relevance for the firm, on the other. The scenario analysis illustrated in this chapter may be seen both as an alternative and a complementary method for measuring exposure. Its advantage relative to regression analysis is that it does not require a large amount of historical data on cash flows. ,

We analyse two kinds of disturbances. First, in Section 2 we assume there is a 10 percent unanticipated increase in the money supply in the host country (the LC-country) of a particular subsidiary for which we wish to evaluate exposure. Thereafter, in Section 3, we assume that there is a fiscal expansion in the same country. For each disturbance we develop a number of scenarios or cases, each corresponding to different views of the macroeconomic adjustment mechanism to the disturbance. Lacking a global macroeconomic model on which everybody agrees it is of value to understand how sensitive cash flows are to different scenarios for macroeconomic development.

VI.2   A SCENARIO ANALYSIS OF AN UNANTICIPATED MONEY SUPPLY INCREASE

In this section all cases have in common an unanticipated increase in the money supply of local currency (LC). The cases differ in terms of the inflation effect of this disturbance, corresponding disturbances in other countries, the degrees to which PPP and LOP hold, relative price changes in the inflation and exchange rate adjustment process, and the degree of indexation of loans. The relative price changes in particular may depend on the type of output which is produced by the firms. The differences can be viewed as differences in relative speeds of adjustment among markets and differences in the degree of efficiency in international goods and financial markets. In addition, the impact of the disturbance on expectations plays an important role.

In Table VI.1 we formulate in general terms the cash flows which were listed in Table V.2 in the previous chapter. Base period figures are the same as well. We distinguish between five components of commercial cash flows, and two components of financial cash flows.

Flows A and B in Table VI.1 are after tax revenues from *export sales* in nominal LC-terms. These and other flows must be deflated by the price level in period *t* in order to obtain a measure of their *real* value evaluated in the host country. Flow C is revenues from *domestic sales* in the host country.

The costs of production are represented by flows D and E: flow D being costs of *imported inputs* from the USA and flow E *wage costs* in the host country. The volume effects applied to costs are the weighted sums of the volume effects on sales.

There are two kinds of volume effects. First, a change in the relative price between the output good and other commodities in each country produces volume changes depending on elasticities ϵ_1^{FC}, ϵ_1^{US} and ϵ_1^{LC}, respectively. Note that these elasticities represent the percentage change in sales volume from a one percent change in the relative price. We assume that relative prices are given by demand effects of the disturbance. The volume effects ϵ_1^{LC}, and ϵ_1^{FC}, and ϵ_1^{US} depend then on the firm's supply response to the relative price change. The second volume effect is due to deviations from LOP, and represent the firm's willingness to increase sales in a foreign country in response to a depreciation of the host country-currency (LC) at constant prices in each country. The (positive) elasticities ϵ_2^{FC} and ϵ_2^{US} capture this type of supply elasticities in the two countries to which the firm exports.

We assume in all cases that $\epsilon_1^{LC} = \epsilon_1^{FC} = \epsilon_1^{US} = .5$, i.e., a one percent increase in the relative price in any country causes an increase in sales volume of one-half percent.

The elasticities ϵ_2^{FC} and ϵ_2^{US} are also cases assumed to be .5, i.e., a one percent appreciation of the importing country's exchange rate at constant prices also induces the firm to increase export supply by one-half percent.

Knowledge of the supply elasticities is obviously crucial for estimating exposure, and analysis of the firm's market over recent history is necessary to obtain this kind of knowledge. If the firm had control over prices then the supply response and the price response would be determined simultaneously by the firm. Our assumption that the firm is a *price taker* makes the examples somewhat simpler. We keep the elasticities constant through the chapter but the reader can easily experiment with other assumptions.

The financial flows are denoted by F and G in Table VI.1. Flow F is expressed in a somewhat.different form as compared to Chapter V. It is simply the amount of LC-debt in the base year (25) multiplied by the percent change in the price level. This amount is the increase in the firm's debt capacity as a result of inflation, which increases the LC-value of all assets. Thus, without changing the financial structure, the firm can borrow more and potentially distribute the loan to shareholders without increasing the cost of capital.

Table VI.1   Cash flows, nominal, in local currency in period t

A. **Nominal sales revenue in FC country**

$$LC(1 - T)\left\{FC\ 20 \cdot P_t^{FC}\left(\frac{OP_t^{FC}}{P_t^{FC}}\right) \cdot e_t^{LC-FC}\left[1 + \left(\frac{OP_t^{FC}}{P_t^{FC}} - 1\right)\epsilon_1^{FC}\right.\right.$$

$$\left.\left. + \left(\frac{OP_t^{FC} \cdot e_t^{LC-FC}}{OP_t^{LC}} - 1\right)\epsilon_2^{FC}\right]\right\}$$

B. **Nominal sales revenue in US**

$$LC(1 - T)\left\{USD\ 30 \cdot P_t^{US}\left(\frac{OP_t^{US}}{P_t^{US}}\right) \cdot e_t^{LC-USD}\left[1 + \left(\frac{OP_t^{US}}{P_t^{US}} - 1\right)\epsilon_1^{US}\right.\right.$$

$$\left.\left. + \left(\frac{OP_t^{US} \cdot e_t^{LC-USD}}{OP_t^{US}} - 1\right)\epsilon_2^{US}\right]\right\}$$

C. **Nominal sales revenue in LC country**

$$LC(1 - T)\ 50 \cdot P_t^{LC} \cdot \frac{OP_t^{LC}}{P_t^{LC}}\left[1 + \left(\frac{OP_t^{LC}}{P_t^{LC}} - 1\right)\epsilon_1^{LC}\right]$$

D. **Costs of imported inputs**

$$LC(1 - T)\left\{USD\ 40 \cdot P_t^{US}\left(\frac{IP_t^{US}}{P_t^{US}}\right) \cdot e_t^{LC-USD}\left[1 + \gamma_1^A + \gamma_2^A\right]\right\}$$

where

$$\gamma_1^A = .2\left(\frac{OP_t^{FC}}{P_t^{FC}} - 1\right)\epsilon_1^{FC} + .3\left(\frac{OP_t^{US}}{P_t^{US}} - 1\right)\epsilon_1^{US} + .5\left(\frac{OP_t^{LC}}{P_t^{LC}} - 1\right)\epsilon_1^{LC}$$

$$\gamma_2^A = .2\left(\frac{OP_t^{FC} \cdot e_t^{LC-FC}}{OP_t^{LC}} - 1\right)\epsilon_2^{FC} + .3\left(\frac{OP_t^{US} \cdot e_t^{LC-USD}}{OP_t^{LC}} - 1\right)\epsilon_2^{US} + .5 \cdot 0$$

are average volume effects due to relative price changes within countries and between countries; respectively (compare Table V.5). Weights .2, .3, and .5, respectively, are base-period sales 20, 30, and 50, respectively, relative to total sales (100).

E. **Wage costs**

$$LC(1 - T)\left\{30 \cdot P_t^{LC} \cdot \frac{WP_t^{LC}}{P_t^{LC}}[1 + \gamma_1^A + \gamma_2^A]\right\}$$

F. **Increase in debt capacity**

$$LC25(P_t^{LC} - 1)$$

Table VI.1 (Cont'd.)

G. Interest costs

$$LC(1 - T) \cdot 25 \cdot i_t^{LC}$$

All prices and exchange rates are measured relative to base year $t-1$.

ϵ_1 = percent change in quantity supplied from a one percent change in relative output price within country.

ϵ_2 = percent change in quantity supplied to export market from a one percent change in relative output price between countries.

T = tax rate.

P_t = price level in t.

OP_t = nominal output price in t.

IP_t = nominal input price in t.

W/P_t = nominal wage cost in t.

e_t^{LC-FC} = LC currency units per unit of FC currency.

Alternatively the inflation gain may be used to reduce debt. Notice that this inflation gain is not taxed. If loans are indexed, then interest costs increase as well, but such cost increases are taxed and appear in flow G. These flows are the after tax interest expenses on LC loans. There are no other loans. It is assumed in the cases in this section that the real interest rate was determined in the previous period. Therefore, unanticipated increases in interest cost happen only if some or all loans are indexed. In the next section for a fiscal disturbance, we consider the case of a flexible real interest rate as well.

The degree of indexation depends on the firm's choice of long-term versus short-term loans and the degree to which changes in inflation are anticipated at the time the interest rate is determined. The shorter the maturity of loans, and the higher the degree to which inflation is anticipated, the higher is the degree of indexation.

It is assumed that period $t-1$ is the base year when all prices are equal to unity, and the base case interest rate is 10 percent. Unanticipated changes occur between period $t-1$ and t. It is naturally possible that certain price changes were anticipated already in the previous period. Therefore, anticipated cash flow effects from sales may also occur in period t. To simplify the exposition we do not include these effects in the analysis. The methodology used here could be used to estimate anticipated cash flows as well. It is possible that changes in prices and interest rates between two previous periods would typically include further adjustment in the period under consideration. It is also possible that cash flow effects beyond period t could be anticipated in t if unanticipated changes occur between $t-1$ and t.

The cases will now be discussed in the order of Table VI.2, which shows values of different variables that are inserted in the formulas in Table VI.1. The results for cash flows are shown in Table VI.3, where positive entries are positive cash flow effects and negative entries are negative cash flow effects relative to the base case.

The *base case* is shown in the far right in Table VI.3 and is identical to flows in Table V.1. The base year commercial cash flows after tax are LC 12, and the financial flows are LC -1 at the 10 percent interest rate. We set depreciation cash flows equal to zero, though with historical cost accounting, inflation has an impact on such flows similar but opposite in sign to the inflation gain on debt. Fifty percent of sales occur abroad and 50 percent in the country. We limit the analysis to changes in the *real* value of the LC-subsidiary's cash flows. These changes capture the impact of disturbances on the subsidiary's ability to remit dividends to shareholders.

Table VI.3 shows also exposure coefficients denoting *the percentage change in commercial, financial, and total cash flows respectively, from a one percent change in selected market price variables*. It is worth noting that in this scenario analysis of one disturbance, it is in some cases questionable, whether a certain cash flow change should be regarded as exposure to, say, exchange rate changes rather than changes in inflation or the interest rate. All changes are due to the original disturbance. Therefore, we can say that a particular cash flow effect depends on, for example, the change in the exchange rate only if the exchange rate change due to another disturbance would have the same cash flow effect. Here, we regard as exchange rate effects those commercial cash flow changes that depend on a deviation from the law of one price (LOP) between countries, while inflation effects are those cash flow effects that are the results of changes in relative prices *within* a country (during the inflation process), and from changes in interest rates due to inflation indexation.

We turn now to discussion of the cases. The specific figures in Table VI.2 are inserted in formulas in Table VI.1 to derive Table VI.3.

Case 2.1.a LC-inflation, PPP, LOP, No Indexation

This case represents a monetarist view of the world. The money market and all goods market clear rapidly. Therefore no relative price changes. There is a 10 percent increase in the price level, and the exchange rate depreciates by the same amount. The real value of commercial cash flows remain unchanged, i.e., cash flows increase in proportion to the price level.

There is a substantial gain on the financial side for contractual flows for interest expense. Interest costs remain unchanged but inflation pays back 10 percent of the loans, i.e, debt capacity increases by 2.5.

Case 2.1.b As 2.1.a but Full Indexation

All commercial flows are identical to the previous case. There is no relative price-effect. The interest rate for the firm increases to 20 percent. There are nevertheless substantial financial gains, since nominal rather than real interest costs are taxed.

We can estimate exposure coefficients as well. These coefficients are calculated as the percent change in commercial, financial, and total cash flows, respectively, from a one percent change in the price level, the exchange rate, and the interest rate, respectively. There is a gain of 2.5 on the real value of debt minus an increase in interest cost equal to one due to indexation. Thus, on 10 percent inflation there is a 150 percent improvement in financial cash flows (1.5/1)·100. The coefficient for the percentage change in financial flows for one percent inflation is accordingly 15. On total flows (11) the gain is (1.5/11)·100 or 13.6 percent. Therefore the inflation exposure coefficient is 1.36. There is no commercial exposure. We can note by comparing with case 2.1.a that the magnitude of inflation exposure depends critically on the degree of indexation of loans, i.e., the degree to which interest costs change with inflation. Exchange rate and interest rate exposures are zero. There are no real effects of exchange rate changes and the real effects of interest rate changes are entirely due to the degree of inflation indexation of loans.

Table VI.2   Assumptions about levels of price variables after a 10 percent increase in LC money supply

In all cases $\hat{M}^{LC} = 10$ percent and firm-specific elasticities are: $\epsilon_1^{LC} = \epsilon_1^{FC} = \epsilon_1^{US}$ and $\epsilon_2^{FC} = \epsilon_2^{US}$. Base case all prices equal to 1.

Case 2.1.a.   LC inflation; PPP; LOP; no indexation.

$P_t^{LC} = 1.1$ (price level in LC country)

$P_t^{FC} = P_t^{US} = 1$

Relative output price $\dfrac{OP_t}{P_t}$ in all countries $= 1$

$$\frac{IP_t^{US}}{P_t^{US}} = \frac{WP_t^{LC}}{P_t^{LC}} = 1$$

$e_t^{LC-FC} = e_t^{LC-USD} = 1.1$

$i_t = 10$ percent or .1

Case 2.1.b.   As 2.1.a but loans fully indexed

$i_t = 20$ percent or .2

Case 2.2.a.   Inflation in all countries; output price rigid; PPP; LOP; half indexation

$\hat{M}^{FC} = \hat{M}^{US} = 10$ percent

$P_t^{LC} = P_t^{FC} = P_t^{US} = 1.1$

Relative output price $\dfrac{OP_t}{P_t} = \dfrac{1}{1.1}$ in all countries

Other relative price $= 1$ in all countries

$e_t^{LC-FC} = e_t^{LC-USD} = 1.1$

Average i_t for firm $= 15$ percent

Case 2.2.b.   As 2.2.a, but loans fully indexed

$i_t = 20$ percent

Case 2.3.   Different inflation rates; PPP; LOP; input prices and wage costs rise faster than inflation; full indexation

$\hat{M}_t^{FC} = \hat{M}_t^{US} = 10$ percent

$P_t^{LC} = 1.08, P_t^{FC} = 1.1, P_t^{US} = 1.08$

Relative output price in each country $= 1$. Thus $OP_t^{LC} = OP_t^{FC} = OP_t^{US} = 1.08$

$\dfrac{IP_t^{US}}{P_t^{US}} = 1.05$; input price rises 5 percent over general price level in US

Table VI.2 (Cont'd.)

$\dfrac{WP_t^{LC}}{P_t^{LC}} = 1.02$. Wage costs rise 2 percent above general price level in LC

$e_t^{LC-FC} = 1.08/1.1$, $e_t^{LC-USD} = 1.0$

$i_t = 18$ percent

Case 2.4. Exchange rate undershooting with LC inflation; no intracountry relative price changes; full indexation

$P_t^{LC} = 1.1$, $P_t^{FC} = P_t^{US} = 1.0$

All relative prices within countries $= 1$

$e_t^{LC-FC} = e_t^{LC-USD} = 1.05$

$\epsilon_2^{FC} = \epsilon_2^{US} = .5$

$i_t = 20$ percent

Case 2.5. Overshooting of exchange rate with LC inflation; no intracountry relative price changes; full indexation

$P_t^{LC} = 1.1$, $P_t^{FC} = P_t^{US} = 1.0$

All relative prices within countries $= 1$

$e_t^{LC-FC} = e_t^{LC-USD} = 1.15$

$\epsilon_2^{FC} = \epsilon_2^{US} = .5$

$i_t^{LC} = 20$ percent

Case 2.6. LC inflation with relative price changes and exchange rate overshooting; full indexation

$P_t^{LC} = 1.05$, $P_t^{FC} = P_t^{US} = 1.0$

$\dfrac{OP_t^{LC}}{P_t^{LC}} = 1.02$, $\dfrac{OP_t^{FC}}{P_t^{FC}} = \dfrac{OP_t^{US}}{P_t^{US}} = 1.0$

$\dfrac{WP_t^{LC}}{P_t^{LC}} = .95$

$e_t^{LC-FC} = e_t^{LC-US} = 1.15$

$i_t = 15$ percent

Table VI.3 Exposure coefficients and real cash flow effects of 10 percent unanticipated LC money supply increase under different macroeconomic scenarios

Case		2.1.a	2.1.b	2.2.a	2.2.b	2.3	2.4	2.5	2.6	Base case levels
Cash flow	A	0	0	-1.06	as 2.2.a	0	-.54	.55	1.08	8
	B	0	0	-1.59	as 2.2.a	0	-.81	.83	1.63	12
	C	0	0	-2.65	as 2.2.a	0	0	0	.20	20
	D	0	0	.73	as 2.2.a	-.8	.90	-.91	-1.93	-16
	E	0	0	.55	as 2.2.a	-.24	.14	-.14	.33	-12
Net commercial A + B + C + D + E		0	0	-4.02	as 2.2.a	-1.04	-.31	.33	1.31	12
	F	2.5	2.5	2.5	as 2.2.a	2.0	2.5	2.5	1.25	0
	G	0	-1	-.5	-1	-.8	-1	-1	-.5	-1
Net financial		2.5	1.5	2.0	1.5	1.2	1.5	1.5	.75	-1
Total		2.5	1.5	-2.02	-2.52	.16	1.19	1.83	2.06	11

Case	2.1.a	2.1.b	2.2.a	2.2.b	2.3	2.4	2.5	2.6	Base case levels
Exposure coefficients for percent change in commercial flows									
$\hat{p}^{FC}$	0	0	−.67	as 2.2.a	0	0	0	0	
$\hat{p}^{US}$	0	0	−1.01	as 2.2.a	−.83	0	0	0	
$\hat{p}^{LC}$	0	0	−1.68	as 2.2.a	−.25	0	0	1.75	
$\hat{e}$	0	0	0	as 2.2.a	0	−.52	.18	.14	
$\hat{\imath}^{LC}$	0	0	0	as 2.2.a	0	0	0	0	
Exposure coefficients for percent change in financial flows									
$\hat{p}^{D}$	25	15	20.0	15	15	15	15	15	
$\hat{e}$	0	0	0	0	0	0	0	0	
$\hat{\imath}^{LC}$	0	0	0	0	0	0	0	0	
Exposure coefficients for percent change in total flows									
$\hat{p}^{LC}$	2.27	1.36	−.01	−.46	1.09	1.30	1.36	3.27	
$\hat{e}$	0	0	0	0	0	−.56	.20	.15	
$\hat{\imath}^{LC}$	0	0	0	0	0	0	0	0	

Case 2.2.a   Inflation in all Countries; Output Price Rigid; PPP; LOP; Half Indexation

In this case the price level increases by 10 percent in *all* countries, and there is no change in the exchange rate (PPP holds). The price of the particular output is rigid or lags in the inflation process due to slow demand response for the firm's products. Therefore, there is a 10 percent fall in the relative price of the firm's output in all countries. In domestic and export markets, sales fall as a result of the supply decrease. The magnitude of the fall in sales depends on the supply elasticities, which in all countries are assumed to be .5. Revenues as well as costs fall.

Inflation exposure coefficients for commercial flows can then be estimated for each country, since the cash flow effect for each country depends on inflation occurring in that country. As an example, cash flows from sales in the USA decrease with an amount equal to 1.59 on the revenue ride. In addition, a share of the cost decrease—proportional to the USA share in the volume of sales—is due to US inflation. We calculate this cost effect as

$$.4(40 + 30) \cdot .3\left(\frac{1}{1.1} - 1\right) \cdot (.5) = -.38$$

The first figure is $(1 - T)$. Real costs of production in the base year are 70 of which a share .3 depends on sales to the USA. The fall in volume is captured by the last two factors: the relative price change and the elasticity. The net commercial cash flow effect due to inflation in the USA is -1.21. Note that in Table VI.3 cost decreases appear as positive numbers. On total commercial cash flows we obtain a coefficient equal to $[(-1.21/12)/10] \cdot 100 = -1.01$. The commercial cash flow effects due to FC inflation are calculated similarly. The net cash flow effect on exports to the FC country is $-.804$. The coefficient for the percentage change in commercial cash flows due to FC inflation becomes $-.67$.

In the host country revenues fall 2.65 while costs fall .64. The commercial cash flow coefficient for LC inflation becomes -1.68.

On the financial sides there is a gain equal to $+2.0$. Interest cost after tax increase $.05 \cdot 25 \cdot .4 = .5$ while the untaxed increase in debt capacity remains 2.5. Finally, the *total* cash flow exposure coefficient for LC inflation is negligible, since commercial cash flows domestically fall 2.01 while financial flows increase 2.0. Thus, the gain on the financial side offsets the loss on the commercial side in the domestic markets. The total cash flow effect in all countries is negative, however. Total cash flow exposure coefficients for FC and US inflation are not included in the table.

Case 2.2.b   As Case 2.2.a but Full Indexation

Commercial flow effects are the same as in case 2.2.a. Financial cash flow effects are the same as in case 2.1.b. The total flow exposure coefficient for LC-inflation depends now on a net loss; $-2.01 + 1.5 = -.51$. The coefficient becomes $-.46$. The large total negative outcome of cases 2.a and 2.b relative to the outcome of cases 1.a and 1.b is due to the output-price rigidity, which would depend on a relative lag in the demand for the product in the aftermath of a money supply increase in every country.

Case 2.3   Different Inflation Rates; PPP; Input Prices Lead Inflation; Full Indexation

In this case there is also a money supply increase in all countries. The money supply increase in the LC country and the US does not lead to immediate adjustment of all prices, but different prices adjust with different speed to a new equilibrium level. On the average the inflation rate in the US and the LC country is 8 percent, while the relative price of the US produced input goods rises 5 percent more in the US. In the LC country wage costs rise faster than prices on the average. As opposed to the previous case there is no real decrease or increases in the demand for the firm's output. Thus, the nominal demand increase due to the increased money supply leads to an output price change equal to the average inflation rate. Markets for inputs and labour are different, however. In both, prices adjust *more* than the average price level. These assumptions are not general. In some commodity markets prices are going to rise faster than the average as a result of a faster demand response when the money supply increases. In others the price is going to lag in the inflation process as in case 2.2. Wages may rise faster or slower than the average rate of inflation, though it may be more common that wages are 'sticky' in the inflation process. At other times wage increases may trigger monetary expansion.

The above relative price effects in the inflation process determine the changes in the real value of commercial cash flows. We assume still that PPP and LOP holds internationally. Financial flows are affected by inflation in the LC country as in cases 1b and 2b with full indexation.

Among commercial flows, revenues remain unchanged in all countries. Costs of imported inputs (flow D) increase as a result of the relative price increase in the USA, and real wage costs (flow E) in the LC country rise in the inflation process. There is obviously a negative commercial cash flow effect of inflation in this case. The coefficient for commercial exposure to US inflation $(-.83)$ depends on the increase in the real costs of inputs (.8 in Table VI.3). Similarly, the coefficient for exposure to LC inflation depends on the increase in real wage costs $(-.24$ in Table VI.3), divided by total commercial cash flows (12). We divide the cash flow effects by eight to obtain the exposure coefficients per unit of inflation in each country.

The total cash flow coefficient for LC-inflation depends on the above wage increase as well as the financial cash flow gains. The latter outweigh the cost increases with the result that the total exposure coefficient for LC-inflation is positive. The financial gain is in fact large enough to offset all cost increases.

Case 2.4   Undershooting of Exchange Rate

In this and the next case we introduce relative price changes between countries, i.e, deviations from LOP and PPP, while inflation *per se* does not cause relative price changes *within* countries. Money supplies in the FC country and the USA remain fixed. In this case, it is assumed that the exchange rate does not depreciate sufficiently to offset the LC-inflation relative to zero inflation in other countries. Thus, there is a 5 percent *real* exchange rate appreciation of the LC currency relative to both the other currencies. As result of the real appreciation, sales fall in the foreign country. In our particular case, we assume that the FC and dollar prices in export markets remain constant so that the firm has to accept an LC-price decrease in export markets relative to the domestic markets. The supply elasticity is .5, i.e, production and sales for export markets are lowered when there is a real appreciation.

The effect on commercial flows is actually rather small in this case. Sales revenues fall in export markets but costs of imported inputs from the USA fall as well, and, since the volume of sales falls, there are additional savings on wage costs. The net loss of commercial flows due to the real exchange rate change is far less than the gain on financial flows due to inflation.

Commercial flow exposure is in this case entirely an exchange rate exposure since the relative prices *between* countries change while relative prices within countries are independent of inflation.

Case 2.5   Overshooting of the Exchange Rate

This case is similar to the previous one but we assume now that there is a real depreciation due to exchange rate overshooting. A number of theoretical macroeconomic models for exchange rate adjustment to monetary disturbances predict this kind of overshooting. LC-inflation is 10 percent but the exchange rate depreciates 15 percent. Money supplies and price levels remain fixed abroad. Elasticities are the same as in case 2.3, and we assume again that the firm is a price taker in the export market.

The commercial cash flow effects of the real exchange rate depreciation are in this case opposite to those in the previous case. Thus, the net commercial cash flow effect is positive and, accordingly, the exchange rate exposure of commercial cash flows enhances the exposure of financial flows to inflation. Since relative prices within countries are constant commercial flows are not exposed to inflation.

Case 2.6   Exchange Rate Overshooting; Output Price Leading Inflation; Wage Costs Lagging Inflation: Full Indexation

This case contains a combination of relative price effects from the previous cases. The domestic price level (P_t^{LC}) increases 5 percent, and foreign price levels are constant, while the exchange rate depreciates 15 percent. Thus, there is a real depreciation which is twice as large as in the previous case. Notice also that the average price level changes less than the money supply, which is realistic for periods as short as a quarter. Wages are now rising less than inflation which also is realistic.

The export revenue flows increase in real terms due to the real depreciation. Foreign currency prices remain constant and LC export prices rise. Domestic sales revenues (C) increase also as a result of the 2 percent increase in the relative output price in the inflation process (all elasticities of supply are .5 as before). Prices in LC on exports rise approximately 8 percent more than prices on domestic sales.

The cost of imported inputs (D) increases as a result of the real depreciation, and due to increased export sales. Wage costs (E) fall, since wages are lagging in the inflation process.

Among changes in commercial cash flows we regard changes in domestic sales and wage costs as caused by inflation in the LC-country which causes domestic relative price changes. Changes in export sales and costs of imported inputs are regarded as caused by the (real) exchange rate changes.

We calculate first the exchange rate exposure coefficient for commercial cash flows. The changes in revenue flows A and B represent a positive impact of the exchange rate equal to 2.71. The cost *increase* due to increased sales abroad is

$$.4 \cdot 35 \cdot \left[1 + \left(\frac{1.15}{1.05 \cdot 1.02} - 1 \right) \cdot .5 \right] - .4 \cdot 35 = .52,$$

where .4 · 35 are the costs after tax of production for exports before the disturbance. The term within parentheses is the change in the relative price between countries, i.e, deviations from LOP.

An additional exchange rate effect is due to the increase in real costs of imported inputs (1.15/1.05). This increase is the LC costs after tax of imported inputs at the new sales volume minus the costs at the old sales volume:

$$.4 \cdot 40 \cdot \frac{1.15}{1.05} \cdot \left[1 + .5 \cdot (1.02 - 1) \cdot (.5) + .5 \left(\frac{1.15}{1.05 \cdot 1.02} - 1 \right) \cdot .5 \right]$$
$$- .4 \cdot 40 = 1.93.$$

The total exchange rate effect is then 2.71 − .52 − 1.93 = .26. The exchange rate exposure coefficient for commercial cash flows becomes $[(.26/12)/15] \cdot 100 = .14$.

We turn now to the effects of LC inflation on commercial cash flows. These effects include changes in domestic revenues as a result of the domestic real price increase, cost increases due to increased domestic sales, and changes in wage costs, The first effect is $+.2$ (C), while changes in real costs (D + E) depend on inflation to the extent the changes are not explained by the exchange rate. The exchange rate effect on cash flows through costs was shown to be $-.52 - 1.93 = -2.45$. The total cash flow effect of cost changes in Table VI.3 is -1.60. Thus, inflation has a positive cash flow effect through costs equal to 0.85. The reason is that real wage costs have fallen. In total the 5 percent inflation causes an increase in commercial cash flows equal to $.85 + .2 = 1.05$ and the commercial cash flow exposure coefficient for LC inflation becomes $[(1.05/12)/5] \cdot 100 = 1.75$.

Given our assumptions about financial flows, the total impact of inflation is a cash flow increase equal to $1.05 + .75 = 1.80$. The total cash flow exposure coefficient for inflation is therefore $[(1.80/11)/5] \cdot 100 = 3.27$.

Comparing the different cases we observe that the inflation gain in debt capacity dominates the commercial flow effects in many cases. If the tax shield on depreciation had been included the inflation gain on nominally contractual flows would have been reduced. When nominal interest costs are rigid, the positive effect of inflation is particularly strong but even with perfect indexation there is a positive effect, since the increase in debt capacity is not taxed. Commercial exposure, on the other hand, depends in sign and magnitude on the nature of relative price adjustment in the inflation process. The strongest negative commercial effect occurs in case 2.2, in which the output price is rigid in the inflation process in each country. Volume of sales falls since profitability decreases substantially. The strongest positive commercial effect occurs in case 2.6, in which the exchange rate overshoots, thereby lowering imported input costs and increasing export sales and price.

We could have made additional assumptions about financial positions in foreign currencies due to borrowing or the use of foreign currency as invoice currency. The expressions developed in Chapter V can easily be applied on such cases but we leave those exercises to the reader.

VI.3   A SCENARIO ANALYSIS OF AN UNANTICIPATED FISCAL EXPANSION IN THE LC COUNTRY

In this section we assume that the fiscal authority in the LC country conducts an expansionary policy increasing nominal aggregate demand in the country by 5 percent. The figures assumed in different cases are described in Table VI.4. In case 3.1 we assume that there is a real demand increase for our firm of the same magnitude while all prices are rigid. This case may be called Keynesian. In Case 3.2 the aggregate demand increase translates into 5 percent inflation as a monetarist model may predict. In the third case there is a mixture of volume and price effects. These differences may reflect the level of employment and capacity utilization in the economy. At full employment an aggregate demand increase would cause inflation.

The cases differ also in their exchange rate effects. In macroeconomic theory it is often found that with high capital mobility a fiscal expansion causes an appreciation of the exchange rate leaving fiscal policy nearly ineffective. Case 3.1 is consistent with this pattern. In case 3.2 the exchange rate remains constant but since there is inflation the *real* exchange rate appreciates in this case as well. In case 3.3 the fiscal expansion causes a depreciation. This pattern is consistent with low capital mobility and may be most relevant for a developing country.

Relative prices may change in the adjustment to fiscal policy as they do with monetary policy. The relative output price may fall or rise depending on the relative demand and supply changes among sectors. In the first 'Keynesian' case the *volume* of demand and sales increase at constant relative prices. In the second case the relative price of the firm's product falls in an inflation process, while in the third case it rises. As we argued in Section VI.2, the speed of the demand response in the firm's product market after an aggregate disturbance determines whether the relative output price will rise or fall. The firm's sales response to relative price changes is described by the same elasticities as in the previous section and the firm is still a price-taker. Changes in the relative price between countries (deviations from LOP) induce a supply response in the foreign market as in the previous section. The figures in Table VI.4 have been inserted in the formulas in Table VI.1. The cash flow effects appear in Table VI.5.

Table VI.4   Assumptions about levels of price variables after a 5 percent increase in aggregate demand due to fiscal policy

All elasticities in all cases = .5. Base case all prices equal to 1.

Case 3.1. Increase in volume of demand and sales at constant relative prices; real interest rate increase; exchange rate appreciation

Aggregate demand effect = 1.05 on sales.
all relative prices = 1
all price levels = 1
e_t = .95 -> LC value of export price falls.
i_t = 12 percent

Case 3.2.a. Inflation; interest rate increase; domestic relative output price falls; nominal exchange rate constant

$P_t^{LC} = 1.05$, $P_t^{FC} = P_t^{US} = 1$

$\dfrac{OP_t^{LC}}{P_t^{LC}} = \dfrac{1.03}{1.05}$, other relative prices = 1

$e_t^{LC-FC} = e_t^{LC-USD} = 1 ->$ LC value of export prices constant

i_t = 12 percent

Case 3.2.b. As 3.2.a but loans fully indexed

i_t = 17 percent

Case 3.3. Both volume of sales and inflation increase; exchange rate depreciation; real interest rate increases; LOP; relative output price increases

Aggregate demand effect: 1.03 on sales

$P_t^{LC} = 1.02$, $P_t^{FC} = P_t^{US} = 1$

$\dfrac{OP_t^{LC}}{P_t^{LC}} = 1.02$

$e_t^{LC-FC} = e_t^{LC-USD} = 1.02$

$OP_t^{LC} = 1.02 \cdot 1.02$ (nominal LC output price)

LOP => $OP_t^{FC} = OP_t^{US} = 1.02$ (assuming LOP; the foreign currency price is the domestic price divided by the exchange rate)

i_t = 12 percent

Case 3.1   Increase in Volume of Demand and Sales at Constant Relative Prices; Real Interest Rate Increase; Exchange Rate Appreciation

In this case fiscal policy has the effect of increasing demand for all products without any domestic price effects. The real interest rate increases from 10 to 12 percent, however, and the exchange rate appreciates 5 percent. As shown in Table VI.5 domestic sales revenues increase while revenues from export sales fall due to the lower profitability of selling abroad. Costs of imported inputs increase (negative cash flow) due to the appreciation while wage costs increase as a result of the higher total sales volume. The net effect on commercial flows is negative since export sales revenues fall both in volume and price. Interest costs increase on the financial side. The total cash flow effect is accordingly negative.

For exposure purposes we may view the increase in domestic demand by 5 percent as associated with the rise in the interest rate, since this price variable is the one most closely linked to fiscal policy. Accordingly, we calculate a coefficient for the percentage change in commercial cash flows from a one percent change in the interest rate. The cash flow effects captured by this coefficient is the 5 percent increase in sales revenue (flow C) after tax $(.4 \cdot .05 \cdot 50) = 1$, plus the associated increase in the cost of production for domestic sales $(.4 \cdot .5 \cdot 70).05 = .7$. The net effect is .3. Since the interest rate has increased 20 percent the commercial flow coefficient for the interest rate becomes $[(.3/12)/20] \cdot 100 = .125$.

The total flow coefficient for this interest rate increase should take into account increased interest costs as well. Since these increase .2, the total cash flow gain due to the interest rate increase is .1. The total interest rate exposure coefficient is then $[(.1/11)/20] \cdot 100 = .05$. Thus, a fiscal policy raising the interest rate ten percent (from say 10 to 11) causes a one-half percent increase in total cash flows.

We turn next to calculation of exposure coefficients for the exchange rate, which falls 5 percent. Export revenues fall 1.47. Costs of imported inputs fall with the appreciation and wage costs related to exports fall as a result of the decline in export volume. Since the total cash flow change due to costs is $-.46$ (a cost increase) and the cost increase related to domestic sales is .7 from above, there is a cost decrease as a result of the exchange rate change equal to .24. The total exchange rate effect is therefore the fall in export revenues (-1.47) plus the cost

Table VI.5 **Exposure coefficients and real cash flow effects of unanticipated expansionary fiscal policy**

Case		3.1	3.2a	3.2b	3.3	Base case levels
Cash flow	A	−.59	−.49	as in 3.2a	.24	8
	B	−.88	−.74	as in 3.2a	.36	12
	C	1.0	−.57	as in 3.2a	1.22	20
	D	−.61	.94	as in 3.2a	−.4	−16
	E	.15	.14	as in 3.2a	−.3	−12
Net commercial: A + B + C + D + E		−.93	−.72	as in 3.2a	1.12	12
	F	0	1.25	as in 3.2a	.50	0
	G	−.20	−.20	−.7	−.20	−1
Net financial F + G		−.2	1.05	.45	.30	−1
Total A–G		−1.13	.33	−.27	1.42	11
Exposure coefficients for percent change in commercial flows						
$\hat{p}^{LC}$		0	−1.20	as in 3.2a	3.92	
$\hat{e}$		2.05	0	as in 3.2a	0	.
$\hat{i}^{LC}$		−.13	0	as in 3.2a	.075	
Exposure coefficients for percent change in financial flows						
$\hat{p}^{LC}$		0	25	15.0	25	
$\hat{e}$		0	0	0	0	
$\hat{i}^{LC}$		−1	−1	−.29	−1	
Exposure coefficients for percent change in total flows						
$\hat{p}^{LC}$		0	.96	.05	6.55	
$\hat{e}$		2.24	0	0	0	
$\hat{i}^{LC}$		.05	−.09	−.03	−.01	

decrease (.24) for a cash flow effect of −1.23. The exchange rate exposure coefficient for commercial flows is $[(-1.23/12)/(-5)] \cdot 100 = 2.05$. On total cash flows the exchange rate exposure coefficient is $[(-1.23/11)/(-5)] \cdot 100 = 2.24$.

Case 3.2.a Inflation, Interest Rate Increase; Domestic Relative Output Price Falls; Nominal Exchange Rate Constant

In this case the economy may be near full employment and accordingly the increase in aggregate demand causes inflation. The firm—a price-taker at home and abroad—experiences no change in the foreign currency prices in export markets while, at the constant exchange rate, the domestic output price rises only 3 percent while other prices rise 5 percent. LOP does not hold in the short run, nor does PPP.

In Table VI.5 we see that revenues in export markets fall. The reason is that for our price-taking firm, the LC value of export prices falls relative to the LC value of domestic sales. Export supply is cut back. Revenues fall in the domestic market as well as a result of the fall in the domestic relative output price.

Imported input costs fall for two reasons. First, there is a decrease in sales volume, and, second, real input costs fall since there is a real appreciation at the constant nominal exchange rate. Real wage costs (E) fall, as well, because of the decrease in sales volume.

Since, in this case, there is no volume effect independent of price changes, and the nominal exchange rate remains constant, we may say that all changes in commercial cash flows occur as a result of domestic inflation. Accordingly we derive a coefficient for the change in commercial cash flows due to domestic inflation equal to $[(-.72/12)/5] \cdot 100 = -1.2$.

For total cash flows the coefficient for inflation should include the decrease in the real value of debt (F). The total effect of inflation is $1.25 - .72 = +.53$, and the inflation exposure coefficient becomes $+.96$. Thus, the positive inflation effect on financial flows outweighs the negative effects on commercial operations.

Real interest costs increase as before (flow G). Therefore the interest rate exposure coefficients for financial and total cash flows are $[(-.2/1)/20] \cdot 100 = -1$ and $[(-.2/11)/20] \cdot 100 = -.09$, respectively. Notice that there is a 20 percent increase in the interest rate.

In cases 3.1 and 3.2 we observe that for this exporting firm commercial cash flows deteriorate. In both cases there is a real appreciation reducing export sales but also reducing imported input costs.

Case 3.2.b: As 3.2.a but Loans Fully Indexed

The commercial flow effects are obviously the same as in case 3.2.a as is the financial gain due to the increase in debt capacity (F). Interest costs increase, however, since the interest rate rises from 10 to 17 percent (a 70 percent increase).

The inflation exposure coefficient is now calculated from the change in net commercial flows ($-.72$), plus the increase in debt capacity ($+1.25$), minus the increase in interest costs due to the indexation ($-.5$). The total effect of inflation is nearly zero or $+.03$, which gives us a total cash flow coefficient for inflation equal to $+.05$. Notice that interest rate coefficients are smaller than in case 3.2.a, since the nominal interest rate increase used to calculate the coefficients is larger.

Case 3.3   Both Volume of Sales and Inflation Increase; Exchange Rate Depreciation; Real Interest Rate Increase, LOP

On the aggregate level this case is a mixture of the previous ones. Fiscal policy has a limited effect domestically on real aggregate demand (3 percent) as well as on inflation (2 percent). We assume that the demand for the firm's product initially increases more than aggregate demand so that the relative output price increases by 2 percent. Due to low capital mobility the fiscal policy causes a depreciation of 2 percent in this case. LOP holds so that the output price in FC and USD becomes $OP_t^{LC}/e^{LC-FC} = 1.02 \cdot 1.02/1.02 = 1.02$. The sales increase in export markets depends on the supply elasticity $= .5$. Thus, the export sales volume increases by one percent. Real export revenues in LC increase .24 in the FC country and .36 in the US. In the domestic market there is a 3 percent volume increase at constant prices plus a one percent volume increase in response to the relative output price increase. In sum, domestic revenues increase 1.22.

Imported input costs per unit and wage costs per unit remain unchanged since in local currency both prices increase with inflation. Thus, production costs increase only as a result of the increase in sales. The volume increase is 2.5 percent ($.5 \cdot .03 + .01$). The first part of this increase is due to the domestic volume effect from fiscal policy at a constant relative price. The second part is the supply response to the relative output price increase. Costs of imported inputs (D) increase .4 while wage costs increase .3. Commercial cash flows increase 1.12.

In order to calculate exposure coefficients we regard the domestic volume increase occurring at a constant relative price—the 3 percent rise in aggregate demand—as interest rate related. Thus, for purposes of estimating the interest rate exposure of commercial cash flows there is a gain of three percent of after tax revenue minus costs for domestic sales (.4·.50·35). This gain amounts to .18 corresponding to a 20 percent rise in the interest rate. Accordingly the interest rate exposure coefficient is .075. The interest rate effect on total cash flows includes the increase in interest costs (−.20) in Table VI.5. Then we obtain an interest rate exposure on total cash flows equal to −.01.

The remaining cash flow effects in this case are due to domestic inflation, as a result of which the relative output price and supply increase. Since PPP and LOP holds there is no exchange rate exposure. We obtain a coefficient for the change in commercial cash flows due to domestic inflation equal to $[(0.94/12)/2] \cdot 100 = 3.92$. With financial indexation there is an additional gain of .50 in debt capacity. Accordingly, the total cash flow coefficient for inflation becomes 6.55.

Comparing the different scenarios for fiscal policy effects on cash flows, we notice that under capital mobility in cases 3.1 and 3.2 the exporting firm faces substantial cash flow losses. The reason is that the real exchange rate appreciates. A simultaneous domestic demand increase as in case 3.1 may offset the loss with a gain in the domestic market. To the extent fiscal policy triggers inflation rather than a real aggregate demand increase at constant prices, the cash flow effect depends largely on whether output prices lead or lag in the inflation process. In addition inflation always has the positive effect of increasing the firm's debt capacity. In the absence of capital mobility the expansionary fiscal policy may cause a devaluation, in which case export revenues rise as well.

VI.4   USING A SCENARIO APPROACH TO ESTIMATE AND HEDGE EXPOSURE

We have mentioned in previous chapters that the regression approach to estimating exposure does not always enable the firm to identify stable exposure coefficients and a large amount of consistent historical data on cash flow is required to obtain estimates. On the other hand there is no need for any deep understanding of macroeconomic relationships for implementing the regression approach.

The scenario approach developed in this chapter has the opposite characteristics. It does not take a lot of historical data to implement, and it can be used to estimate exposure even when exposure coefficients are unstable over time as a result of changes in the macroeconomic structure. It can also be used for sensitivity analysis in order to identify variables to which the firm's cash flows are sensitive. The disadvantage of the scenario approach is that detailed knowledge and understanding of macroeconomic relationships among exchange rates, interest rates, price levels, and relative prices are necessary requirements for useful implementations.

The exposure coefficients derived in this chapter may be used for hedging cash flow exposure along the lines we discussed in Chapter IV. Exchange rate; interest rate; and inflation exposure coefficients are useful guides for hedging, if these coefficients are independent of whether the underlying disturbance is monetary or real. For example, a certain exchange rate exposure coefficient in Table VI.3 for monetary disturbances is useful for calculating the size of a hedging contract if *either* the coefficient calculated in Table VI.5 for the monetary disturbances is the same as the one calculated for the a fiscal disturbance, *or* there is substantial uncertainty about only one kind of disturbance. When these conditions are not satisfied, exposures should be defined in terms of monetary, fiscal or other real disturbances. In Chapter IV we showed that the size of, for example, a hedging contract for monetary exposure would depend on the exchange rate's sensitivity to the same disturbance.

Take as a simple example of this approach to hedging, Case 2.5 in Table VI.3 above. There, a 10 percent money supply change causes an increase of .20 in total cash flows. Thus, the money supply exposure coefficient becomes $[(.20/11)/10] \cdot 100 = .18$, i.e., a one percent change in the money supply causes a .18 percent increase in cash flows. At the same time it is known that the same money supply increase causes a 15 percent change in the exchange rate. Thus, a one percent change in the money supply causes a 1.5 percent increase (depreciation) of the exchange rate. With this knowledge the forward market could be used to hedge against cash flow effects of unanticipated money supply changes. Based on the analysis in Chapter IV a contract should be taken such that, if the money supply increases by one percent, and expected cash flows are $100, there should be a loss on the forward contract of $.18. With such a contract a one percent fall in the money supply would cause a gain of $.18 on the forward contract offsetting a loss of $.18 and the firm would be hedged against money supply exposure.

Using the scenario approach in order to analyse the sensitivity of the firm's cash flow to different kinds of disturbances, it may be desirable to extend the analysis beyond the near future. Cash flow effects over several quarters should then be included in the analysis. Macroeconomic adjustment over this longer period could accordingly be important.

In the analysis we made specific assumptions in each case about the relative price effects in one period after a disturbance. However, one would expect that after monetary disturbances, relative prices and real exchange rates would return to their original level after some time. Therefore, in order to implement a longer term scenario approach, one must specify time paths of relative prices and exchange rates after different disturbances. It is especially important to form judgement about how long a time it will take for relative prices to return to equilibrium and for PPP and LOP to be restored.

Once a time path of relative prices, exchange rates, and interest rates to monetary, fiscal, and other possible disturbances have been specified the scenario approach can be implemented over several periods. Expected cash flows for a number of periods should be expressed in terms of price variables as in Table VI.1. Then, assuming disturbances of different kinds of magnitudes, the levels for all price variables are estimated for each period under each scenario. Thereafter, the figures for prices under each scenario are inserted in the expression for cash flows for each period. The result is a range of cash flow outcomes for several periods over a range of disturbances. Applying the scenario approach will help the firm identify the critical assumptions for its 'worst case' outcome.

VII

EVALUATION AND FEEDBACK

VII.1 INTRODUCTION

We mentioned in Chapter II that managers can be considered stakeholders in a firm and therefore their attitude towards risk influences the firm's choice of exposure to different macroeconomic risks. Managers' risk-attitude depends strongly on the internal evaluation of individuals' performances with respect to risk-taking and return on financial and operating decisions. Therefore, it is important that the system of evaluation induces managers to act consistently with the objective of the firm with respect to other stakeholders, and in particular to shareholders. In Chapter II we argued that the interest of the latter group as reflected in stockmarket value may be a reasonable weighted average of other external stakeholders' concerns.

A conflict between the objective of managers and the objective of external stakeholders is often referred to as a principle-agent problem. It is no doubt an important concern. For example, it is often argued that the time-horizon of American firms is 'irrationally' short or that they are excessively risk-averse. As a result, their investments are 'too low' to remain competitive with, for example, Japanese firms (see e.g., Ellsworth, 1985). It is not always clear whether this argument refers to an irrationality relative to the social interest or relative to shareholders and other external stakeholders. The argument is sometimes supported by the more or less well-founded opinion that firms in the USA seem preoccupied with near-term accounting income and its stability as opposed to economic value. In that case firms would not act in the interest of most of its stakeholders. In other words, there would be a principal-agent problem in the form of an excessively short time horizon or excessively high risk-aversion on the part of managers.

Exposure management can not be made consistent with the firms overall objective, unless systems for budgeting, evaluation, and feedback are developed independent of or complementary to the regular accounting system. The reason is that accounting rules may be misleading relative to economic objectives as we noted in Chapter III. The consistency between *incentives of managers* at different levels and the *firm's objective* has two aspects. First, manager's *risk-return trade-off* must be made consistent with *stakeholders* risk-return trade-off, and, second, managers must be held *responsible* only for decisions for which they have actual *authority*. We discuss these issues in Section VII.2.

Once the incentive/objective problem is resolved the firm's concern would turn to actual data to be used for evaluation and feedback. We discuss in Section VII.3 the distinction between *realized* and *unrealized* gains/losses, which causes a problem in comparing loans of different currency-denominations, since, for example the timing of interest payments may differ from that of exchange rate gains and losses. A second data problem for evaluation arises from the distinction between *anticipated* and *unanticipated* changes in different variables, which is also discussed in Section 7.3. A third data problem for evaluation is due to the fact that most accounting and reporting is in *nominal* terms while shareholders' concern is with the *purchasing power* of their dividend income and wealth. This issue is discussed in Section VII.4. We will not go into the specifics of how firms should design their internal reporting and accounting to obtain relevant information. Oxelheim (1985) contains a more detailed discussion of corporate reporting systems.

In addition to evaluation of managers at different levels relative to given objectives, it is necessary to evaluate whether the overall strategy for exposure management achieves its desired objectives relative to alternative strategies. For example, one could ask whether a minimize variance strategy actually reduces variance below the level which would have been obtained with a laissez faire strategy. We discuss this issue in Section VII.5. Finally in Section VII.6 we discuss briefly arguments for centralization versus decentralization of exposure management.

VII.2 MANAGER'S INCENTIVES AND THE FIRM'S OBJECTIVE

The evaluation of a manager at any level influences the person's behaviour and motivation. Before discussing principles for evaluation we illustrate in Table VII.1 the levels of management involved in exposure management and the type of decision that would be made at each level. A complete evaluation programme must include all levels.

Top management—the board of directors or the managing director—determines the overall strategy. In Chapter V we distinguished between laissez faire, minimum risk, maximum expected return, and risk/return trade-off strategies. In Section VII.5 we return to the evaluation of strategies which may involve a self-evaluation by top management as well as shareholders' evaluation.

Table VII.1 Decisions and evaluations at different levels

	In charge	Example of choice	Evaluation
Policy level	Board Managing Dir.	Laissez faire Minimum variance Maximum return Risk/return trade-off	Self evaluation or shareholders' evaluation
Tactical level	Head of Finance Head of Sales	Balance sheet vs forward market hedges. Options. Shifting sales among countries. Indexing of contracts	Level and variance of cost of financing, of cash flows from sales, etc.
Operational level	Treasurer	Timing of forward contracts and options. Minimum costs of contracts	Minimum cost of obtaining desired contracts

Top management would also evaluate the performance of decisions made at the *tactical level*. This level is represented, for example, by the head of finance and head of sales. These persons would decide, for instance, *how* the variance of cash flows of different types can be minimized by means of balance sheet hedges, forward contracts, leads and lags, and options for financial exchange rate exposures and by means of shifting sales from one country to another (through, for example, pricing), or by adapting contracts for commercial exchange rate exposures. Since the commercial non-contractual exposure typically becomes a financial contractual exposure at delivery as shown in Figure III.2, it is an important task for the top level to determine how tactical decisions should be distributed between, for example, the sales and finance functions. Firms differ naturally in terms of the length of contract period and the degree to which they have a choice of invoice currency and payment conditions. In some firms with flexibility in pricing and payment terms exposures are non-contractual to a large extent. Then tactical decisions for the head of sales refer to pricing and sales in different currencies and countries, the choice of invoice currency, and payment terms, while the finance function is limited to entering financial contracts of different types in order to reduce the residual exposure. In this case the tactical decision for the head of finance is to determine whether the risk-return objective imposed from above is best met by internal or external hedging transactions, and whether options or forward markets should be employed, etc. Interest costs, expected exchange rate changes and other costs associated with different contracts should be considered.

The third, *operating level* chooses, for example, the exact timing of contracts, bank connections, and the type of security to issue or invest excess cash in with the purpose of minimizing outright costs of implementing tactical decisions.

The operating level is in principle easy to evaluate since its objective can be stated in terms of costs or return. No risk-return trade-off is determined at this level. The tactical level on the other hand may face an objective which includes variance reduction as well as cost and profit aspects. Then evaluation should include the same factors. We turn now to a more detailed discussion of the evaluation of the tactical level.

Any evaluation must have a *reference point*. Though the budget may have many purposes we consider for the sake of discussion the situation when the firm creates a budget as some kind of forecast and thereafter managers are evaluated relative to this budget. The evaluation of subsidiaries' performance can take many different forms. Cash flows or accounting profits may be used. The evaluation may be based on outcomes in foreign currency or in the parent's currency using different exchange rates. Translation gains and losses may or may not be considered.

Lessard and Lorange (1977) have discussed what exchange rate to use for budget and evaluation, respectively, in order to induce local managers at the subsidiary level, and heads of sales and finance in any firm to (1) behave in accordance with the firm's objective and (2) to restrict themselves to decisions for which they have the expertise. Lessard and Lorange limit their discussion to the case when the firm wants to maximize profits, and distinguish between the following exchange rates in budgeting and evaluation of subsidiary performance and the performance of subunits (e.g., export sales) within a firm.

1. The actual rate at the time of the budget.
2. A forecast exchange rate such as the forward rate.
3. The end of period exchange rate, which for the budget is a continuously updated actual rate.

If different rates are used for budget and evaluation, respectively, such as the rate at the time of the budget for the budgeting and the end of period exchange rate for evaluation, then managers are induced to form their own forecast of exchange rate changes. If the expertise lies elsewhere, then this situation may lead to inferior decisions about sales in different countries. Furthermore, the managers are induced to try to make exchange rate gains by means of changes in currency of invoice and other means by which positions in different currencies could be influenced. A further drawback of using the rate at the time of the budget for budgeting is that production and planned sales levels in different countries would not take anticipated exchange rate changes into account. Using an *internal rate* based on a forecast resolves this problem. This problem is also resolved by the continuous updating of the budget rate, *if* production levels and sales can be adjusted continuously on short notice. The need to plan production and sales from a forecast is then reduced.

Assume now that exposure objectives are determined at the top level and that these objectives include risk in addition to return considerations for planned sales decisions as well as financial decisions, i.e, for non-contractual and contractual cash flows. Then, if the firm uses end of period rates for evaluation and budget (i.e., the continuously updated rate), local managers are induced to *maximize profits* at actual exchange rates. The overall objective that includes exposure of cash flows from sales as well as financial flows calls for giving up some profit for reduced risk, however. For cash flows from sales, such an objective can only be fulfilled if, say, local managers are induced to behave in a risk averse manner. Using end of period rates for evaluation, local managers would have to be constrained in terms of quantity sold in different currency areas. But then, they are no longer evaluated on decisions over which they have authority.

Given the exposure objective it is clearly desirable to create a budget as well as carry out evaluation at an *internal exchange rate*. Not only would centralized expertise be used to forecast exchange rates, but it would also be possible to use the internal rate to induce local managers to avoid sales in 'risky' currencies and countries. Such risk-reduction can be achieved by adjusting an exchange rate forecast with a risk-premium. The profitability in 'risky' currencies can be made to appear lower so that managers are induced to avoid sales in those currencies and countries.

The same reasoning as for the exchange rate can be applied on other macroeconomic price variables such as interest rates and price levels. Internal forecasting provides future prices at which expected cash flows, as described in the regression equations in Chapters IV and V, are evaluated. Exposure objectives with respect to different variables can then be induced for decentralized decisions by adjusting each market price forecast with a risk-premium based on the firm's exposure to unanticipated changes in exchange rates, interest rates, and price levels. Evaluation of managers must then be carried out at *the same* adjusted internal market prices. Otherwise their incentives do not coincide with the firm's objective as expressed in these internal prices.

Many firms have centralized the finance function and financial exposure management, while leaving production and sales decisions decentralized at the local level. Furthermore, it is common that exposure and risk avoidance concerns only financial decision. In this case, the internal prices, interest-rates, and exchange-rates for budget and evaluation of local *sales* decisions can be the forecast ones, while the central finance function determines financial exposure. As we noted in previous chapters, neglecting so called non-contractual exposure on cash flows from sales could be inconsistent with the risk-averse firms objective, however. It is of course possible to estimate this non-contractual exposure and allow the central finance function to hedge such exposure, while local managers maximize cash flows from sales. In Chapter V such a procedure was shown to be consistent with a world in which Fisher Open (FO) holds.

The use of risk adjusted internal prices and rates that deviate from forecast ones in budget and evaluation could allow the central finance function to focus on financial exposure while sales and purchase divisions adjust activities to take risk into account. As noted in Chapter V both commercial operations and financial positions should be adjusted for risk when the firm is risk-averse and FO is not believed to hold. Similarly, if employment fluctuations are considered costly, then it is desirable that sales managers are induced to reduce fluctuations in sales.

In this connection we should note that forward exchange rates in particular and also interest rates, may include market risk-premia. Specifically, the forward premium/discount and the interest rate differential between currencies may include the market's evaluation of the risk of holding one currency relative to another. In this case, there would typically be deviations from the FO relationship (see Appendix III.3) and the forward rate would be a biased forecast of the future exchange rate. Therefore, if we believe that participants in international financial markets are risk-averse, *and* our risk-evaluation of different currencies is similar to the market's, then the forward rate could be used as an internal future rate, i.e., a risk-adjusted forecast of the future exchange rate. The same reasoning applies to future interest rates.

The risk-premium contained in the forward premium/discount on a currency, compensates for risk on financial positions over a particular time-horizon. For the firm concerned about output variability rather than pure cash-flow or profit variability, risk-evaluation might be highly firm-specific, however, and not related to the risk-premium contained in interest rates and the forward premium/discount.

Even in the case when top management is risk-averse with respect to financial decisions as well, and does not believe in FO, tactical decisions by the head of finance may have to be based on firm-specific internal rates, unless existing forward rates include an acceptable risk-premium on different currencies. Top management would have to determine such firm specific internal forward rates based on forecast and its risk-evaluation of currencies. If this method for taking risk into account is not feasible, tactical decisions by the finance function may have to be constrained. Then quantitative rules for selective hedging have to be determined. These rules may be limits on positions in strong and weak-currencies based on forecasting and evaluation of currency risk. It is inevitable that more specific decisions will have to be taken at a higher level, if risk-premia cannot be incorporated in internal prices.

VII.3 REALIZED VERSUS UNREALIZED AND ANTICIPATED VERSUS UNANTICIPATED GAINS/LOSSES

In the late 1960s and early 1970s long-term interest rates in Great Britain hovered around or over 15 percent while in Switzerland they were as low as 5 or 6 percent. Many British firms chose to borrow long-term in Swiss francs. Then over a five-year period the pound depreciated by 100 percent. Thus, even on a before tax basis, the Swiss franc loans became extremely expensive relative to pound loans. In addition, British tax authorities did not allow deductions for exchange rate losses, while outright interest costs were tax-deductible. On these grounds, the Swiss franc loans became the downfall of a number of firms, and of an even larger number of managers who were responsible for the Swiss franc loans.

Were persons responsible for taking loans denominated in Swiss francs appropriately fired? The answer would depend on what these individuals could have been expected to foresee. The non-deductability of exchange losses is a heavy burden, even if interest rate differentials exactly offset anticipated exchange rate differentials. This fact does not speak in favour of those taking Swiss-franc loans. Neglecting taxes, however, it could be argued that the pound depreciation in excess of the interest rate differential was completely unanticipated. Then the ex ante likelihood that the Swiss franc loan would be better than the pound loan was as large as the likelihood that it would be worse. Under these circumstances it is necessary that managers are evaluated in hindsight only on what could reasonably have been anticipated. Strong risk-averse or even risk-paranoid behaviour may otherwise be induced to the detriment of the firm.

What if those seeking Swiss franc loans considered only interest costs, neglecting even expected exchange rate changes? That would have been a serious error, but, given many firms' reporting systems, reasonable behaviour from an individual's point of view. Interest costs show up as an outright expense each period but exchange losses are not realized until the loan is repaid. Therefore, the manager choosing the Swiss franc loan would be burdened with lower outright costs of financing for a long period and may have left the company with good recommendations before the moment of truth. Most accounting methods referred to in Chapter III would have shown translation losses of the pound depreciation but these may not be clearly associated with the loan in the evaluation of costs of financing. One reason is that they are not realized and another reason is that they do not appear in all firms as costs of financing together with interest costs.

It is clearly important to recognize the connection between interest rate and exchange rate changes in long-term decisions just as it is important to recognize the connection between nominal interest rates and inflation. Oxelheim (1985) shows that it may take a long time for interest rate differentials to be offset by exchange rate changes and that in some cases it never happens. However, on the average for many loan decisions and many currencies we expect that the only difference in loan costs among currencies would correspond to deviations from FO on an expected basis (Appendix III.3). Such deviations would correspond to risk premia which typically are small.

There is still disagreement about the appropriate timing of accounting for unrealized exchange rate gains and losses, and there is not one 'correct' solution to the problem. Under fixed or pegged but adjustable exchange rates, one can reasonably expect exchange rate changes to cause realized gain or losses in the future. Thus, such exchange rate changes should be taken into consideration when evaluating the cost of a loan by distributing the exchange gain or loss over the period of the loan. Under flexible exchange rates, however, there are wide fluctuations from month to month or week to week. Thus, many exchange rate changes are temporary and will never cause realized gains or losses. Such exchange rate changes should accordingly not be included when evaluating the relative cost of loans. It is naturally hard to determine whether an exchange rate change is permanent or temporary. The firm would need some guidance towards evaluation of a more long-term average exchange rate at a point in time and use such a rate to obtain exchange rate adjusted costs of loans in different currency denomination. We noted in Chapter III that a PPP rate may serve as a measure of a long-term exchange rate but given the long periods over which there are deviations from PPP a moving average of rates over some time or a forward rate at the beginning of the year may be superior translation rates.

Similar problems arise when evaluating in hindsight the choice of long-term versus short-term borrowing and fixed rate versus flexible rate loans in one currency. To what extent could interest rate changes, with the result that, for example, a long-term loan became relatively expensive, have been anticipated? Are interest rate changes permanent enough to properly induce the refinancing at lower rates or with a series of short-term loans? Are changes in bond-values due to changes in interest rates permanent or temporary?

The distinction between anticipated and unanticipated changes are important for evaluating specific cover and hedge transactions as well. We mentioned in Chapter III that the cost of cover is sometimes seen as the forward premium on the forward rate relative to today's rate. If a manager were evaluated on costs of covering transactions in this way, the manager would be induced to cover foreign currency receivables when the foreign currency is more expensive in the forward market than in today's spot market. However, when there is a choice between cover and no cover, the relevant comparison is between the forward rate and the anticipated future spot rate. This difference expresses the anticipated *opportunity cost* of covering.

Using the *ex post* spot rate relative to the forward rate for evaluation would induce the manager to create a personal forecast, for which expertise lies elsewhere (see also Dufey and Giddy, 1978). If *ex post* spot rates are used in evaluation of covers, then it is important to obtain a sufficient *number* of observations in order to determine whether the manager systematically makes costly cover and hedge decisions. Otherwise, the poor predictive power of the forward rate could imply occasional large *ex post* opportunity costs of covering. In order to avoid such losses a manager could be induced to be risk-averse even when this is not called for.

VII.4 NOMINAL VERSUS REAL MAGNITUDES

External as well as internal accounting systems do not generally correct for inflation. In some hyperinflationary countries, such as Brazil, balance sheets and income statements are corrected for inflation and in other countries it may be necessary to take note of inflation effects on the net worth in annual statements.

Maximizing nominal cash flows in a currency is equivalent to maximizing real (the purchasing power of) cash flows. However, risk in nominal terms is not the same as risk in real terms when there is inflation uncertainty. We have noted that nominal interest rate fluctuations may simply correspond to expected inflation variance. Then large fluctuations in unanticipated nominal interest costs, which are often associated with floating rate loans and short-term financing, may be the consequence of a sensible policy of reducing unanticipated fluctuations in real financial cash flows. Similarly, exchange rate changes are often associated with differential inflationary developments among countries, and taking a position in a foreign currency can in fact reduce the firm's sensitivity to domestic inflation (see Chapter V). Estimating exposure in nominal terms can accordingly be seriously misleading, especially over longer time periods over which exchange rates are more likely to offset inflation differentials.

Neglecting inflation exposure would correspond to estimating exposure of nominal cash flows in the regression equations IV.1 and IV.3 in Chapter IV, and among independent variables price level changes would not appear. Exchange rate exposure measures and interest rate exposure measures could then be seriously exaggerated, since nominal cash flow changes related to inflation may simultaneously be related to exchange rate and/or interest rate changes. Exposure coefficients for the exchange rate and interest rates would be biased and, if hedging contracts described in Chapter IV are based on these coefficients, seemingly hedged positions would in fact leave the firm exposed to inflation risk.

VII.5 EVALUATION OF STRATEGIES

In Chapter V we argued that the choice of exposure management strategy among laissez faire, minimum variance, maximum expected return, and risk-return trade-off would be based on top management's view of the world with respect to the validity of market equilibrium relationship in goods and financial markets and its perception of what risk-attitude and time perspective best serve shareholders' interest. The evaluation of an implemented strategy could take the form of indirectly testing for purchasing power parity in goods markets, FO in international financial markets, and the impact of cash flow variance on the firm's stock-market price. However, top management could also test directly whether the implementation of a particular strategy has been successful by comparing in hindsight the result of a certain strategy with alternative strategies. In essence, such tests are indirect tests of whether top management's view of goods and financial market price relationships are valid. These tests would also enable managers to evaluate how much is gained by choosing a strategy that is perfectly consistent with the firm's objective, but one that may be costly to implement in terms of employee time. We suggested in Chapter V that a simplified strategy may cause small deviations from exposure management objectives but also reduce the costs of exposure management.

   To illustrate our reasoning, assume that a firm, which is risk-averse, has chosen to minimize the variance of all cash flows by instructing both head of sales and head of finance to reduce cash flow variance in their areas as much as possible. Management wishes to evaluate this strategy relative to a laissez faire strategy under which it does not engage in any transactions with the purpose of reducing cash flow variance.

One straightforward method of evaluating alternative strategies in this case would consist of a few relatively simple steps. First, it is necessary to estimate total cash flows each period under the actual method used and the total cash flows that would have been incurred if no hedging and covering transactions had been performed. Transactions cost to banks and other external agencies should be included. If both FO and PPP hold we would expect that cash flows following a risk-minimizing strategy and a laissez faire strategy, respectively, would *on average* differ only by an amount equal to transaction costs for hedging. If the difference systematically is larger or smaller, then FO and PPP assumptions may be questioned. Notice that it is necessary to include a sufficient number of periods in the comparison, since within each period there may be exchange gains or losses under a laissez faire strategy, which exceed the interest differential between positions in different currency denominations.

The second step in the comparison would be to estimate the variance of cash flows under the actual strategy pursued with the variance that would have existed had a laissez faire strategy been pursued. It is necessary to evaluate the variance of *real* cash flows, i.e., nominal cash flows should be adjusted for inflation in each period. In order to evaluate variance *ex post*, it is again necessary to use data for a number of periods (at least six) to obtain one variance observation.

The third step in the evaluation process would be to summarize return and variance for different strategies as in Table VII.2. The table allows management to compare returns and variances and to evaluate whether the differential is consistent with the views of Fisher Open and purchasing power parity and whether the differential is large enough to motivate expenses in terms of employee time for implementing the chosen strategy. In the table we have extended the comparison to include a maximize return as well as a selective hedging strategy. The example – comparison in Table VII.2 shows that including costs of time and costs of contracts, the laissez faire strategy results in a higher firm value than the minimize variance strategy, but the variance of cash flows is also higher. In the absence of costs of time and contracts the values become the same indicating that PPP and FO hold on average. In this situation when there is some variance reduction it is a question of whether the costs of achieving this reduction are justified.

Table VII.2 shows also that the outcome could be improved by following strategies of maximizing return or by selectively employing hedging. This result implies that for commercial flows there were profit opportunities in forecasting deviations from LOP and PPP. Possibly there were also profit opportunities in financial markets. We assume, however, that management believes strongly in FO and regards the profit opportunities as caused by real exchange changes and deviations from LOP. The selective hedging strategy gave a slightly worse outcome and a slight variance reduction compared to the maximize return strategy.

The implication of this comparison is that none of the four strategies in the table may be the best. Instead, as we noted in Chapter V, the firm could employ a strategy of maximizing the outcome for commercial flows while minimizing the variance of *total* commercial and financial cash flows by means of financial transactions alone. Such a strategy is consistent with the belief in FO. The commercial transactions would then be based on forecasting of real exchange rates and deviations from LOP, and financial positions would depend on the resulting commercial exposure.

Table VII.2   Comparison of strategies for exposure management

Strategy	Outcomes in period				Present value of outcomes	Present value minus transaction costs	Variance of outcomes
	1	2	3	... 12			
Laissez faire (never cover)	5	7	6	8	72	72	4
Minimize-variance*	6	6	6	6	72	71	0
Maximize return	7	8	6	8	78	78	5
Trade-off return/ variance (selective cover)*	6.5	7.5	6	8	77.5	77	3

* Under the assumption that variance of both commercial and financial cash flows are minimized or reduced.

Management must still ask, however, whether employee time and contract costs are low enough to justify the expense to reduce variance.

Another method for evaluating strategies would be to follow up on the regression approach to exposure developed in Chapter IV. A regression for total cash flows could be run in order to obtain measures for exposure to different variables given the firm's strategy. Thereafter, adjustable cash flows are removed from total cash flows, and a regression for non-adjustable flows is run in order to evaluate whether exposure of non-adjustable cash flows have been offset by the implemented strategy. Finally, it is necessary to evaluate the contribution of adjustable cash flows before any adjustment such as hedging or cover is made.

The implementation of the regression approach demands observations from a larger number of periods than the previous approach to evaluation. Furthermore, we emphasize again that it is essential to distinguish between anticipated and unanticipated changes in variables.

Anticipated exchange rates, inflation rates, and interest rates for each period are represented by the forecast the firm used in previous periods for commercial and financial decision-making. These forecasts should also be evaluated since the actual outcome of both cash flows and their variance would depend on the particular forecasts used. Thus, another step in this evaluation is to analyse whether the strategy's success or failure depend on the actual forecasts. Alternative forecasts of, for example, exchange rates can be obtained *ex post* from forward rates, interest rate differentials of different kinds such as Euro-currency rate differentials, treasury bill rate differentials, representative money market rate differentials, etc., and forecasts obtained from banks and advisory services. It has also been argued by, for example, Oxelheim (1985) that a forecast can be constructed as a weighted average of forecasts from different sources. Such averages have been shown to perform well. This evaluation of different forecasts should also take into account that the firm would have behaved differently under alternative forecasts.

Finally, we should emphasize that an important part of the evaluation would be to identify the reasons for a potential failure of a strategy to improve on results relative to alternative strategies. As we have mentioned, the failure may depend on bad forecasting or false assumptions about market relationships such as FO, PPP and LOP for particular products. The failure may naturally also depend on poor decisions on the tactical and operational levels, where a particular strategy is implemented. Before changing a strategy it is essential to check whether the assigned strategy has been implemented in an efficient way on different levels. It is, however, important to have realistic views of what can possibly be implemented, and this depends on the way markets work. For example, top management may have the view that the forward rate can be beaten by specific forecasting efforts in the firm. A strategy based on this view may fail either because the actual forecasters perform poorly or because markets work efficiently and the forward rate is the best predictor. In the latter case top management must design the evaluation in such a way that the reason for the strategies failure can be identified. In the first case personnel should be changed but in the second case the strategy should be changed.

VII.6 CENTRALIZATION VERSUS DECENTRALIZATION OF EXPOSURE MANAGEMENT AND EVALUATION

We mentioned in Chapter III that there has been an increased tendency towards centralization of exposure management and that this tendency may be explained by scale advantages when buying and selling currencies, the scarcity on local levels of expertise and advantages in global tax planning and exchange control avoidance at a centralized level. Furthermore, centralization may help the firm take advantage of differences in transaction costs among markets. The focus in many firms on translation exposure of the consolidated balance sheet may also explain the tendency towards centralization.

Part of an evaluation program for macroeconomic exposure management should naturally include an evaluation of its organization, and how objectives are best met with different degrees of centralization. Advantages of centralization from the point of view of the firm's objective may be offset, as noted in Chapter III, by decreased motivation when responsibilities are removed from local decision-makers.

In principle it is possible to achieve any kind of objective with centralized as well as decentralized management. On the face of it centralization would seem advantageous when the firm is risk-averse since cash flow or market value variance should be reduced for the firm as a whole and a local unit's contribution to the variance can only be evaluated at a central level. However, as we discussed in Section VII.1, internal pricing schemes for currencies can be used to induce local managers to choose currency positions so as to take into account the central evaluation of risk. Internal exchange rates should for this purpose include an adjustment for the centrally perceived risk. Similarly, risk-aversion on the local level can be induced in commercial operations by risk-adjusted internal good prices or by risk-adjusting the required rate of return on sales in different markets. The exact methods for designing such pricing schemes cannot be discussed here. Ideally they require a rather elaborate analysis, but even in the absence of such an analysis, practical pricing schemes may be developed in a firm by trial and error of risk-adjustment based on managers' intuition.

The evaluation of macroeconomic exposure of different kinds for different types of cash flows cannot be decentralized. The exposure of any cash flow would depend on other flows in the firm, assuming that the firm's objective includes the variance of its own cash flows rather than stockholders' portfolio variance. In the latter case, a particular flow's contribution to portfolio risk is independent of the contribution of other flows of the firm but depends instead on the composition of shareholders' portfolios.

The evaluation of different types of risk should also be done on the centralized level for the risk-averse firm, since we wish to identify the *independent* contribution of exchange rates, interest rates, price levels and relative prices to cash flow variance. Once this evaluation is complete the above principles for decentralization of decision-making by means of internal pricing are valid.

In the absence of internal pricing schemes it would seem as if centralization of exposure management would be advantageous. However, there are also advantages of decentralization. For example, it may be advantageous to decentralize decisions to a unit at which relevant information is quickly available. Guidelines for exposure management in this unit, such as limits to particular positions in currencies or short-term debt, should then be given based on the degree to which its cash flow exposures are regularly offset by cash flow exposures in other units. Another advantage of decentralization is that the quality of centralized decisions is reduced by the inability or unwillingness of subsidiaries to report on time relevant information. Furthermore, motivation and morale of subsidiary managers may be reduced when important profitability related tools are beyond their control. There are ways around the second problem. For example, subsidiaries may themselves decide on whether they wish to cover *internally* their exposures. Headquarters may then decide the extent to which it wants to hedge externally the *sum* of all subsidiaries' exposure, provided that headquarters obtain up-to-date information on subsidiaries' total cash flows in different currencies.

The desirability of centralization depends also on the dividend remittance policy of the corporation. In most large corporations subsidiaries are not simple 'cash cows'. There is substantial flexibility in the remittance policy for subsidiaries and the timing of remittances may be adjusted so that they occur at relatively favourable real exchange rates. The larger this flexibility is, and the higher the extent to which real exchange rates can be forecast, the stronger is the case for at least partial decentralization. One example of how partial decentralization can be carried out is to obtain from local managers information about total expected *real* local cash flows and their variance. Local managers can be asked to *maximize* the real value of cash flows in their respective host currencies. At the parent level, the implied total variance of cash flows from all subsidiaries can then be estimated. The timing of remittances could then be adjusted in such a way that the firm's objective with respect to total variance is fulfilled.

A more common simplification and decentralization by firms is to manage the exposure on financial flows (including contractual commercial cash flows) separately, i.e., without taking into account the elasticities of the commercial side of the firm. Sales and purchase departments may on their own deal with exchange rate related effects on price and volume of sales and purchases of goods. As we have argued, this kind of simplification may increase or reduce the total exposure of the firm, however. Assume, for example that a firm loses on its operations from a real appreciation of a foreign currency. To offset such exposure, the financial position in the foreign currency should be negative. Losses on commercial operations would then be offset by gains on the financial position. Independent action by the finance function may lead to partial covering of a foreign liability position which could increase the fluctuations of the subsidiary's earning.

In this connection we should emphasize the importance of clarifying within the firm the exposure management task of the financial versus sales and purchases divisions. We have emphasized that exchange rates have an impact on the firm in a variety of ways. If the financial function of the firm bears responsibility for managing total exposure, which, as we have seen, is rational if FO holds, then sales and purchase divisions must not perform its own exposure management. They should make purchase decisions, as well as decisions on credit terms and invoice currency with the objective of maximizing cash flows or value but it is also important that they provide the relevant information to the finance function for the latter to determine the net financial position in different currencies. Thus, it is possible for a firm to have the finance function responsible for covering and hedging and still take a more complete view of exposure. A good 'on-line' information system is required, however. The finance function would have to obtain information about the sensitivity of *non-contractual flows* to exchange rate changes and other variables in order to estimate the financial positions in each currency that would offset total non-contractual exposure. These positions would provide zero-exposure benchmarks.

We touched above on information requirements for the finance function in order for it to perform its task under a minimum variance strategy. In general, an important aspect of the organization is the choice of hardware and information system. The choice of information system depends naturally on which parts of the organization need to communicate, and in which ways and with what data they need to communicate. As noted, the need for a local sales department to transfer sales forecast information about currency of invoice and credit terms to other units such as the central finance function depends on the exposure management strategy, and its degree of centralization. The degree of centralization as well as the strategy would in turn depend on the ability to transfer relevant data to a central finance function. Computer based information systems enable the firm to communicate internally, quickly, and improve centralized decisions. Many types of information are often integrated with exposure information. For example, information with respect to tax planning, long-term financial planning and accounting systems are all part of the central finance function's information requirements.

It is obvious that a large amount of non-quantifiable but nevertheless relevant information may never reach the level at which decisions are made in a centralized system. Even if information can be transmitted to a centralized level the ability of managers to act on the information and to comprehend it is limited. This limitation necessarily induces the decision-maker to simplify the final information output. It could be tempting to use, for example, available accounting information to determine exposure, since an economic evaluation creates the need for a large amount of additional information at a centralized level. We point again to the possibility that the accounting system allows the evaluation of traditionally measured exchange rate losses on contractual transactions but it may not recognize that losses are offset by gains in the form of increased sales since these gains are not clearly related to particular price and exchange rate changes in the accounting system.

When the central finance function is a profit centre it becomes essential to obtain rapid information about profit opportunities in financial markets. These profit opportunities would typically not last long. It is therefore desirable that positions created by decentralized activities become known to the central function rapidly by means of an 'on-line' information system. Similarly, the feedback of information to subsidiaries becomes important. For example, the company may save on transactions cost, if a subsidiary can be induced to invoice in a particular currency rather than having the central finance function entering forward contracts to offset nondesirable currency positions.

Improved information systems may also be helpful in a process of decentralization. For example, up-to-date exchange rate forecasts and risk-evaluation information can more easily be made available at local levels to improve decentralized exposure decisions. Similarly, when internal transfer prices are used to provide incentives for local managers, the communication system is important for transferring up-to-date information.

VIII

CONCLUDING REMARKS

VIII.1 INTRODUCTION

In this chapter we summarize the main points in the previous chapters. We compare the information requirements of alternative methods for measuring macroeconomic exposures. Thereafter, we summarize the major elements which are required to develop an effective exposure management programme.

VIII.2 MEASURING MACROECONOMIC EXPOSURE

We have discussed five approaches to measuring macroeconomic exposures. In Chapter III traditional methods were summarized. In particular, we analysed the limitations of transaction and translation exposures. We developed in Chapter IV a regression approach to measuring exposures in which regression coefficients are interpreted as exposure or sensitivity coefficients. These coefficients can be estimated either for market price variables such as exchange rates, price levels, and interest rates, or for policy and non-policy disturbances like money supply changes, changes in budget deficits, and oil price changes. In Chapter V we argued that sensitivity coefficients could be estimated or at least approximated without applying a formal regression analysis, by using internal knowledge about the structure of cash flows and the impact of macro-events on these flows. Finally, in Chapter VI a scenario analysis of exposure was developed.

The different methods for exposure measurement require different kinds of information as inputs. Therefore, the relative advantage of each depends largely on the costs and availability of relevant information. The traditional methods in Chapter III have the additional disadvantage of not recognizing the interdependence among different macroeconomic exposures.

Figure VIII.1 demonstrates how different approaches would be chosen depending on the availability of information. On the far left we state the common objective of all methods; to measure macroeconomic exposures. Thereafter, we make a major distinction based on the availability of historical cash flow data. These data could be detailed cash flow figures for financial and commercial cash flows by product line, country of sales, currency of denomination, and other characteristics discussed in Chapters IV and V. They should exist on a quarterly basis for a minimum of five years.

If historical data of this kind are available then regression analysis can be performed. However, the resulting exposure coefficients are stable over time and applicable on future periods only if there is some stability in policy authorities' behaviour. We distinguish between stability of policy regime and stability in the relative frequency with which different disturbances occur.

Regression analysis on money supply and other macroeconomic disturbances can be applied, if there is stability of policy regime. This kind of stability implies that the exchange rate regime does not change and that central banks' and fiscal authorities' responses to economic events remain unchanged over time. For example, if central banks move from interest rate targeting to money supply targeting there is a regime shift. Uncertainty about policy regime is a *political risk*. When this risk is substantial exposure coefficients for money supply disturbances and other events are unreliable guides for future effects of disturbances on cash flows.

With the existence of political risk of the above nature, it could still be possible to measure exposures to exchange rates, price level and other market price variables by means of regression analysis. Exposure coefficients so derived can easily be used for hedging decisions if so desired (see Chapter IV). The coefficients for these price variables may be unstable as well, however. Specifically, if there is wide fluctuations in the frequencies with which money supply changes, fiscal policy shifts and non-policy disturbances occur, the exposure coefficients may not be reliable guides for future exposures. The reason is that each type of disturbance has its specific impact on the market price variables and cash flows. The relationship between, say, the exchange rate and cash flows depends therefore on which kind of disturbance is most frequent.

Moving downwards in Figure VIII.1 we see that in the absence of policy stability, either in terms of regime or relative frequency of disturbances, alternatives to regression analysis must be found. Under the assumption that historical cash flow data exist, regression analysis can be supplemented with current information of relevance for exposure coefficients. For example, coefficients may have been estimated for periods with different types of policy behaviour. The relevant coefficients can then be inferred by judgement about future policy behaviour. Alternatively, as suggested in Chapter V, coefficients can be approximated, given knowledge in the firm of how different kinds of cash flows are influenced by disturbances about which there is uncertainty.

We should emphasize here even if regression analysis is not directly applicable or reliable, the definition of exposure coefficents within regression equations, provides useful *guidance for the exposure measures a firm should try to arrive at by any method*. Regression coefficients are summary figures for the economic impact on cash flows of different disturbances through a whole variety of more or less obvious channels.

Internal knowledge about the impact of different kinds of disturbances on cash flows may be more or less detailed. The knowledge may be based on judgment and experience or it may be based on explicit formulation of macroeconomic relationships among disturbances and relative prices as well as market conditions of relevance for a firm. In the former case relatively loose judgment about exposure coefficients as defined in Chapter V could be formed. In the latter case a scenario analysis of the type we developed in Chapter VI is useful.

An advantage of the scenario analysis is that it does not rely heavily on historical cash flow data. Its disadvantage is that relatively detailed judgment about macroeconomic structure is required.

Figure VIII.1 Conditions for use of different methods for measuring macroeconomic exposure

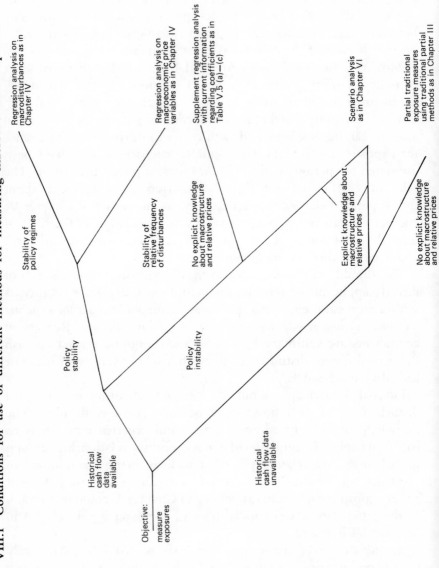

The scenario analysis is a useful tool for sensitivity analysis as well as in the budget process. Many different assumptions can be made and the events to which cash flows are particularly sensitive can be identified. Budget alternatives may be analysed under different forecasts about macroeconomic events. Sensitivity analysis would refer to sensitivity to unanticipated macroeconomic events, while in the budget process the cash flow effects of anticipated events are analysed.

Finally, in Figure VIII.1, we have traditional exposure measures from Chapter III, such as transaction and translation exposures to exchange rate changes. The disadvantages of these measures have been discussed at several occasions in this book. They are partial in terms of coverage of cash flows and their implied assumption that prices, interest rates, and exchange rates move independently is usually not valid. Nevertheless, lacking historical cash flow data and lacking knowledge about the macroeconomic structure of relevance for the firm these measures are still readily available. Understanding alternative exposure measures is nevertheless useful, since they enable management to improve traditional partial measures and potentially form judgment on their validity.

Though we have presented the different exposure measures as substitutes, it is obvious that from management's perspective they are complementary. Ideal measures are hard to obtain. Political as well as data problems and other econometric problems discussed in Chapter IV make regression exposure coefficients unreliable under some circumstances. The scenario approach, on the other hand, requires assumptions about macroeconomic structure about which there is substantial disagreement. Therefore, the different exposure measures could be applied simultaneously. If the results are similar under each method they are highly credible. On the other hand, if results become different, there is reason to check underlying assumptions of each method in order to evaluate its relative validity.

VIII.3 ELEMENTS OF AN EXPOSURE MANAGEMENT PROGRAMME

Much of the discussion in this book has covered the measurement of exposure. However in Chapter V we also analysed how an exposure management strategy could be determined to be consistent with stakeholders' objectives. Information requirements to implement strategies were derived in the same chapter. We discussed also conditions under which strategies could be simplified and operationalized by reducing information requirements. In Chapter VII evaluation, feedback, and some aspects of organization of exposure management were discussed.

We summarize these parts of the book in Table VIII.1 which contains the elements that should enter into a comprehensive programme for exposure management. The table lists first the required inputs to determine a strategy. These inputs were discussed in Chapter V. They include (1) an analysis of how cash flows of different kinds depend on price levels, exchange rates, and interest rates. We emphasized that the *real* value of cash flows should be analysed. Inputs include also (2) the firm's objective relative to stakeholders. Thereby, the *target variable* can be selected. This variable may be near-term cash flows, economic value, market value or accounting value. We argue that cash flows or economic value should be chosen. The *time perspective* of the firm is one aspect of the choice between these two variables. The *risk-attitude* of management on behalf of the stakeholders determines whether the

---

Table VIII.1   Elements in exposure management programme

Inputs for determining exposure management strategy

1. Character of cash flows.
2. Firm objective; target variable, risk–attitude, time-perspective.
3. Goods and financial market pricing relationships (PPP, LOP, FO).

Information

4. Current organization and information system.
5. Availability of information and expertise to implement desired strategy at different levels (exposure measures and forecasts).

Operational management

6. Possible reorganization and information system development.
7. Specification and delegation of responsibilities to tactical and operational decision levels.

Evaluation and feedback

8. Accounting and reporting systems.
9. Evaluation of exposure management strategy.

---

variance of the target variable should be part of the objective. Finally, among inputs we discussed the *pricing relationships* in international goods and financial market (3). For example, if *purchasing power parity* holds there is no exchange rate risk, and if *Fisher Open* holds the expected costs of borrowing in different currencies are equal. The validity of the latter relationship enables the firm to select highly simplified strategies even when variance of cash flow and value are considered important. Sales and purchase divisions can then be run with the objective of maximizing cash flows or value while the responsibility of minimizing variance is taken over by the finance function.

Next we turn to information available to implement a strategy. The current organization and information system (4) could constrain the implementation of a desired strategy. Furthermore, the relevant information and expertise for estimating exposure and obtain forecast may not exist (5).

In order to operationalize, the desired strategy reorganization and new information systems may be required (6). Alternatively, management would have to determine what strategy is feasible and the extent to which desired objectives are compromised by a feasible strategy. We discussed possible simplifications in Chapter V.

In order to operationalize the strategy, responsibilities must be delegated to tactical and operational levels in the firm (7). The specific tasks of head of sales, head of purchase, and head of finance on the tactical level vary depending on the strategy. For example, if Fisher Open is considered valid, and a minimize variance strategy has been selected, heads of sales and purchase need not consider cash flow variance even though management is willing to sacrifice return in order to reduce variance.

Delegation of authority was discussed in Chapter VII, where we also discussed the evaluation of management on different levels. The incentives to fulfil the firm's objective on each level of authority depend strongly on evaluation systems. It is therefore necessary that delegation of authority is determined consistent with the evaluation system and consistent with overall objectives.

In order to perform evaluation and obtain information feedback among different levels of authority, accounting and reporting systems (8) must be developed if not already satisfactory for the chosen strategy. Managers must be evaluated with the relevant information. Oxelheim (1985) discusses these aspects in more detail but we noted, for example, in Chapter VII that, when evaluating loans in different currencies, it is an important issue to determine how a specific exchange rate change should be allocated over the loan-period. Furthermore, we argued that effects on sales of changes in exchange rates or interest rates may not be reported as related to these variables. The result is that exposure managers are evaluated on too narrow a range of cash flows.

We discussed finally in Chapter VII the overall evaluation of the exposure management strategy (9). A selected strategy should be compared to alternative strategies in order to determine, for example, the actual costs of obtaining a certain desired decrease in variance. This type of evaluation would show whether assumptions made about goods and financial market relationships were correct. It may then be revealed to a risk-averse firm that deviations from, say, Fisher Open are not large enough to justify the firm's expense on variance reduction of both commercial and financial cash flows, or that real exchange rate fluctuations are so predictable or unimportant that a strategy of never hedging would lead to substantial savings without a substantial increase in the variance of cash flows.

BIBLIOGRAPHY _____

Adler, M. and B. Dumas (1980), in B. Antl (Ed.), *Currency Risk and the Corporation*. London: Euromoney Publications, pp. 145–158.

Adler, M. and B. Dumas (1983), International portfolio choice and corporation finance; A synthesis. *Journal of Finance*, **38**, 3, June, 925–984.

Aliber, R. Z. and C. Stickney (1975), Accounting measure of foreign exchange exposure; the long and short of it, *The Accounting Review*, Jan, 44–57.

Aliber, R. Z. (1978), *Exchange Risk and Corporate International Finance*, Macmillan, London.

Artus, J. R. and A. McGuire (1982). A revised version of the multilateral exchange rate model, *IMF Staff Papers*.

Bank for International Settlements (1985), *Annual Report*, Basle.

Bird, G. (1986), New approaches to country risk, *Lloyds Bank Review*, **162**, Oct.

Boyd, W. (1801), *A Letter to the Rt. Hon. William Pitt on the Influence of the Stoppage of Specie*, London.

Carter, E. and R. Rodriguez (1978), What 40 US multinationals think, *Euromoney*, March.

Cassel, G. (1922), *Money and Foreign Exchanges after 1914*, Constable, London.

Clarke, P. B. (1973), Uncertainty, exchange risk, and the level of international trade, *Western Economic Journal*, Sept.

Cornell, W. B. (1980), Inflation, relative prices and exchange risk, *Financial Management*, **9**, Autumn, 30–34.

Dooley, M. and P. Isard (1980), Capital controls, political risks and deviations from interest-rate parity, *Journal of Political Economy*, **88**, April, 370–384.

Dornbusch, R. and P. Krugman (1976), Flexible exchange rates in the short run, *Brookings Papers on Economic Activity*, **3**.

Doukas, P. (1983), *The Exposure of U.S. Multinational Corporations to Foreign Exchange Fluctuations Arising From the Translation of the Financial Statements of Their Foreign Subsidiaries*. PhD Dissertation, Dept. of Economics, New York University.

Dufey, G. and I. Giddy (1978), International financial planning. The use of market-based forecasts, *California Management Review*, **21**, 1, Fall.

Dufey, G. and I. Giddy (1984), Eurocurrency deposit risk, *Journal of Banking and Finance*, **8**, Dec, 567–589.

Dufey, G. and S. L. Srinivasulu (1983), The case for corporate management of foreign exchange risk, *Financial Management*, Winter.

239

Edwards, S. (1984), LDC foreign borrowing and default risk: An empirical investigation 1976–80, *American Economic Review*, **74**, 726–734.

Eiteman, D. K. and A. I. Stonehill (1982), *Multinational Business Finance*, Addison-Wesley Publishing Co., Reading, Massachusetts.

Ellsworth, R. R. (1985), Capital markets and competitive decline, *Harvard Business Review*, Sept/Oct, 5, 171–183.

Einzig, P. (1962), *The History of Foreign Exchange*, Macmillan, London.

Evans, P., M. Folks Jr. and M. Jilling (1978), *The Impact of Statement of Financial Standards No. 8 on the Foreign Exchange Risk Management Practices of American Multinationals, Financial Accounting Standards Board*, Stamford.

Fama, E. (1984), Forward and spot exchange rates. *Journal of Monetary Economics*, **14**, 319–338.

Feder, G. and R. E. Just (1977), A study of debt servicing capacity applying logit analysis, *Journal of Development Economics*, **4**, 23–58.

Feiger, G. and B. Jacquillat (1982), *International Finance—Text and Cases*, Allyn and Bacon, Boston.

Financial Accounting Standards Board (1975), *Accounting Research Bulletin*, No. 51, FASB; Stamford.

Fisher, I. (1896), Appreciation and interest, *Publications of the American Economic Association*, **11**, 331–442.

Frank, C. and W. Cline (1971), Measurement of debt servicing capacity: An application of discriminant analysis, *Journal of International Economics*, March.

Frankel, J. (1979), The diversifiability of exchange risk, *Journal of International Economics*, 9, Aug, 379–394.

Frenkel, J. (1981), The collapse of purchasing power parities during the 1970s, *European Economic Review*, **16**, May, 145–165.

Frenkel, J. and R. M. Levich (1975), Covered interest arbitrage: unexploited profits? *Journal of Political Economy*, **83**, April, 325–338.

Frydman, R. (1982), Towards an understanding of market processes: individual expectations, learning and convergence to rational expectations equilibrium, *American Economic Review*, **72**, Sept, 652–668.

Garner, K. and A. Shapiro (1984) A practical method of assessing foreign exchange risk, *Midland Corporate Finance Journal*, Fall, 6–17.

Giddy, I. (1976), An integrated theory of exchange rate equilibrium, *Journal of Financial and Quantitative Analysis*, **9**, Dec, 883–92.

Glick, R. (1986), Market neutrality conditions and valuation of a foreign affiliate, *Journal of Business Finance and Accounting*, **13**, Summer, 239–299.

Grauer, F. L., R. H. Litzenberger, and R. Stehle (1976), Sharing rules and equilibrium in an international capital market under uncertainty, *Journal of Financial Economics*, **3**, 233–256.

Hekman, C. R. (1985), A financial model of foreign exchange exposure, *Journal of International Business Studies*, Summer, 83–94.

Hodder, J. E. (1982), Exposure to exchange rate movements, *Journal of International Economics*, Nov, 375–386.

Huang, R. (1984), Exchange rate and relative monetary expansions: The case of simultaneous hyperinflation and rational expectations, *European Economic Review*, **24**, 2, March, 189–195.

Jacque, L. L. (1978), *Management of Foreign Exchange Risk*, Lexington Books, D. C. Heath and Company, Lexington, Massachusetts.

Keynes, J. M: (1923), *A Tract on Monetary Reform*, Macmillan, London.

Kobrin, S. J., (1979), Political risk: a review and reconsideration, *Journal of*

International Business Studies, **10**, Spring/Summer, 67–80.

Korth, C. M. (1979), Developing a country risk analysis system, *Journal of Commercial Bank Lending*, December.

Lessard, D. R. (1979), Financial management of international operations, introduction, in Lessand, D. R. (Ed), *International Financial Management, Theory and Application*, Warren, Gorham and Lamont, Boston.

Lessard, D. R. and J. B. Lightstone (1986), Volatile exchange rates can put operations at risk, *Harvard Business Review*, **64** (4) July–August.

Lessard, D. R. and P. Lorange (1977), Currency changes and management control: resolving the centralization/decentralization dilemma, *Accounting Review*, July, 628–637.

Levi, M. (1983), *International Finance—Financial Management and the International Economy*, McGraw-Hill, New York.

Levich, R. M. (1979), *The International Money Market*, JAI Press, New York.

Levich, R. M. (1980), Forecasting exchange rate advisory services, in Levich, R. M. and C. Wihlborg (Eds), *Exchange Risk and Exposure*, Lexington Books, D. C. Heath and Company.

Lintner, J. (1965), The valuation of risk assets and the selection of risky investments in stock portfolios and capital budgets, *Review of Economics and Statistics*, **47**, February, 13–37.

Lucas, R. E. (1976), Econometric policy evaluation: A critique, in K. Brunner and A. H. Meltzer (Eds), *Carnegie-Mellon Conference Series on Public Policy*, **1**, North Holland, Amsterdam.

Markowitz, H. (1959), *Portfolio Selection. Efficient Diversification of Investments*, Wiley, New York.

McKinnon, R. (1979), *Money in International Exchange*, Oxford University Press, Oxford.

Meese, R. A. and K. Rogoff (1983), Empirical exchange rate models of the seventies—do they fit out of sample? *Journal of International Economics*, **14**, Jan, 3–24.

Mossin, J. (1966), Equilibrium in a capital asset market, *Econometrica*, **34**, October, 768–783.

Mussa, M. (1982), A model of exchange rate dynamics, *Journal of Political Economy*, **90**, Feb, 74–104.

Officer, L. (1982), *Purchasing Power Parity and Exchange Rates: Theory, Evidence and Relevance*. JAI Press, New York.

OPTICA Report 2 (1977), Inflation and Exchange Rates, *Evidence Guidelines for the European Community*, Brussels, Febr.

Oxelheim, L. (1981), *Företagens utlandslån – Valuta- och redovisningsaspekter* (Corporate Foreign Loans – Currencies and Accounting Aspects), Liber, Stockholm (in Swedish with summary in English).

Oxelheim, L. (1983), Proposals for new accounting standards for foreign monetary items, *Journal of Business Finance and Accounting*, **10**, 2, Summer.

Oxelheim, L. (1984a), *Foreign Exchange Risk Management in the Modern Company—A Total Perspective*. Scandinavian Institute for Foreign Exchange Research, Stockholm, June.

Oxelheim, L. (1984b), Country risks and industrial structure in a Nordic perspective, *Unitas*, Helsingfors, Dec.

Oxelheim, L. (1985), *International Financial Market Fluctuations*, Wiley, Chichester.

Oxelheim, L. and C. Wihlborg (1986), Exchange rate related exposures in a macroeconomic perspective. In Ghosh and Khoury (Eds), *Recent Developments in International Banking and Finance*, Lexington Books, D. C. Heath and Company.

Pigott, C. and R. J. Sweeney (1985), Purchasing power parity and exchange rate dynamics: some empirical results, in S. W. Arndt, R. J. Sweeney and T. D. Willett (Eds), *Exchange Rates, Trade and the U.S. Economy*, Ballinger, Cambridge, Massachusetts.

Prindle, A. R. (1976), *Foreign Exchange Risk*, Wiley, London.

Rao, R. and S. Magee (1980), The currency of denomination of international trade contracts, in R. M. Levich, and C. Wihlborg (Eds), *Exchange Risk and Exposure*, Lexington Books, D. C. Heath and Co., Lexington, Massachusetts.

Ricks, D. A. (1978), *International Dimensions of Corporate Finance*, Prentice Hall, Englewood Cliffs, New Jersey.

Rodriguez, R. (1980), *Foreign Exchange Management in US Multinationals*, Lexington Books, Lexington, Massachusetts.

Rodriguez, R. and E. Carter (1976), *International Financial Management*, Prentice Hall, Englewood Cliffs, New Jersey.

Roll, R. (1979), Violations of purchasing power parity and their implications for efficient international commodity markets, in M. Sarnat and G. P. Szego (Eds), *International Finance and Trade*, Ballinger, Cambridge, Massachusetts.

Ross, S. A. (1976), The arbitrage theory of capital asset pricing, *Journal of Economic Theory*, **13**, Dec, 341–60.

Sachs, J. (1982), LDC debt in the 1980's: risk and reforms, in P. Wachtel (Ed), *Crises in the Economic and Financial Structure*, Lexington Books, D. C. Heath and Co., Lexington, Massachusetts.

Shapiro, A. C. (1983). *Multinational Financial Management*, Allyn and Bacon, Boston.

Shapiro, A. C. (1984), Currency risk and relative price risk, *Journal of Financial and Quantitative Analysis*, Dec, 365–373.

Shapiro, A. C. and S. Titman (1984), An integrated view of risk management, *Working Paper*, University of Southern California, December.

Sharpe, W. F. (1964), Capital asset prices: A theory of market equilibrium under conditions of risk, *Journal of Finance*, **19**, Sept, 425–442.

Thygesen, N. (1977), Inflation and exchange rates, *Journal of International Economics*, **8**, 301–317.

Tobin, J. (1958), Liquidity preference as behavior towards risk, *Review of Economic Studies*, Feb, 65–86.

Treynor, J. (1965), *Towards a Theory of the Market Value of Risky Assets*. Unpublished.

Wihlborg, C. (1978), Currency risks in international financial markets, *Princeton Studies in International Finance*, 44, Princeton University, December.

Wihlborg, C. (1980a), Currency exposure—taxonomy and theory, in R. M. Levich and C. Wihlborg (Eds.), *Exchange Risk and Exposure*, Lexington Books, D. C. Heath and Company, Lexington, Massachusetts.

Wihlborg, C. (1980b), Economics of exposure management of foreign subsidiaries of multinational corporations, *Journal of International Business Studies*, **11**, Winter, 9–18.

Wihlborg, C. (1982), The effectiveness of exchange controls on financial capital flows, *Columbia Journal of World Business*, Winter, 1–10.

Willett, T. D. (1986), Exchange rate volatility, international trade, and resource allocation: a perspective on recent research, *Journal of International Money and Finance*, **5**, supplement, March, 101–112.

AUTHOR INDEX

SUBJECT INDEX